the tribes of the person-centred nation

an introduction to the schools of therapy related to the person-centred approach

edited by

pete sanders

PCCS BOOKS

Ross-on-Wye

First published in 2004

PCCS BOOKS
Llangarron
Ross-on-Wye
HR9 6PT
Tel (01989) 77 07 07
Fax (01989) 77 07 00
www.pccs-books.co.uk

The Tribes of the Person-Centred Nation: An introduction to the schools of therapy related
to the Person-Centred Approach

ISBN 1 898059 60 8

Cover design by Old Dog Graphics
Printed by Bath Press Ltd, Bath, UK.

contents

preface

Pete Sanders

My original training in therapy in 1974 was person-centred at heart and, tellingly, it was many years before I found out about Focusing. I have been learning about the many ways in which practitioners express their person-centredness ever since. On many occasions in the past 15 years or so I have been made aware of the differences between people in the person-centred 'family' more than the similarities between us — at times there was a real sense that the person-centred nation might fragment.

It also became clear that changes were taking place in counselling and psychotherapy around the world. 'Evidence-based practice' was causing funding to shift towards short-term cognitive therapies and furthermore I believed that if the person-centred nation continued its internecine fighting, we might disappear altogether. However, in 2000, at the ICCCEP conference in Chicago, several people presented similar papers quite independently and the keynote speakers were inclusive rather than divisive. In 2002 at the Durham BAPCA 'Dialogues' conference there was again an inclusive atmosphere in which practitioners talked freely about their differences. This book was conceived in the bar at the Durham conference. I wanted a gathering of the tribes of the person-centred nation in print in the UK where we might respectfully share, listen and learn from each other.

The fifth International Conference for Client-Centered and Experiential Psychotherapy (ICCCEP) was held in Chicago. I think it is significant that the World Association for Person-Centered and Experiential Psychotherapy and Counseling (WAPCEPC) had its inaugural meeting at this conference.

British Association for the Person-Centred Approach (BAPCA).

At the same time, I do not want to diminish the real concern that some practitioners have that the term 'person-centred' and Rogers' discoveries are being hi-jacked. Carl Rogers was mocked for putting empathy at the centre of his approach in the 1940s. Now everyone, even cognitive therapists, wants to be empathic (and respectful, and real). Those therapists that mindfully hold these ideas at the centre of their philosophy, theory and practice should join forces and talk, not build walls. I want to actively promote this process, which is why I have brought these colleagues together.

I wear the colours of the classical tribe and in this regard have been publicly called a 'dinosaur', a 'fundamentalist', 'immature' and

I write this with only a trace of irony. Anyone who knows me will know that I have always defended free speech to the end, I love a debate and I remain confident that 'the facts are friendly'. Our person-centred nation offers the world a moral, humane paradigm for change. Person-Centred Therapies try to do (as John Shlien urged) not only what is effective, but also what is right. We can start by listening to each other.

'rigid' over the years. So it is with great pleasure that I introduce this book because I know that our nation of many tribes will be all the stronger when we listen, learn, debate and organise together.

The process of writing this book has had the contributors looking at, and commenting on, each other's work as we have worked to practise this process of dialogue. It has taken a degree of courage for them to take part in this adventure and submit their work to scrutiny in this way. I sincerely believe that this is the constructive way forward for us all. It has also been a treat for me — I have learned a huge amount by working with these talented people. At the logistical level, chaos was only a moment away at any point. I applaud them all, Tony, Campbell, Nick, Mick and Richard — congratulations, three cheers and thanks.

Tony Merry

I was first introduced to Carl Rogers' work in the mid-1970s, and I subsequently trained in Client-Centred Therapy from 1981 to 1984. I also had some contact with other therapeutic methods, including Gestalt and Transactional Analysis, and I had some quite extensive experience of various forms of group encounter, some of which I found helpful, some entertaining and some downright offensive.

Meeting and working with Rogers towards the end of his life were very affirming experiences. It seemed to me that the close, empathic attention that Rogers both espoused and 'lived' was the most gently powerful factor in creating opportunities for positive change in both myself and in others. I became a follower of Rogers' approach and, later, an advocate for it. However, I have never viewed Client-Centred Therapy with anything other than a critical eye. I am, by nature, a sceptical person with a questioning outlook on life generally. I have a great desire to understand and to create my own 'sense' and meaning from what I read and experience, and I am not easily persuaded of any particular 'truth'. One of the most enduring things I learned from my undergraduate biological science training (which in most other respects was old-fashioned and alienating) was to question the nature of 'evidence' and to remain open-minded to the existence of other explanations and models.

In this sense, I don't regard my position as a 'classical' client-centred therapist as the correct position, and other positions as wrong. It is simply that, in my experience, understanding and individual meaning-making, this classical position is most consistent with what I observe in myself and others about how human relationships can most reliably become constructive and creative. In the 'classical' position, I see all the elements required to make psychotherapy effective. I see in it, a deep respect for and trust in the positive potentials present within human persons, even though these potentials may have become so damaged that their recovery and expression are threatened sometimes, it seems, beyond endurance.

I see the 'classical' position as attending to the whole person — with equal respect for content and process, feeling and thinking, and being and becoming. Whilst I have certainly been influenced by the other models and approaches described in this book, I see much of what they say as being already present within the 'classical' approach, either implicitly or explicitly. There are, of course, some divisions between us, some more obvious than others, but I don't see this book as representing a competition between the various approaches described here. How these divisions can be resolved, if indeed some of them can be, is a matter for each reader.

Campbell Purton

I first learned about Focusing around 1986, on my initial person-centred training course. I found it interesting but did not follow it up. Several years later, at the ICCCEP Conference in Gmunden I was fascinated by a presentation about the work of the Japanese therapist Fujio Tomoda. Tomoda's work is little known in the West, but someone told me that there were similarities with Focusing. I went along to some of the Focusing presentations at the conference and knew that I had to learn more about this. I then did a Focusing training course with Barbara McGavin, and began to read Gendlin's work.

International Conference for Client-Centered and Experiential Psychotherapy (ICCCEP), Gmunden, Austria, 1994.

My original training, like his, was in philosophy, and reading his work threw a whole new light on person-centred theory for me. I attended some of the international Focusing conferences, one of Gendlin's workshops in New York, was fortunate to have a Focusing partnership with Rob Foxcroft, from whom I have learned much, introduced more Focusing-oriented material into our Counselling Diploma at the University of East Anglia, and with much help and support from Judy Moore have recently been setting up our Diploma and MA course in Focusing and Experiential Psychotherapy. Focusing, in spite of being so simple, can be curiously difficult to learn, but as it becomes better appreciated, and people are helped by it (as I have been) I think that there will be an increasing interest in the deeply original philosophy which lies behind it. I hope my chapter can make some small contribution to these developments in the Person-Centred Approach.

Nick Baker

I have worked as a counsellor, supervisor and primarily a counsellor educator for nearly 20 years, and for most of that time I have felt myself to be a *practitioner*: someone who defines himself through his actual relational work. Writing was the province of others. That started to change when I began working at St Martin's College, Lancaster in 2000. Then the BAPCA 'Dialogues' Conference at Durham, mentioned in my chapter, made me realise that how I work was not being recognised. I could either shrug my shoulders and feel that I was somehow *still* not 'proper', or I could 'come out'! With the support of my family and my colleagues at work, I have done just that.

There have been two big influences on my person-centredness. Prior to my undertaking my Diploma in Counselling course at Wigan, I worked as an educational counsellor for the Open University and, as part of that work , I was a counsellor at numerous Summer Schools. I learnt there that what was important to me were not the external aspects of life for the hard-pressed O.U. students, but how they were experiencing everything that was happening for them. Moreover, with only a week to work with them, I had to learn ways of establishing quick and strong connections. That has always stayed with me. The second big influence was the work of Gendlin. He spoke to me in ways that both made sense of how I was working, but also pointed me towards a more formalised way of working with *experiencing*. And to achieve this with an article cumbersomely entitled *Subverbal Communication and Therapist Expressivity*, is no mean feat.

Gendlin, E.T. (1967). 'Subverbal communication and Therapist Expressivity: Trends in Client-Centered Therapy with Schizophrenics.' In C.R. Rogers and B. Stevens (eds.) *Person To Person: The Problem of Being Human*. New York: Souvenir Press, pp. 119–28.

Reading the chapters written by my fellow authors, I think my 'newness' to writing is very apparent. They all write with great aplomb and panache as well as with enthusiasm, whereas I write with just enthusiasm. That is quite alright with me; I hope it is with you.

This chapter has come about with the encouragement of my

wife, Jay, and the support of my colleagues Trudy Johnston, Rosie Wenner and Sandra Taylor at College, and Liz Muir, my supervisor. I know I am also indebted to all the students, clients and supervisees with whom I have spent such precious time over the years, which has helped me to get this far in my work.

I would be pleased to hear from you if you want to discuss any part of my chapter.

Mick Cooper

Although my first experience of a counselling course was a person-centred certificate, I subsequently trained for four years in existential psychotherapy. I loved the values of the Person-Centred Approach, but got unbearably frustrated with the lack of structure on my person-centred certificate, where it felt like we would spend interminable hours deciding whether to have our lunch breaks at 12.30 or 12.45! In my existential training, I think I also came to experience a deeper acceptance of the intense feelings of anxiety, panic and mournfulness that I had experienced from childhood, and continue to experience. Here, these feelings were not construed as blocks to actualisation and growth, but as expressions of a very meaningful and valid perception of the reality of my, and human, existence. On completing my existential training, however, I returned to the person-centred fold, and much of the reason for this was to do with the greater feeling of community, warmth and 'relational depth' that I experienced within this world, and continue to experience in my work as a Senior Lecturer in Counselling at the University of Strathclyde's Counselling Unit. Today, however, I continue to see myself as someone who straddles the person-centred and existential worlds; and in my more recent writings — including my chapter for this book — I have attempted to look at ways in which the best of the latter can be brought into the best of the former.

Straddling two worlds, however, feels like quite a comfortable position for me, and perhaps it is because I seem to have a great desire to challenge and deconstruct any fixed, 'all-encompassing' model of how people come to be the way they are, and how they can be helped by therapy. In my recent book, *Existential Therapies* (Cooper, 2003), for instance, I argued that there was no, one way of practising existential therapy. Rather, I tried to show the great richness-in-diversity of this approach. Alongside this desire to deconstruct is a desire to dialogue: to exchange ideas across people

Cooper, M. (2003). *Existential Therapies.* London: Sage.

and disciplines, and to move forward together in our understandings. For me, then, this book is a great opportunity to further the Person-Centred Approach: to move away from fixed and dogmatic notions of what Person-Centred Therapy is, and to celebrate the great diversity of our field and the possibility of dialogue across differences.

Richard Worsley

When I was first described as integrative person-centred in my approach to therapy I felt ill-at-ease, even a little offended. I was just, I thought, being myself.

My chapter is born out of a number of years of teaching Person-Centred Therapy at diploma level, before moving on to my present job as a University Counsellor at the University of Warwick. Being a teacher of counselling taught me to look hard at all theory as useful insight, but at the same time to challenge my students to find out what it was for each of *them* to be person-centred. I could not tell them. They had to find out. I sometimes worry that person-centred training courses can become dogmatic about person-centredness. This willed openness is at the heart of my chapter. After a number of years, I knew that I had to move on to a place where I could work with a range of people at high volume and pressure. (That sounds like a physics lab!) The sheer variety and challenge of working with students and staff in a Russell-group University with all of its pressure has made me face like nothing else what it is for me to be genuine, myself. I face working from deep within the intuitive self to contact people. I improvise. I take risks, and need to assess them for my clients' sake. I strive to be person-centred in its full, ethical sense. Above all, I have met a growing sense of what it really is for Richard to be person-centred.

My hope is that my chapter conveys some of the excitement and puzzlement of this journey. I am grateful to those — colleagues, clients, supervisees — who have shared it with me so far. I have explored many of the issues here in my *Process Work in Person-Centred Therapy: Phenomenological and existential perspectives* (Worsley, 2002). I continue to pursue a parallel interest in the relationship of philosophy and counselling, which is in turn rooted in work I have done in philosophical theology and through my life as an Anglican parish priest.

Worsley, R. (2002). *Process Work in Person-Centred Therapy: Phenomenological and existential perspectives.* Basingstoke: Palgrave.

introduction — read this first

pete sanders

Reading this book

Before we get properly under way, I wanted to say a word or two about the layout of the book, mainly regarding the second column on each page. This is entirely my responsibility. There are several ideas behind the second column. First, that apart from the occasional cross-references to other chapters, you will not have to go off the page to get references. Second, it allows some additional information, asides from the authors, or definitions of terms, without breaking up the flow of the text too much. Third, it provides a space for comments from the remaining contributors where they might take a different view to a point of theory. I hope it works.

In particular I wanted to give an impression of dialogue, rather than a series of monologues, and I really dislike having to turn to the end of a book to find the full reference.

There is one peculiar convention I have adopted with the references. That is that if a full reference in column two relates to a name and date in the text (e.g. Rogers, 1951), the name and date in column two will be in bold. This should help when column two gets crowded and you want to quickly find the right reference. Otherwise names and dates in column two will be in normal text.

Rogers, C.R. (1951). *Client-Centered Therapy: Its current practice, implications and theory.* Boston: Houghton Mifflin.

I think it is safe to say that the writing of this book has been an adventure for all concerned. All the contributors have learned something from the process of doing it, and at some stage we each had the thought that we would have appreciated such a book during our own training. We hope you find it as encouraging and exciting an experience as we have.

What is a tribe?

The answer to this question is somewhat arbitrary and parochial. Arbitrary in the sense that there is no set of criteria 'out there' against which my selection can be measured. Parochial in that this is a UK book, with a UK slant — written by UK authors about what is (or might be) available in the UK. At the same time it is a book with a mission. Our mission is to bring the UK person-centred community into a more intimate relationship with its natural 'family' — some of the other tribes of our nation. I say

I have taken the analogy of 'tribes' and the terms from Margaret Warner's (2000) paper: 'Person-centered Psychotherapy: One Nation, Many Tribes.' *Person-Centered Journal,* 7 (1): 28–39.

this because in many trainings, Client-Centred and Person-Centred Therapy (CCT and PCT) are aligned with psychodynamic or other humanistic approaches with scant regard for compatibility in history, philosophy, theory or practice. At the same time, the natural family of CCT and PCT is unknown to, or little-understood by, many UK trainees and practitioners.

Along the way I had to make a decision about what was to be in the book and what was to be excluded. My criteria for inclusion are as follows:

1. The approach must be a 'primary' therapeutic approach. By this I mean that it would be considered to be appropriate for professional, diploma-level training. It would not *necessarily* be an 'option' or a 'bolt-on' element (although it *might* feature in some training in this way). The theoretical base, then, must be primary — working up from first principles — not secondary, i.e., resting as a secondary layer of theory on, say, classical client-centred therapy.

2. There must be a theoretical base for the approach which both distinguishes it from classical client-centred *and* puts it in relation to classical client-centred therapy, in the same stream of theory.

3. There must be training opportunities available in the UK, either as a specialist training, or as a significant proportion of existing person-centred trainings.

4. There must be literature available in the UK which lays out the basic elements of the approach.

Not all of these criteria have been met by all approaches represented in this book. It seemed reasonable to bend the rules a little since one part of our mission is to encourage and give support to fledgling practitioners in the UK to demand training and literature in approaches which in mainland Europe are taken for granted. For example, whilst there is no training exclusively devoted to experiential therapy, it is given substantial coverage in some courses and specialist Focusing-Oriented Psychotherapy training will be available in the UK in the not too distant future. Some readers might consider it ironic, then, that 'integrative' training is available almost everywhere, yet we worry about the quality. The message in Richard Worsley's chapter is clear: integrative training without discipline, thorough theoretical grounding and rigorous self-examination is not training with integrity. It should probably take longer to become a good integrative therapist than a specialist in one approach by this account. Yet we know that much integrative training is a 'marriage of convenience' — assembled, sometimes

Chapter 6, pp. 125–48.

annually, on the basis of the mix of approaches available in the staff team.

I suspect that most readers of this book will have only a patchy understanding of what I sometimes refer to as the 'turf wars' in the Person-Centred Approach. I am talking about the tensions which occur when any new strand of theory and practice emerges in any area of human endeavour. These tensions are to do with ownership of the ideas, whether they are *correct*, what happens when and if they are amended, superseded or added to as a result of new thinking or new evidence. This book is an attempt to answer these questions. You may have thought that there is only one 'person-centred therapy', but by the time you have read the next chapter, you will probably understand what Art Bohart (Bohart, 1995) meant when he said 'will the real person-centred therapy please stand up?'

The history of psychotherapy is the history of big ideas, developments, disagreements and splits. The world of Client-Centred/Person-Centred Therapy is no different. Carl Rogers had a big idea which threw down the gauntlet in the shape of his 'if-then' hypothesis regarding the six 'necessary and sufficient' conditions. There have been developments, and vigorous disagreements, and a following of different paths, but practitioners world-wide seem dedicated to working together, uncomfortable though that might be, to further refine their understanding and practice in the service of clients. This book is about that history and the ideas that form the strands, the members of the 'family' or, as Margaret Warner has it, the 'tribes' of the 'nation' of the person-centred approaches to psychotherapy.

A gathering of the tribes

We present this book as an opportunity for UK readers interested in person-centred approaches to counselling and psychotherapy to find out about the history of the ideas and how they developed into stand-alone approaches. Our hope is that this will not only enrich your current learning, but also better inform any choices of further training that you might make. The authors of the various chapters have covered the value-base and philosophical roots of each theory to help readers decide where they stand. They are not presenting a cast-iron definition of each 'tribe'. Each chapter is the author's own interpretation of the approach they represent. Readers will find overlap and disagreement. This is as it should be, since we are swimming in muddy waters. If tolerating discomfort whilst struggling for meaning and clarity isn't to your

Some argue that defining what is *correct* is just a matter of applying 'rational thought' to the 'evidence'. If it were this simple, there would be only one type of psychotherapy and you might imagine that that one type would probably be a matter of applying the right method to the particular type of distress suffered. I could then point out that embedded in even these two sentences are the assumptions that:
(a) mental distress is best thought of as an 'illness',
(b) that this illness is best thought of and dealt with in the same way we deal with physical illness,
(c) that we have reliable and valid ways of understanding what 'evidence' is and how to collect and interpret it.
Learning about any therapy is to constantly challenge these assumptions.

Bohart, A.C. (1995). 'The Person-Centered Psychotherapies.' In A. Gurman and S. Messer (eds.) *Essential Psychotherapies: Theory and Practice.* New York: Guilford, pp 85–127.

The formation of the World Association for Person-Centered and Experiential Psychotherapy and Counseling (WAPCEPC) in Chicago in 2000 is the most hopeful evidence of the 'gathering of the tribes'.

At each turn, the authors encourage students of the Person-Centred Approach to read widely. It should go without saying that none of these chapters are the 'last word' on any of the approaches represented.

Authors recommend a UK-published book at the end of each chapter. Do try to read them. Wherever you do your training, ask the library to stock these books and others referenced here.

taste, then you may find the reading difficult. The approaches chosen are as follows:

Classical Client-Centred Therapy

This is the 'original' approach, the starting point of it all as described in Carl Rogers' early writings.

Focusing

Springing from the work of Eugene Gendlin, Carl Rogers' close colleague.

Experiential Therapy

Developments which embrace ideas from both Rogers and Gendlin, infused with cognitive psychology and Gestalt Therapy.

Existential Therapies

Based on the work of European Existential philosophers.

Integrative Person-Centred Therapy

Presented here as a way of approaching therapy from a person-centred base of values, philosophy and theory.

Already, some will take issue with this list. They will argue that existential therapies aren't person-centred and integrative therapy isn't an approach. Although this is 'technically correct' they are included here because,

1. Carl Rogers was clearly influenced by existential writers. He included existential ideas in client-centred theory from the start. The two therapeutic traditions grew up in parallel and now we are beginning to understand the relationships between the two much better. Knowing more about existential therapies has enriched my understanding of Client-Centred Therapy and I believe building bridges between the two can only benefit both.

2. *Technical eclecticism* (the ad hoc collection of techniques to fit a client's problem(s) as diagnosed by the therapist) is not being proposed here. Although there is no single 'school' called 'integrative therapy', we want to acknowledge that many practitioners integrate many elements of their experience into the therapeutic moment. This is not an assembly governed by the content of training or the latest weekend workshop, but an acknowledgement that the self is the therapist's instrument.

Whether or not it is 'correct' to include these approaches, at least now you, the reader, will be better able to judge. Having said that, I did decide to exclude certain developments and at the same time decided to allow myself half of a get out clause in this introduction.

What is not a tribe?

There are long and short answers to this question. The long one would entail lists of approaches and justifications for excluding them. The short answer is presented here. I have chosen this because it enabled me to include a brief introduction to methods and ideas which I have excluded, even though they have been associated with the Person-Centred Approach for many years. Maybe I am wrong and will regret it. I fully expect that subsequent editions of this book (if there are any) will be amended to include other approaches. As self-appointed arbiter I am not claiming any authority, just an attempt to present a realistic picture of what is available. If you know different, please let me know.

This is not necessarily a book about developments or 'evolutions' in person-centred theory. A 'tribe' is not simply a new idea (however elegant or however it might revolutionise our practice). Dave Mearns' 'configurations of self' and Margaret Warner's 'dissociative and fragile process' are important new ideas, but they are unlikely to spawn a new school of theory or a new strand of practice which will develop its own identity.

> I do not mean to be pejorative when I say 'simply'. I do not mean 'merely' — heaven knows that a genuine new idea is rare enough and hard to come by.

This section is not about new ideas in that narrow sense. It is here to present the reader with brief résumés of two approaches to therapy which clearly spring from the well of person-centred theory and practice. The reason they are not considered to be tribes differs in each case, although some might argue that each has a strong case to be included as a 'tribe'. They are, in alphabetical order:

Expressive Therapy is not considered by me to be a 'primary' training. I believe it is best considered as an advanced training or a progression from the basics once they are mastered. It also has no theoretical 'roots' in CCT or the PCA — expressive arts theory lies outside the realm of therapy, although it may be *associated* with personal development, maturity and mental good health through creativity. This means that expressive therapy is not now and never would be considered a 'tribe' of the PCA. It is modal application of the PCA. Most therapists (regardless of theoretical orientation) practise in a particular and somewhat constrained verbal mode. Expressive therapy applies given therapeutic theories to other modes of expression that are not necessarily dependent upon speaking — making marks, structures, music and movements.

Pre-Therapy is not usually viewed as a therapeutic approach in its own right (although I will actually argue that we might consider it to be). It is, in Prouty's own terms, a 'pre' therapeutic endeavour. In addition, there is no dedicated Pre-Therapy training available in the UK and, as we go to press, it does not form a significant element in any professional training programme that we know of. This means that Pre-Therapy could soon become a 'tribe', in the parochial terms of this book, should its practitioners demonstrate that it is a therapeutic approach in its own right and clinical-level Pre-Therapy training is provided in the UK.

In this chapter I aim to provide a 'taster', an 'in a nutshell' answer to the frequently-asked question: 'What exactly *is* Expressive therapy/Pre-Therapy?' The idea is to provide the briefest of introductions so that the interested reader can follow-up either by reading a key text introducing the approach or by seeking out brief training opportunities or workshops. You will not find comprehensive or in-depth coverage here, just summaries and signposts.

Expressive Therapy
Even as I wrote that sub-heading, I toyed with the idea of using the term 'Expressive *Therapies*' — plural — to indicate that there is not just *one* expressive therapy. In this country, there are many idiosyncratic ways of incorporating the use of the expressive arts into person-centred practice. A definition of an expressive therapy is 'the application of creative/expressive arts to therapeutic relationships, whether with individuals or with groups'. The theoretical orientation of the practitioner will determine exactly how the creative/expressive art mode will be translated and applied in the therapeutic situation. A crude example might be that in a person-centred setting, a client would be non-directively helped or facilitated to understand any meaning in their art-work. In a psychodynamic setting, the client's art-work will be interpreted by the therapist.

Although this example implies an expressive art approach that yields a product (like a painting, sculpture, collage or piece of writing), it still applies to, for example, voice work, drama or movement.

There has been a growth in expressive therapy associated with the Person-Centred Approach over the past 15 years and this has led to the careful exploration of the position of expressive therapies in relation to classical Client-Centred Therapy. To summarise the points of debate:

1. Does the application of creative/expressive arts methods imply that Rogers' six conditions are necessary but not sufficient, i.e. in need of supplementation with creative techniques?
2. Are arts modes simply methods of communication, helping

Paul Wilkins (person-centred psychodrama) and Tony Merry debated some of these points in 1994: see Wilkins, P. (1994). 'Can Psychodrama be Person-

access essentially the same material but through non-verbal channels? Is symbolisation of experience accessible (or maybe *better* accessible) through non-verbal modes of expression, like movement, painting, sculpture? Do non-verbal modes of experiencing and expression complement, add to and amplify verbal expressions?

3. Many theorists across several therapeutic approaches testify to the health-promoting characteristics of creativity. In the PCA, expressive therapy theory generally suggests that creativity is an essential feature of the human actualising tendency.

4. Since Client/Person-Centred Therapy is holistic, some argue that only when the client is offered a range of expressive possibilities (music, movement, painting, sculpting, etc.), not just the verbal, can we claim truly to be working with the whole person.

5. Are artistic creative methods better at working with edge-of-awareness material than 'traditional' verbal methods?

5. Can the offering of creative/expressive arts methods be done in such a way as to honour the non-directive principle of classical CCT practice?

In the UK, readers are most likely to come across the published work of Natalie Rogers and Liesl Silverstone in relation to creative/expressive approaches and the PCA, although there have been many individuals who have ploughed their own furrows over the years; adapting and applying PCA theory and practice to art therapy.

Natalie Rogers developed her expressive therapy approach in the early 1980s. Her approach is known as *person-centered expressive therapy* and incorporates a range of expressive arts modes in what she calls the Creative Connection (Rogers, N., 2000). This is the opening up of an inner core of experiencing through creative self-expression. Movement, music, voice work, sculpture, painting and writing are all integrated into a developmental therapeutic approach which draws on shamanic practice.

Natalie Rogers suggests that a mental life exclusively governed by verbal, cognitive processes is unhealthy and unfulfilling. Emancipation of the creative aspects of self is the key to full healthy functioning. She also argues that 'edge-of-awareness material', especially organismic needs not admitted to awareness (she uses the Jungian term *shadow*), are better accessed by expressive arts methods — and are then possibly less threatening.

Centred?' *Person-Centred Practice, 2* (2): 14–18; and Merry, T. (1994). Editorial. *Person-Centred Practice, 2* (1): 1–4. Both reprinted in T. Merry (2000)(ed.) *Person-Centred Practice: The BAPCA Reader.* Ross-on-Wye: PCCS Books. Coverage of other elements can be found in Rogers, N. (2000). *Creative Connection: Expressive arts as healing.* Ross-on-Wye: PCCS Books; and Silverstone, L. (1997). *Art Therapy The Person-Centred Way.* 2nd Edn. London: Jessica Kingsley.

Rogers, N. (2000). *Creative Connection: Expressive arts as healing.* Ross-on-Wye: PCCS Books.

More information about person-centred expressive therapy and Natalie Rogers' work can be obtained by visiting <www.nrogers.com>.

Carl Rogers' six 'necessary and sufficient conditions' for therapeutic personality change are listed in Chapter 1, pp. 5–6, this volume.

Silverstone, L. (1997). *Art Therapy The Person-Centred Way.* 2nd Edn. London: Jessica Kingsley.

More information about Liesl Silverstone's work can be viewed on <www.person-centred-art-therapy.com>.

Rogers, C.R. (1957). 'The necessary and sufficient conditions for therapeutic personality change.' *J. Consulting Psychology.*
Rogers, C.R. (1959). 'A theory of therapy, personality and interpersonal relationships as developed in the client-centred framework.' In S. Koch (ed.) *Psychology: A Study of a Science.* New York: McGraw-Hill, pp. 184–256. Abridged and reprinted in H. Kirschenbaum and V.L. Henderson (eds.) (1990). *The Carl Rogers Reader.* London: Constable, pp. 236–57.

It's difficult to imagine a psychotherapy approach which does not have psychological contact as a prerequisite. It is possible that some transpersonal approaches might have a very different view of what constitutes contact, but therapeutic change without some sort of contact between practitioner and client is hard to imagine.

There is not enough space here to evaluate the relationship of Natalie Rogers' work to classical CCT. Suffice to say that it is founded on Carl Rogers' therapeutic conditions and is integrative in nature. Although much of the method is client-self-directed, there is tension with the non-directive principle since the therapist *does* make process suggestions as therapy progresses.

Liesl Silverstone, based in the UK, has developed her own variant of person-centred art therapy (Silverstone, 1997). The underpinning philosophy is humanistic and creative-holistic, in that Silverstone also argues that the human creative core is a sort of healing antidote to the constrained cognitive processes typical of western culture. She advocates the person-centred notion of *integration* of verbal and non-verbal, the cognitive and the affective, rather than suggesting that one form of processing is better than another. She also points (as does Natalie Rogers) to the durability of some of the products of art therapy work, which clients can keep and continue to use in therapy long after the session in which the original work was done.

In positioning her variation of person-centred art therapy, Liesl Silverstone emphasises the non-directive nature of her process, and contrasts it with the interpretation required in traditional Freudian-informed art therapy.

Pre-Therapy

American psychologist Garry Prouty first published his ideas in the 1970s, although he had been gestating them for over ten years before that. Prouty's work turns the spotlight on Carl Rogers' first therapeutic condition, namely *psychological contact* (Rogers, 1957). It is no exaggeration to say that unless psychological contact with the client is made, therapeutic change cannot take place. In his original work (Rogers, 1957, 1959), Rogers suggested that psychological contact is a prerequisite for the other therapeutic conditions or possibly a conduit through which they can flow. Prouty reminded therapists that this cannot be taken for granted.

Garry Prouty reiterates Rogers' position that in order for psychotherapy to take place psychological contact *must* be established. This is particularly important with those clients who have their ability to establish and maintain psychological contact with another human being impaired by illness or injury, organic or psychological. Prouty challenges the view that psychological contact is a binary on-off affair — we are either in contact or we are not. His theory involves three types of contact: contact with self, contact with the environment and social contact (or contact with others). I have described this elsewhere (Wyatt and Sanders, 2002) as a *cascade* of contact, with the whole process being critically impaired if an element is missing. So, the internal economy of contact between self and experience is as important as contact between self and other, before therapy can be effective.

Prouty (Prouty, Van Werde and Pörtner, 2002) and his associates explain how contact can break down (and can be re-established) in various psychotic symptoms such as hallucination. They postulate that, under certain circumstances, a combination of internal and external experiential isolation causes pathological withdrawal. The person becomes 'pre-expressive', by which Prouty means that underlying the symptoms of autism, psychosis, brain damage, or whatever, 'there is somebody in there' (Prouty, 1998). Pre-Therapy, then, according to Prouty, 'points at the concrete' re-establishing the connection between sensation, experience and self — isolation is reduced and a bridge is built over the gulf of contact-impairment.

The therapeutic method of Pre-Therapy is deceptively simple. In practical terms it is a continual re-presentation of elements of shared reality. This encourages contact with self, reality and others. Prouty describes the elements of Pre-Therapy as follows:
• Contact Functions (the client's process)
• Contact Reflections (the therapist's responses)
• Contact Behaviours (the client's behaviour)

Contact Functions
• Reality Contact (awareness of the 'world', specifically people, places, things and events)
• Affective Contact (awareness of moods, feelings and emotions)
• Communicative Contact (symbolisation of world and affect to others — using words or sentences)

Contact Reflections
• *Situational* Reflections (SR) Reflecting aspects of the shared environment.
• *Facial* Reflections (FR) Reflecting verbally or by 'mimicking' the facial expressions of the client.
• *Body* Reflections (BR) Reflecting, verbally or posturally, the gestures, movement and postures of the client.
• *Word-for-word* Reflections (WWR) Repeating back what the client says word for word.
• *Reiterative* Reflections (RR) Remaking contact by repetition of

Wyatt, G. and Sanders, P. (2001). *Rogers' Therapeutic Conditions. Volume 4: Contact and Perception.* Ross-on-Wye: PCCS Books.

Prouty, G., Van Werde, D. and Pörtner, M. (2002). *Pre-Therapy: Reaching contact-impaired clients.* Ross-on-Wye: PCCS Books.

Prouty, G. (1998). 'Pre-Therapy and the Pre-Expressive Self.' *Person-Centred Practice, 6* (2): 80–8. Reprinted in T. Merry (2000)(ed.) *Person-Centred Practice: The BAPCA Reader.* Ross-on-Wye: PCCS Books, pp. 68–76.

This is a huge understatement. I feel obliged to point out that without *at least* reading one of the references below, it is simply impossible to get even the slightest flavour of what Pre-Therapy is all about. The best introduction to Prouty's work is Prouty, G., Van Werde, D. and Pörtner, M. (2002). *Pre-Therapy: Reaching contact-impaired clients.* Ross-on-Wye: PCCS Books.

A Brief summary of Pre-Therapy can be found in Mearns, D. (2003). *Developing Person-Centred Counselling.* 2nd edition. London: Sage.
My personal recommendation is that anyone interested in Pre-Therapy should attend a workshop, preferably run by Garry Prouty or one of his associates. Dion Van Werde runs workshops in the UK from time to time.

For more information visit http:// web.tiscali.it/no-redirect-tiscali/ Pretherapy/

previous reflections that showed an effect.

Pre-Therapy has significant implications for therapy theory and practice:
1. Therapists should no longer gratuitously assume that psychological contact is a 'given'.
2. Psychological contact may be viewed as existing in a range of degrees, although there is a logical cut-off point where a person is out of contact and pre-expressive.
3. Therapists now have a strategy for being with a wide range of contact-impaired clients, including those suffering from:
    (i) psychotic symptoms
    (ii) dissociation and depersonalisation
    (iii) dementia, including degenerative brain disease
    (iv) learning disabilities
    (v) brain damage

When contact is restored, the therapist may then build a relationship with the client to help with a range of problems from restoring everyday personal functioning through to psychotherapy.

Training

At one stage in the preparation of this book, I thought it would be a good idea to point readers in the direction of training opportunities in the approaches described herein. It soon became clear that it was not possible to do this for a number of reasons. First, authors were reticent when it came to recommending particular institutions, lest anyone think they might be responsible for the quality of the training. Second, whenever such a list is compiled, it is immediately out of date. New courses are commissioned and occasionally established ones disappear. Third, training is always a personal choice.

In the spirit of the latter point, I thought it might be more helpful to make some general points on choosing training:
1. Before you embark on professional (diploma) or masters training, be sure you know what theoretical orientation you want to be trained in (including, if you decide upon a 'person-centred' training, the 'tribe' of the approach that best fits you).
2. Find out about the course methods, i.e. whether the course has a fixed timetable, lectures, etc. and who sets and assesses the assignments. Person-centred training should follow person-centred methods, i.e. be student-centred, with the students' learning managed by the students themselves.

It is a tricky line to tread without becoming patronising and/or banal with this 'advice'. It is nevertheless surprising how many people do not realise that they can choose and since counselling training is costly in terms of time, personal commitment and money, it is no less than essential to make an informed decision.

We hope that one of the consequences of reading this book will be that prospective students will be more clear about the type of therapist they want to become, and so stand a better chance of accessing the type of training that will best suit their needs.

We acknowledge that despite the best intentions of the staff, institutions and validating bodies increasingly insist upon instructional modes of learning and tutor-led or even external assessment. Whichever way you look at it these methods are not person-centred. Prospective students, however, may have little or no choice in the area where they live. For more information on learning to be a counsellor, the following books might help:

3. If at all possible, resist the temptation to simply go to the college or institute closest to where you live. For many people this is, of course, the only option.

4. Talk to the tutors on the telephone if possible, insist on an interview. It is your opportunity to interview the staff — do they have experience and qualifications in the approach which is being trained? Look at the facilities — not just the training rooms, but also the library, do they take relevant journals, for example?

5. Is the course accredited or validated by the BACP or a university or the UKCP?

6. If possible, meet with, and talk to, current or previous trainees for an inside opinion on the course.

7. Wherever you decide to go, you will be spending two years or so as a student, forging learning relationships with the staff and fellow students. Regardless of the reputation of the institution, does it feel like the right place for you?

In summary, the best practice is to research the training opportunities thoroughly. Get information from a wide variety of sources. The internet is the best source of up-to-date information from professional bodies and special interest organisations:

• British Association for Counselling and Psychotherapy:
    http://www.bacp.co.uk

• Independent Practitioners' Network:
    http://ipnosis.postle.net/pages/princproc.htm

• British Association for the Person-Centred Approach:
    http://www.bapca.org.uk

• Focusing Institute:
    http://www.focusing.org

• United Kingdom Council for Psychotherapy:
    http://www.psychotherapy.org.uk

The following are books for students or prospective students and contain information about the *process* of person-centred training:

• Buchanan, L. and Hughes, R. (2000). *Experiences of Person-Centred Counselling Training: A compendium of case studies to assist prospective applicants.* Ross-on-Wye: PCCS Books.

• Merry, T. (2002). *Learning and Being in Person-Centred Counselling.* 2nd edition. Ross-on-Wye: PCCS Books.

• Sanders, P. (2003). *Step in to Study Counselling.* 2nd edition. Ross-on-Wye: PCCS Books.

Although written for trainers, this is a very informative book if you can get hold of a copy from a library:
Mearns, D. (1997). *Person-Centred Counselling Training.* London: Sage.

history of cct and the pca: events, dates and ideas

pete sanders

1

Introduction

The first national BAPCA conference held at Durham in September 2002 was titled 'Dialogues' and featured dialogues between 'classical' Client-Centred Therapy (CCT), Gendlin's 'Focusing', and existential therapies. Those of you embarking on training in CCT or Person-Centred Therapy (PCT) might wonder what it was all about. You may think that the term 'Client-Centred Therapy' was dropped many years ago and that now everyone knows that there is one unitary (if fairly broad) 'school' of Person-Centred Therapy. It is more complicated than that. I hope you will find a quick tour of the history of events and ideas in the tradition of CCT and PCT will not only bring you up to date regarding the strands of thinking in the approach (the identities of the 'tribes' of the person-centred 'nation'), but also help you understand person-centred theory in general. It might also help you identify the subtle variations of person-centred theory as taught in your own training and help you decide to which tribe you wish to belong (or if at all).

An ongoing debate regarding the range of approaches claiming to be 'person-centred' has been bubbling away for many years in books, journals, unpublished papers, seminars, cafes, and hotel bars at international conferences. This continued with renewed vigour in the 2003 Person-Centred and Experiential Psychotherapies Conference at Egmond aan Zee in the Netherlands in July 2003.

In this chapter I will try to outline the debate as a backdrop to, or even the *raison d'être* of, this book. Those of you finishing a certificate in counselling or just starting a diploma might think that the history of Client-Centred Therapy and the Person-Centred Approach is fairly simple and straightforward, and that it might go something like this:

Carl Rogers thought up the basic idea in the 1940s, called it 'client-centred' to shift the emphasis of psychotherapy from an expert therapist-based affair to an enterprise in which the patient (Rogers, importantly, called this person the 'client') and their

BAPCA — The British Association for the Person-Centred Approach

As noted in the introduction to this book on page i, the terms are taken from Margaret Warner's (2000) paper: 'Person-centered Psychotherapy: One Nation, Many Tribes.' *Person-Centered Journal 7* (1), pp. 28–39.

Person-Centered and Experiential (PCE) conference sponsored for the first time by the new World Association for Person-Centered and Experiential Psychotherapy and Counseling (WAPCEPC).

Each of the other contributors to this book also give accounts of the history of the approach they are representing and where it intersects with the history of CCT and the PCA. In particular, Nick Baker on page 68 presents Hart's (1970) account of the phases of development of CCT and the PCA.
Hart, J.T. (1970). 'The Development of Client-Centred Therapy.' In J.T. Hart and T.M. Tomlinson (eds.) *New Directions in Client-Centered Therapy.* Boston: Houghton Mifflin, pp. 3–21

needs were put at the centre. His ideas culminated in his 'necessary and sufficient conditions' writings in 1957 and 1959. Then after moving to California in the 1960s he changed the name of the therapy to 'person-centred' to further de-emphasise the formal medical/clinical nature of the proceedings, restoring more qualities of equality and person-hood to the helping relationship. Rogers then went on to invent encounter groups and work towards world peace until his death in the mid-eighties. The end.

Kirschenbaum, H. (1979). *On Becoming Carl Rogers.* New York: Delacorte.
Thorne, B. (2003). *Carl Rogers.* 2nd Edition. London: Sage.

Barrett-Lennard, G.T. (1998). *Carl Rogers' Helping System: Journey and Substance.* London: Sage. In his substantial book, Barrett-Lennard not only gives an account of the history of ideas in CCT/PCA, but also embeds them in the social and political context of the US at the time. Anyone wanting to understand the PCA and Rogers' work in its social and historical context would do well to read this book.

In particular, Rogers was influenced by the developments emanating from the Pennsylvania School of Social Work and Philadelphia Child Guidance Clinic. Here the work of Otto Rank (a psychoanalyst) and his student Jessie Taft caught Rogers' attention. Taft's 1937 book, *The Dynamics of Therapy in a Controlled Relationship* is cited by Rogers several times in his early work, up to *Client-Centered Therapy* (1951), Boston: Houghton Mifflin.

Rogers, C.R. (1939). *The Clinical Treatment of the Problem Child.* New York: Houghton Mifflin.

When deliberately abbreviated like this, I am sure that all readers will realise that there is much more to the story. At the personal level in Rogers' life, the gaps can be filled by reading a decent biography of Rogers (e.g. Kirschenbaum, 1979; Thorne, 2003). In this chapter my aim is to fill in some of the gaps in the history of the development of the ideas. This is something of a tall order, given the space available, but hopefully it will be a good foundation for your understanding of the different ways the person-centred approach to therapy has differentiated and diverged rather like a piece of string: first being woven from, then fraying into different strands. Other books (e.g. Barrett-Lennard, 1998) give a much fuller account.

Non-Directive Therapy

In 1928, aged 26, Carl Rogers joined the Child Study Department of the Rochester Society for the Prevention of Cruelty to Children. During his time there he moved away from the psychometric measuring approach of professional psychology and became more interested in the practical approach to helping children and parents practised by social workers.

He published his first book in 1939: *The Clinical Treatment of the Problem Child.* Even in this early book, the seeds of his later work are clearly evident. He realised that a good relationship with the parents of the problem child was one of the keys to success and he listed the factors that he found to be important:

1. It only works with parents who want to be helped.
2. The *relationship* between the helper and the parent is the 'essential feature . . . The worker endeavours to provide an atmosphere in which the parent can come freely to experience and realise his own attitudes . . .'
3. The effect on the parent is to help clarify their feelings and bring about self-acceptance.
4. It relies on the parents themselves to independently arrive at their own parenting solutions.

5. Its essence is one of non-interference.
6. It relies on the '. . . individual's own tendency toward growth . . .'

In 1939 Rogers moved to Ohio State University as a full professor. In the following year he gave a talk at the University of Minnesota titled 'Newer concepts in psychotherapy' that caused something of a stir and Rogers knew he was on to something. Rogers' second book *Counseling and Psychotherapy: Newer concepts in practice*, was published in 1942. In it he presented, for the first time ever, the verbatim transcripts of real therapy sessions. The book even included a transcript of an entire eight-session case — the case of Herbert Bryan — complete with notes and analysis. This was nothing short of a revolution in the study and understanding of the previously mysterious world of psychotherapy.

In addition to his revolutionary use of the new technology of wax-disc recordings, Rogers continued to draw together further elements of the framework of what he was soon to call *non-directive therapy*. The title emphasised the key feature that distinguished it from other therapeutic approaches, namely the reliance on the client's own self-directed growth processes rather than the expertness of the therapist. The client was their own expert.

It is important to appreciate that these ideas did not descend upon Rogers out of the blue. He was renowned as an integrator of ideas, taking influences from many leading-edge theorists and practitioners (e.g. Otto Rank and Jessie Taft, above, but also Karen Horney) and from his early graduate students (e.g. Richard Hogan (threat and defence) and most notably Stanley Standal (UPR)).

University of Chicago — Client-Centered Therapy

Rogers moved to the University of Chicago in 1945 where he set up the influential Counseling Center. He gathered around him a group of staff all of whom have been extremely influential either in association with Rogers or in their own right. This group included Virginia Axline, Godfrey Barrett-Lennard, Eugene Gendlin, Thomas Gordon, Nathaniel Raskin, Julius Seeman, John Shlien and Fred Zimring. Later generations of Counseling Center staff included Barbara Brodley and Ned Gaylin.

In 1948 Nat Raskin described the development of the University of Chicago Counseling Center approach under Rogers in his paper *The development of non-directive therapy*, but within a couple of years Rogers changed the name of the approach to *Client-Centred*

This presentation, given on 11 December 1940, is seen by some as the birth of Client-Centred Therapy.

Rogers, C.R. (1942). *Counseling and Psychotherapy: Newer concepts in practice.* Boston: Houghton Mifflin.

Rank, O. (1945). *Will Therapy.* New York: Knopf.
Taft, J. (1937). *The Dynamics of Therapy in a Controlled Relationship.* New York: Macmillan.
Horney, K. (1942). *Self Analysis.* New York: Norton.
Hogan's unpublished 1948 PhD thesis figured strongly in Rogers' formulation of propositions XVI and XVII (Rogers, C.R. (1951). *Client-Centered Therapy.* Boston: Houghton Mifflin, pp. 516–7). Standal, another of Rogers' PhD students, contributed the concept of Unconditional Positive Regard to CCT in his unpublished 1954 thesis. According to Barrett-Lennard, Rogers first used the term UPR in 1956. (Barrett-Lennard, G.T. (1998). *Carl Rogers' Helping System: Journey and substance.* London: Sage, p. 65.) Standal's thesis is evaluated in Moon, K., Rice, B. and Schneider, C. (2001). 'Stanley W. Standal and the Need for Positive Regard.' In J.D.Bozarth and P.Wilkins (eds.) *Rogers' Therapeutic Conditions: Vol. 1. Unconditional Positive Regard.* Ross-on-Wye: PCCS Books, pp. 19–34.

Raskin, N.J. (1948). 'The development of non-directive therapy.' *Journal of Consulting Psychology* (12): 92–110.

Rogers, C.R. (1951). *Client-Centered Therapy: Its current practice, implications and theory.* Boston: Houghton Mifflin.

Non-psychologists finding the language of *Client-Centered Therapy* difficult, may have even more difficulty finding a 'translation' into more everyday English. Barrett-Lennard's 1998 book (*Carl Rogers' Helping System: Journey and Substance.* London: Sage) might be manageable, but for an accessible introduction try Merry, T. (2002). *Learning and Being in Person-Centred Therapy.* Ross-on-Wye: PCCS Books. It covers the 19 propositions in everyday language.

Phenomenology is a philosophical approach in which understanding of the world is rooted in the immediate experience of the individual (contrasted with an understanding of the world based on religious doctrine or scientific analysis). Edmund Husserl (1859–1938) is credited with developing contemporary phenomenology. Each individual perceives events and gives them meaning — in order to understand the behaviour of another, we need to understand the meanings *she* gives to events. Hence Rogers proposed *empathy* as a core factor in effective therapy (contrasted with the behaviourists' search for meaning in external, objective, categories of events and the psychoanalysts' search for meaning in Freud's categories of symbols to allow expert analysis by the therapist).

Existentialism is explained more fully in Mick Cooper's Chapter 5, this volume.

Raskin, N.J. (1949). 'The development of the "parallel studies" project.' *Journal of Counseling Psychology,* 13: 206–19.
Seeman, J. and Raskin, N. J. (1953). 'Research perspectives in client-centered therapy.' In H.O. Mowrer (ed.) *Psychotherapy: Theory and Research.* New York: Ronald Press.
Rogers, C.R. and Dymond, R.F. (1954). *Psychotherapy and Personality Change.* Chicago: University of Chicago Press.

Therapy. The approach was announced and explained in the comprehensive, impressive 1951 volume *Client-Centered Therapy: Its current practice, implications and theory.* This book not only described the theory and practice of therapy, but it also had a theory of personality and applications of Client-Centred Therapy principles in the fields of play therapy, group therapy, teaching and counsellor education. It was very well received then, and is still considered by many to be the best starting-point for understanding this approach. It presents a problem for the non-psychologist reader in that it was written (as was entirely appropriate for its intended readership) in the language of 1950s academic psychology. This can be pretty daunting (or downright impenetrable) without some form of translation or very patient reading. Nevertheless, it was, and remains, a formidable and revolutionary text.

Chapter 11 of this work included Rogers' 19 propositions which represent the first systematic outline of his theory of personality, motivation and change. Whether Rogers was influenced by *phenomenology* as a philosophy (or indeed ever read Husserl) at this stage in his theorising remains a moot point, but he made repeated references to the 'phenomenal field' and his opening proposition 'Every individual exists in a continually changing world of experience of which he is the center' (1951, p. 483) leaves little in doubt. It was not until the late fifties and early sixties that Rogers more formally acknowledged phenomenology and *existentialism.*

During the 1950s, the University of Chicago was definitely the place to be. Rogers developed the first ever research programme to investigate the effectiveness of psychotherapy. He and his team attracted large grants and a huge amount of research was done, not least in the area of trying to develop appropriate methods of study, since no one had attempted to evaluate psychotherapy in such a systematic way before. The team published their results widely (see, for example, Raskin, 1949; Seeman and Raskin, 1953; and Rogers and Dymond, 1954) and the first body of empirical research into psychotherapy was, as a consequence, almost entirely client-centred, and one of the principle distinguishing features of the approach was its inherently *non-directive* nature. This first flush of research was almost universally enthusiastically received by the therapeutic community.

Kirschenbaum noted:

> When Rogers first entertained the idea of undertaking research in psychotherapy, there were no precedents for him to follow.

. . . Recording or transcribing actual interviews was unheard of. One had only the psychotherapist's word as to whether a particular method was effective or not . . . It was, indeed, to use Rogers' phrase 'an art which made a pretense of being a science'. (1979, p. 205)

Another feature of the Chicago team was that Rogers had deliberately made it as egalitarian as possible with a flat management structure. John Shlien, in a private conversation, recalled his astonishment, when arriving at his first faculty meeting, to find Carl Rogers writing the entire staff's salary (with his own at the top) on the chalkboard and asking the assembled staff whether everyone was happy with the rates of pay and the differentials between each grade. Organising the faculty in such a way had a profound, indeed, life-long impact on many of the members of staff. New ideas in theory and research were circulated as *University of Chicago Counseling Center Discussion Papers*, a system formalised by Jack Butler. Many of the theory developments and key research projects which advanced Client-Centred Therapy can be found in the discussion papers as germs of ideas. The academic environment was vibrant and everyone was encouraged to share, co-operate and support.

Whilst at Chicago, Rogers read, 'not only read but really studied' (*ibid.*) the work of psychologists, of Karl Marx and, of particular interest here, existential writers Kierkegaard and Sartre. Of Kierkegaard he wrote 'Though Kierkegaard lived one hundred years ago, I cannot help but think of him as a sensitive and highly perceptive friend. I think this paper shows my indebtedness to him . . .' (Rogers, 1961, pp. 199–200). In the late 1950s, Rogers began using Kierkegaard's phrase 'to be the self one truly is' and adopted Kierkergaard's 'this is true for me but I realise it may not be true for a lot of other people' (Rogers and Russell, 2002, p. 170) style of writing in *On Becoming a Person*. It seems that during this time, Rogers' reading 'caught up' with his earlier ideas. His theorising to date had distinct touches of existentialism and phenomenology, but now he was more systematically integrating some strands of these traditions.

The work of Rogers and the team at Chicago culminated in his seminal 'necessary and sufficient conditions' works published in 1957 in the *Journal of Consulting Psychology,* and in the prestigious collection *Psychology: A study of a science* edited by Sigmund Koch in 1959. Gill Wyatt distinguished between the two versions by putting the 1957 additional wording in italics.

Kirschenbaum, H. (1979). *On Becoming Carl Rogers.* New York: Delacorte.

The interested reader will have difficulty in getting hold of University of Chicago Counseling Center Discussion Papers. They are kept jointly by the Person-Centered Archive, kept by Alberto Segrera at the Universidad Iberoamericana, Mexico and in Chicago, USA, by the ex staff of the now-disbanded Counseling Center.

Ibid.

Rogers, C.R. (1961). *On Becoming a Person: A therapist's view of psychotherapy.* Boston: Houghton Mifflin. This book is peppered with existential influences including the Kierkegaard phrase, in several places.

Rogers, C.R. and Russell, D.E. (2002). *Carl Rogers The Quiet Revolutionary: An oral history.* Roseville, CA: Penmarin Books.

Rogers, C.R. (1957). 'The necessary and sufficient conditions for therapeutic personality change.' *J. Consulting Psychology.*
Rogers, C.R. (1959). 'A theory of therapy, personality and interpersonal relationships as developed in the client-centred framework.' In S. Koch (ed.) *Psychology: A Study of a Science.* New York: McGraw-Hill, pp. 184–256. Abridged and reprinted in H. Kirschenbaum and V.L. Henderson (eds.) (1990). *The Carl Rogers Reader.* London: Constable, pp. 236–57.

There has been much speculation over the importance of the slight variations in the wording between the two papers — is one a development of the other? Things are not helped when we discover that the 1959 chapter was actually *written before* the 1957 paper (in 1954), but got held up in the book publication process. Rogers put the conditions in the form of a hypothesis that *if* these conditions were present *then* the client would improve. This 'if-then' formulation was the sort of hypothesis that research could put to the test.

Wyatt, G. (2001). *Rogers' Therapeutic Conditions. Volume 1: Congruence.* Ross-on-Wye: PCCS Books.

Rogers considered his chapter in the Koch volume (above) to be the best, most complete and comprehensive formulation of his theory — until he revised it in the light of experience or research. However, he never did revise the theory to any notable extent. He might have extended it or elaborated it in the sense of considering some areas in more detail, but there were never changes in the basic tenets.
Readers will have difficulty in obtaining the complete text of the 1959 chapter, although an incomplete version appears in H. Kirschenbaum and V.L. Henderson (eds.) (1990). *The Carl Rogers Reader.* London: Constable, pp. 236–57. The 1957 paper also appears in this collection.

Positivism is a theory of knowledge which takes into account only scientifically determined data and excludes metaphysical sources of understanding of the nature of things. More narrowly it asserts that the validity of knowledge is based on *experimental* science.

1. That two persons are in (*psychological)* contact.
2. That the first person, whom we shall term the client, is in a state of incongruence, being vulnerable, or anxious.
3. That the second person, whom we shall term the therapist, is congruent (*or integrated*) in the relationship.
4. That the therapist is experiencing unconditional positive regard toward the client.
5. That the therapist is experiencing an empathic understanding of the client's internal frame of reference (*and endeavours to communicate this to the client*).
6. That the client perceives, at least to a minimal degree, conditions 4 and 5, the unconditional positive regard of the therapist for him, and the empathic understanding of the therapist. (*The communication to the client of the therapist's empathic understanding and unconditional positive regard is to a minimal degree achieved*).
   (No other conditions are necessary. If these six conditions exist, and continue over a period of time, this is sufficient. The process of constructive personality change will follow (Rogers, 1957).) (Wyatt, 2001.)

This statement was one of the pivotal writings in psychotherapy in the second half of the twentieth century. Rogers had deliberately set about demystifying, decoding and operationalising those aspects of a human relationship which might facilitate constructive personality change. It was nothing less than revolutionary for a number of reasons:

1. It uncovered the previously arcane world of therapy — exposing it to public scrutiny.
2. It made the relationship between therapist and client the agent for change.
3. It presented the factors required for change as an 'if–then' predictive hypothesis, i.e. *if* such and such is present, *then* such and such will happen.
4. It made the whole area of psychotherapy amenable (for the first time) to *positivist* research; some thought this to be a mistake.
5. It declared that *no other conditions are necessary.* This is a direct challenge to approaches based on the theoretical knowledge or expertise of the therapist, or those predicated on the accurate diagnosis of symptoms and the application of targeted techniques.
6. It was, and still is, deeply counter-cultural, since in the pseudo-medical-scientific world of psychotherapy it was (and still is by many) seen as imperative to mimic medical science wherein

the knowledge, expertise and scientific application of skilled techniques are the hallmarks of 'quality'.

When combined with Rogers' previous statements on non-directivity and motivation (the healing potential of the actualising tendency), and personality (the idea that incongruence between the self-concept and experience causes psychological tension), the revolution was complete, since Rogers clearly made the client the locus of the healing process, including the nature and direction of change. The client was at the centre of a self-directed process facilitated by another (the therapist) and experts were effectively written out. This did not go down too well in most circles in the psychological therapies. This challenge to psychological therapies was all the more threatening because the team at Chicago were producing work at a prodigious rate. Research was continuing on many fronts and the Counseling Center attracted funding and had recruited research specialists such as Jules Seeman to help develop and validate new methodologies for the emerging discipline of psychotherapy research.

At the height of the Chicago Counseling Center success, Rogers left to take up a new challenge at the University of Wisconsin in 1957. He was 'head hunted' and joined, uniquely, as professor in both psychology and psychiatry, and soon attracted substantial funding for research. He invited some of the Chicago Counseling Center team to join him and along with Charles Truax and others he undertook research at the Mendota State Hospital. Rogers wanted the research to silence those who criticised the Chicago research for being too small scale, or using clients whose symptoms were not 'severe'. In his own words (Rogers and Russell, 2002) it was to be 'the research to end all research'.

In brief, the aim of the study was to evaluate the hypothesis that the conditions proposed by Rogers would determine the outcome of therapy with people diagnosed with schizophrenia and confined to a state mental hospital. Simply put: if therapists provided high levels of the conditions the patients should improve more than if the therapists provided low levels of the conditions.

In order to anticipate imagined criticisms of the methodology and make it as perfect as possible, the design became overelaborate to the point of being practically unmanageable. Even though 'there were no precedents for him to follow' (Kirschenbaum, 1979, p. 205), the 'Wisconsin project', as it is sometimes referred to, is considered by some to be a heroic failure — overambitious and

When I say 'the revolution was complete', I mean that the sense of turning the world of psychotherapy upside-down was complete. Of course, no theory is complete, and CCT was/is no exception. In particular CCT was/is light on developmental theory. Rogers devoted less than a page in his 1959 chapter to 'Postulated characteristics of the human infant'. (Rogers, C.R. (1959). 'A theory of therapy, personality and interpersonal relationships as developed in the client-centred framework.' In S. Koch (ed.) *Psychology: A Study of Science*. New York: McGraw-Hill. Abridged and reprinted in H. Kirschenbaum and V.L. Henderson (eds.) (1990). *The Carl Rogers Reader.* London: Constable, pp. 236–57.) There, Rogers emphasises that human personality is a *process*, not a series of stages, phases or achievements. Recently, writers such as Margaret Warner have added to this brief early theory, see Warner, M.S. (2000). 'Person-Centred Therapy at the difficult edge: a developmentally based model of fragile and dissociated process.' In D. Mearns and B. Thorne *Person-Centred Therapy Today*. London: Sage, pp. 147–50.

Rogers invited Eugene Gendlin, Philippa Mathieu, Donald Kiesler and Joseph Hart to join him from Chicago. Charles Truax was a graduate student at Wisconsin when Rogers arrived.

Rogers, C.R. and Russell, D.E. (2002). *Carl Rogers The Quiet Revolutionary: An Oral History.* Roseville, CA: Penmarin Books.

The Wisconsin project method and results were finally written up, mainly by Rogers, after he left for California — see sidenote this chapter p. 8.

Kirschenbaum, H. (1979). *On Becoming Carl Rogers*. New York: Delacorte.

The positive points of the project include
• the development of counsellor rating scales by Truax,
• the use of Barrett-Lennard's Relationship Inventory to measure the client's perception of the relationship and
• a greater focus on the therapeutic role of congruence.

Rogers and colleagues final report of the project may be of interest to some readers. Although it is difficult to get hold of, it is not impossible (good training providers should have a copy, or get hold of it through interlibrary loans). **Rogers, C.R., Gendlin, E.T., Kiesler, D.J. and Truax, C.B. (1967).** *The Therapeutic Relationship And It's Impact: A study of psychotherapy with schizophrenics*. Madison: University of Wisconsin Press.

Rogers, C.R. (1961). *On Becoming a Person: A therapist's view of psychotherapy.* Boston: Houghton Mifflin. Chapter 7 pp. 125–59.

A *construct* is an idea, notion, *constructed* by the mind. A personal construct is a constructed notion about oneself.

Gendlin's contribution to the research project was significant: he was director of research, was the theoretical driving-force behind the development of the Experiencing Scale and wrote or co-wrote eight chapters of the final report.

Although there are disputes as to the detail of history, Gendlin and Rogers (see above) appeared to develop a simultaneous interest in the internal experience of the client during therapy. Whether one led and the other followed is of little importance now — Gendlin's thinking and writing on experiencing took it's own path. **Gendlin, E.T. (1962/97).** *Experiencing and the Creation of Meaning.* Second edition. New York: Free Press. Evanston, Illinois: Northwestern University Press, 1997. **Gendlin, E.T. (1974).** 'Client-centered and Experiential Psychotherapy.' In D.A. Wexler and L.N. Rice (eds.) *Innovations in Client-Centered Therapy.* New York: John Wiley, pp. 211–46.

flawed in its design and inconclusive in its results. Others thought that the whole effort was both groundbreaking *and* disappointing, it did have successes and leave a positive legacy. Whatever your position on the Wisconsin project (Rogers, Gendlin, Kiesler and Truax, 1967), it is universally seen as a great opportunity lost and a professional disaster.

It was during his time at Wisconsin, however, that Rogers worked most closely with Eugene Gendlin. Gendlin had been a student of Rogers and staff member at Chicago and Rogers had invited him to join the Wisconsin team. This continued association influenced the development of Client-Centred Therapy in important ways. Gendlin was developing his theory of experiencing, and Rogers was giving much thought to the process within the client during therapy. Although there are differing versions of history at this point, to begin with, it appears that Gendlin's ideas were seminal, and then followed a short phase in which each influenced the other. Rogers presented his ideas (in his 1957 address to the American Psychological Association upon the award of the Distinguished Scientific Contribution Award) as his emerging 'process conception of psychotherapy'. This later surfaced as Chapter 7 in *On Becoming a Person* (Rogers, 1961). Rogers presented a seven-stage process of change within the client along a series of loose dimensions such as openness to experience, positive self-regard, flexibility of personal *constructs* and greater emotional expressiveness. In summary the client moved from separateness to integration in structure and from rigidity to flexibility in internal process.

The Wisconsin project design required the measurement of movement in the client as well as the counsellor-provided conditions and Gendlin as research director of the project turned his attention to client process and its measurement. This represented but one strand of Gendlin's prodigious thinking on experiencing. He went on to develop an entire theory of human experiencing and how this intersected with therapeutic change. This was the first genuine new thinking from one of the Client-Centred Therapy group which grew up around Rogers in Chicago and after. Springing from a shared interest in what was happening in the experience of the client during the change process, Gendlin elaborated his theory of experiencing into a formal description of (a) the moments of change which occurred as the client contacted their present experiencing, and (b) the resultant change (Gendlin, 1962/97; 1974). He called this process 'Focusing'.

This work on how the client touches their inner stream of

experience in the present moment released a proverbial genie from the bottle. There was no getting it back. There were now two tribes (Focusing and Client-Centred Therapy) and soon there would be three as 'experiential' therapy was born along with the debates and disagreements which exercise the person-centred nation to this day. In the space of a few years from around 1958 to 1964 the original client-centred river had divided into three streams which would each become rivers in their own right, yet travelling in parallel, still linked to, and fed by, the same source.

Non-Directive Client-Centred Therapy (NDCCT)

The source continued to be refined by Rogers, but he added little new theory after the early 1960s. There was an increase in the influence of existential philosophy and Rogers continued to extend the application of the basic concepts to areas other than one-to-one psychotherapy, and there were changes in emphasis along the way, but no substantial new theory.

This 'tribe' is described and discussed by Tony Merry in Chapter 2.

Some of Rogers' students and colleagues from Chicago contributed to the refinement and subtle adaptation of the original client-centred theory. These included Jules Seeman (on personality integration and psychological health), Fred Zimring (on the application of cognitive theory to person-centred practice) and John Shlien (on the existential edge of internal congruence and consistency). Others developed wider applications of the ideas, most notably Thomas Gordon (Parent Effectiveness Training and Teacher Effectiveness Training).

Seeman, J. (1983). *Personality Integration.* New York: Human Sciences Press. Zimring, F.M. (1974). 'Theory and Practice of Client-Centered Therapy: A Cognitive View.' In D.A. Wexler and L.N. Rice (eds.) *Innovations in Client-Centered Therapy.* New York: John Wiley, pp. 117–37. Shlien, J.M. (2003). *To Lead an Honorable Life: Invitations to think about Client-Centered Therapy and the Person-Centered Approach.* Ross-on-Wye: PCCS Books.

Focusing

During and after the Wisconsin project, Eugene Gendlin continued to set his own course with Focusing, the practical application of his theory of experiencing. Gendlin was responsible for a piece of clear, original thinking when he unpacked the therapeutic process in the experience of the client. He looked at the course that successful therapy took and tried to describe the process. He believed that the same process happened in all cases where therapy was successful, even though it would be uniquely experienced and expressed by each client, and uniquely facilitated by each therapist. His attempt to write down the process as a formula or series of steps divided the client-centred community. The objections to Focusing included:

This 'tribe' is described and discussed by Campbell Purton in Chapter 3.

Gendlin, E.T. (1978/2003). *Focusing.* New York: Everest House. (New British edition, London: Rider, 2003.) Gendlin, E.T. (1996). *Focusing-oriented Psychotherapy.* New York: Guilford Press.

• Gendlin's description of this process in terms of six 'steps' was seen by the NDCCT therapists as a crucial move away from the non-directive dictum at the core of the approach, since it seemed that Gendlin was advocating *instructing* the client in the focusing steps and directing their progress through the steps.

- Making a description of a possible process into a general rule by saying that the steps were followed in all cases, albeit uniquely, was also deeply unpopular with some in the NDCCT community, since, in principle, it irons out the change process into a 'one size fits all', regardless of whether we all do it differently. The NDCCT therapists believed that individual clients' processes would each be unique *both* in the 'steps' of the process, if indeed there were any, *and* in the expression of the process.

Part of the mission of this book is to disentangle the polemical positions that have been taken up over the years. What is Focusing-Oriented Psychotherapy *really*, and what is its *real* relation to NDCCT? Campbell Purton's chapter will help us answer those questions.

Experiential psychotherapy

For some, Gendlin's descriptions of the process of experience opened a new door of possibilities. Rather than follow Gendlin and focusing, they took the idea of contacting the internal flow of experience and looked for interventions which may assist the client in accessing it. This was a much broader palette than focusing and soon became a river of its own, neither Focusing, nor client-centred. Experiential psychotherapy springs from Gendlin's experiential work, yet is rooted in the egalitarian, non-interpretative tradition of CCT with the client and their actualising tendency at the centre of the therapeutic process. The approach also sought to integrate ideas and methods which aim to put the client in contact with their flow of experience in the present. It distinguishes between directing the content of the client's world and assisting, guiding or directing the client's process in a collaborative manner. All of this smacked too much of diagnosis and application of discrete treatment methods for the NDCCT practitioners. For this reason some call their version of the approach *process experiential psychotherapy*.

It is difficult to pick out the most influential proponents of experiential psychotherapy, but Leslie Greenberg and his associates in North America made their mark in *Patterns of Change* published in 1984. In Europe, Germain Lietaer has been advocating and developing experiential therapy for over 20 years.

This 'tribe' is described and discussed by Nick Baker in Chapter 4.

Some readers may have come across the work of Alvin Mahrer in connection with the term 'experiential therapy'. Although he mentions Rogers and Gendlin as influences, Mahrer's work is very different from the experiential work covered in this chapter. Interested readers can find out more by visiting the website: http://www.cam.org/~howardg/mahrer02.html

In particular Leslie Greenberg and his associates, Laura North Rice and Robert Elliott have used the terms *process experiential, process directive and process guiding* in describing a therapeutic approach and nuances within it. This is covered by Nick Baker in Chapter 4.

Rice, L.N. and Greenberg, L.S. (1984). *Patterns of Change: Intensive analysis of psychotherapy process.* New York: Guilford Press.
Germain Lietaer's contribution is more fully covered by Nick Baker on pages 86–7, this volume.

Things fall apart in Wisconsin

Possibly Rogers' most popular and influential book *On Becoming a Person: A therapist's view of psychotherapy,* was compiled and published whilst he was at Wisconsin. It was a collection of over 20 papers which he drew together, edited and linked to present as a complete book. In it, Rogers hit just the right note: a balance between the personal and the professional/theoretical. The book was well received and proved tremendously popular amongst a very wide range of readers. There was plenty of theory and indeed, philosophy of both human nature and science, but what came through in the relaxed style of writing, was Rogers' personal involvement in the material. True to the title, Rogers the person was there. It was, uncharacteristically for psychology texts at the time, personally reflective and revealing.

The research at Mendota State Hospital, however, was not going well. Whatever developments in theory sprung from the discussions and association at the Wisconsin project, relationships between the members of the team were tense as the project lost steam and direction. Rogers believed that the problems arose because he 'failed to take the time and care needed to allow the Psychotherapy Research Group to become a truly group-centred, self-directing group' (Kirschenbaum, 1979, p. 281). Others in the group thought the basic problem was Rogers' lack of leadership — indeed by the time of the writing-up phase of the project Rogers had already gone. The tensions reached their final messy and tragic conclusions after Rogers had left for California in 1964.

Rogers was not having a happy time at the University of Wisconsin either, which he found too rigid and wedded to a view of academic credibility based almost entirely on passing exams and failing those who did not make the grade. Rogers preferred to encourage individual creative thinking in a much more relaxed environment. He did not favour relaxing the academic standards, but began to believe that the narrow academic tramlines within which the graduate students were expected to keep, strangled original thought and creative learning. He sent memos to the academic hierarchy and the exchanges became increasingly ill-tempered as Rogers wrote papers on his views on the best conditions for graduate education. He resigned from the University to take up a position at the Western Behavioral Sciences Institute (which he earlier had a hand in founding) to work with his old friend and former student from Chicago, Richard Farson.

Rogers, C.R. (1961). *On Becoming a Person: A therapist's view of psychotherapy.* Boston: Houghton Mifflin.

Rogers' keenness to test out his ideas away from the middle-class world of academia in the University of Chicago, whilst admirable in itself, was not enough to maintain the project in all its necessary thoroughness against the myriad of other pressures. These were, most notably, the decision of the Project team to give up much of their control over which patients were to be involved in the interviews and the disappearance of crucial data. In addition, the researchers, who included Gendlin, were not able to function effectively as a team, and with Rogers later moving out to the Californian coast, the team became fractured. The best account of Rogers' troubled time in Wisconsin can be found in Kirschenbaum, H. (1979). *On Becoming Carl Rogers.* New York: Delacorte.

This line of thinking eventually resulted in the publication of *Freedom to Learn: A view of what education might become.* Columbus, Ohio: Charles E. Merrill, in 1969.

Rogers had also spent a year (1963) away from Wisconsin at Stanford University as fellow at the Center for Advanced Study in the Behavioral Sciences. Here he met philosopher Michael Polanyi, another professional association that influenced his subsequent thinking.

Whilst at Stanford, Rogers had time to carefully consider his options. He clearly was not happy with the tight regime at the University of Wisconsin, so he suggested to Richard Farson, Director of the independent research and consultancy service in California, Western Behavioral Sciences Institute, that he (Rogers) join the WBSI full-time. This appointment gave Rogers practically complete freedom to pursue whatever avenue of interest he desired.

It may be interesting for readers to note that Rogers was still using the term 'Client-Centred' as the title of the therapeutic approach right up to the months before his death. See next page.

Rogers, C.R. (1969). *Freedom to Learn: A View of What Education Might Become.* Columbus Ohio: Charles E. Merrill.

Rogers, C.R. and Coulson, W.R. (eds.) (1968). *Man and the Science of Man.* Columbus, Ohio: Charles E. Merrill.

And get back together again in California

Rogers moved to La Jolla, a small town in the northern outskirts of San Diego, California in 1964 and stayed there until his death in 1987. In biographies and notes on Rogers' life, accounts of these years often use the term 'freedom' to describe this period in personal and professional terms. Rogers had freed himself from the strictures of academic life and was able to pursue his interests with little or no hindrance.

Some see this move as the beginning of the end for CCT as a mainstream school of thought in American universities, and that Rogers was running away from the difficulties at Wisconsin, both at the University and at the Psychotherapy Research Project. Others believed that he was so deeply affected by the professional disappointment at the University and disaster at the research project that he initially simply retreated to reconsider his options. He was 61 years old and in what many at that age would consider to be the twilight of an illustrious career — peaceful retirement beckoned. There was no real need for him to break new ground and tread new paths in the application of humanistic psychology, but that is exactly what he did.

Once settled in California Rogers carried the development of the applications of Client-Centred Therapy into new areas. He was encouraged to do this as a result of several influences:
• his discontent with the rather rigid, narrow approach to graduate education at Wisconsin encouraged him to develop his ideas on education resulting in the 1969 publication of *Freedom to Learn.*
• meeting Michael Polanyi at Stanford University stimulated his interest in the philosophy of science and human nature. He increasingly included thoughts on science and humankind in his publications and a dialogue with Polanyi was featured in *Man and the Science of Man* in 1968.
• shortly after arriving in California Rogers acted as consultant to a group of world-renowned physicists at California Institute of Technology, including Murray Gellman and Nobel Prize-winner Richard P. Feynman. This experience no doubt helped Rogers regain confidence after his experiences at Wisconsin.
• whether Rogers was disenchanted with individual therapy is debatable, but he turned his attention to the application of CCT principles in groups. He was not so much interested in *therapy groups* as unstructured, non-directive groups which encouraged congruent, empathic exchanges between participants. These

came to be called *encounter groups* and Rogers wrote the definitive book *Encounter Groups* published in 1970.

• He was able to turn his attention to one of his long-term dreams: using Client-Centred Therapy principles to help reduce international tensions. He had been interested in conflict resolution in social settings for a very long time, and now he became interested in using the approach to foster world peace. The Peace Project — co-ordinated from the Center for Studies of the Person by director, Gay Swenson (Barfield) — involved large group meetings in, amongst other places, Central America, Europe, South Africa and the USSR.

Rogers, C.R. (1970). *Carl Rogers on encounter groups.* New York: Harper & Row.

An account of this work can be found in Rogers, C.R. and Russell, D.E. (2002). *Carl Rogers The Quiet Revolutionary: An Oral History.* Roseville, CA: Penmarin Books. Also Swenson, G.L. (1987), 'When personal and political processes meet: The Rust Workshop.' *Journal of Humanistic Psychology, 27:* 309–32.

Client-Centred — Person-Centred

It was some time in the very late 1970s that Rogers started using the term 'person-centred' to describe his work. In the UK we are used to using the terms *person-centred counselling* or *Person-Centred Therapy* and also *Person-Centred Approach*. Often, we use these terms interchangeably since, in the first place, most therapists following Rogers' general approach see no difference between the processes of counselling and psychotherapy. Second, given the central place of the PCA in the development of counselling outside of medical settings in the UK, the term 'person-centred' was quickly preferred to the term 'client-centred' to indicate the egalitarian, non-expert nature of the helping relationship. This then encouraged only a weak distinction between the notions of the therapeutic and non-therapeutic applications of Rogers' work in terms of nomenclature.

Although it was during this time in California that Rogers started using the term 'person-centred', he used it almost exclusively to describe the application of his ideas to fields other than therapy. In his last book *A Way of Being*, Chapter 6 was titled 'The Foundations of a Person-Centered Approach'. He wrote in the introduction:

> the old concept of 'client-centered therapy' has been transformed into the 'person-centered approach'. In other words, I am no longer talking simply about psychotherapy, but about a point of view, a philosophy, an approach to life, a way of being which fits any situation where *growth* — of a person, a group or a community — is part of the goal. (p. ix)

In all of his later publications, including his biographies, he consistently calls his approach to therapy, 'client-centred'. In the months before he died, in interviews with David Russell, he

Rogers, C.R. (1980). *A Way of Being.* Boston: Houghton Mifflin.

In contrast to what developed in the UK, Rogers was careful to use the terms to delineate between the therapeutic aspects of his approach (CCT) and the broader non-therapeutic (but still obviously change-oriented) philosophy and applications (the PCA, including encounter groups, education, peace project, etc.).

My use of the terms 'person-centred', client-centred', 'approach' and 'therapy' (in various permutations) in this chapter is not intended to convey any 'best practice in usage'. I am simply trying to use the historically appropriate term in the right context. However, readers will come to appreciate that such a simple aim is actually rather difficult to achieve. I hope that readers at least realise that when imprecise definitions, loose usage and cultural traditions collide we are left with a mess. My personal attempt to encourage a simplified nomenclature can be found in the appendix to this book, pp. 149-62.

Volume 2, Number 3 of the journal *Person-Centered Review* was dedicated to Carl Rogers' life. It contained over sixty tributes, eulogies and remembrances.

The journal *Person-Centred Review* was founded in 1986 by David J. Cain and edited by him until its demise in 1990. It was important in the communication of CCT/PCA ideas and maintaining a presence in academic circles. It was dropped by the publisher due to poor circulation figures, but a collection of articles from irs 5-year history is available: Cain, D.J. (2002).(Ed.) *Classics in the Person-Centred Approach*. Ross-on-Wye: PCCS Books.

John Shlien (unpublished interview) believed that making the 'Gloria' film re-awakened Rogers' interest in one-to-one therapy, which had been somewhat in decline in the aftermath of the Wisconsin project. According to Shlien, Rogers was very nervous before the filming and uncomfortable under the hot lights and worried that he might not be able to give a good demonstration of CCT. Apparently, Rogers telephoned Shlien immediately upon his return from the filming saying that he felt he had done a good job. His confidence was restored.

continued to use the term *client-centred* when referring to one-to-one therapy.

It is not altogether clear why in the UK, the majority seem to prefer using the term *person-centred* in relation to *therapy* as opposed to wider applications of Rogers' ideas. For some, the term *person-centred* is preferred because it is less associated with what might be perceived to be the rigid, purist or fundamental *client-centred* position. UK practitioners had, to all intents and purposes, stopped using the term *Client-Centred Therapy*, by the 1990s. In the twenty-first century, however, a small but increasing number of practitioners are again describing themselves as client-centred, possibly to associate their practice with Rogers' early work or the classical position described in Chapter 2 by Tony Merry.

Carl Rogers 1902–1987

When Carl Rogers died in 1987, Client-Centred Therapy and the Person-Centred Approach had been established throughout the world. In some countries, he was best known for his work as a psychotherapist, in others for his work in conflict resolution, cross-cultural work and international peace efforts.

During his time in California, Rogers turned his attention almost exclusively to applications other than individual therapy, i.e. encounter groups, education, politics and peace. Since this book is concerned with therapeutic applications of Client-Centred Therapy, with individuals, families and groups, you can now see why, in this 'history' of events and ideas, we have concentrated mainly on the period before he went to California. To all intents and purposes, Carl Rogers stopped working as a therapist when he left Wisconsin.

Some readers may have seen films or videotapes of Carl Rogers working with individual clients. He is famous (along with Albert Ellis and Fritz Perls) for the *Three Approaches to Psychotherapy* series featuring the client 'Gloria'. This was followed by a second *Three Approaches* series featuring the client 'Kathy' and therapists Arnold Lazarus and Everett Shostrom. In addition, he continued to do 'demonstration' interviews at workshops where the 'clients' were workshop participants or staff. However we look at it, these occasional, one-off, single-sessions would not be considered to be work as a therapist.

One of the consequences of Rogers' turning his attention away from one-to-one therapy is that for those who looked only to Rogers for innovation, Client-Centred Therapy theory effectively stood still for over 20 years between the mid-sixties and the late-eighties. He published brief, occasional essays related to therapy in this time, but none presented *new* theory. Similarly his two books *Carl Rogers on Personal Power* and *A Way of Being* were both overwhelmingly concerned with other applications of his ideas. Some believe the chapter on empathy in the latter book presented no new theory, rather it was an attempt to 'rescue' the beleaguered concept of empathy after it had been so often ridiculed by other psychologists as wooden parrotting. Even Rogers himself had turned away from empathy as a result of this criticism, but he returned to it as a key concept in therapeutic relationships at the very end of his life.

Rogers, C.R. (1977). *Carl Rogers on Personal Power: Inner strength and its revolutionary impact.* New York: Delacorte.
Rogers, C.R. (1980). *A Way of Being.* Boston: Houghton Mifflin.

On the point of new theory, Nick Baker, amongst others, takes a different view. He argues strongly that Rogers' chapter in *A Way of Being* (originally published in 1975 in *The Counseling Psychologist,* 5 (2): 2–10) did indeed present new theory. See Nick's chapter in this volume, pp. 75–6.

'Presence'

As Carl Rogers gave his attention to these extensions and applications of person-centred principles, most would agree that he did not *advance* the theory in the sense of adding new elements or changing existing ones. There is one possible exception to this, when in 1986 he referred to a particular quality of some relationships:

> when I am at my best, as a group facilitator or a therapist . . . when I am closest to my inner intuitive self, when I am somehow in touch with the unknown in me, when perhaps I am in a slightly altered state of consciousness in the relationship, then whatever I seem to do seems full of healing. Then simply my *presence* is releasing and helpful. There is nothing I can do to force this experience, but when I can relax and be close to the transcendental core of me . . . at those moments it seems that my inner spirit has reached out and touched the inner spirit of the other. (pp. 198–9)

Rogers, C.R. (1986). 'A Client-centered/person-centered approach to therapy.' In I.L. Kutash and A. Wolf (eds.) *Psychotherapist's Casebook.* San Francisco: Jossey-Bass, pp. 197–208. Reprinted in H. Kirschenbaum and V.L. Henderson (eds.) (1990). *The Carl Rogers Reader.* London: Constable, pp. 135–52.

This must be one of the most frequently-quoted passages from Rogers' work in recent years. It seems that again, Rogers' sharing of his personal experiences in therapy struck a chord with a large number of people. It can certainly be taken many ways (and has been). Two frequent interpretations are as follows: First, it was read by many as the latest evidence in Rogers' writing that he was, in his later years, acknowledging a spiritual dimension to human existence. This view is probably best elaborated in the work of Brian Thorne. In terms of the development of PCT and the PCA, Rogers had given voice to an unspoken dimension of the lives of many therapists as Person-Centred Therapy embraced the spiritual.

See Thorne, B. (1991). *Person-Centred Counselling: Therapeutic and Spiritual Dimensions.* London: Whurr.
Thorne, B. (1998). *Person-Centred Counselling and Christian Spirituality: The Secular and the Holy.* London: Whurr.
Thorne, B. (2002). *The Mystical Power of Person-Centred Therapy: Hope Beyond Despair.* London: Whurr.

Second, it has caused some speculation regarding whether Rogers was suggesting a further condition — that of 'presence'. Some argue that presence is a transitory, somewhat enhanced type of interpersonal contact between people that happens in 'mature' relationships. It seems to happen in therapeutic relationships characterised by a depth of relating facilitated by high levels of trust, therapist congruence and ability to stay with processing in the present. Another view is that presence is another condition of successful therapy but may not be necessary. Others take Rogers' quote to emphasise the point, central to Client-Centred Therapy, that it is the *relationship* that is the key, not the skills or abilities of the therapist, and furthermore that this relationship is *co-created* by the therapist and client.

The PCA finds its heart

This latter view draws attention to a 'maturing' of Person-Centred Therapy during Rogers' time in California. Theory and practice were not *advanced*, but the PCA deepened, consolidated, and, as Mearns and Thorne (2000, p. 89) have it, 'genuinely found its "heart" during that time'. This grew into a greater, more sharply defined, notion of the *relational* nature of PCT. The emphasis became:

- The human qualities of the therapist, rather than the skilled 'doing' of therapy.
- The idea of therapist congruence as the taking of the whole self of the therapist into the relationship, rather than 'using' congruence as a 'technique'.
- Therapy as a co-created relationship, rather than the application of therapist-provided conditions.

These ideas, increasingly evident in Rogers' writing, shifted the leading-edge emphasis slowly but surely towards other themes and elements which would only come to fruition after his death.

Nearly two decades later . . .

The tribes of the person-centred nation continue to develop and diverge at the start of the new millennium. There are now many variations of therapeutic approach which trace their origins back to the work of Carl Rogers.

In 1989 the first International Conference for Client-Centered and Experiential Psychotherapy (ICCCEP) was held in Leuven, Belgium. This was the first gathering of the tribes. The ICCCEP has been held roughly every third year since and in 2003 became

Mearns, D. and Thorne, B. (2000). *Person-Centred Therapy Today: New frontiers in theory and practice.* London: Sage.

Nick Baker points out that a new emphasis on congruence dates back to the Wisconsin project (see the sidenote on page 8). There are many 'theories' as to why Rogers appeared to shift emphasis from empathy to congruence around the time of the Wisconsin project.

The ICCCEP conferences were held in Leuven, Belgium, 1989; Stirling, Scotland, 1991; Gmunden, Austria, 1994; Lisbon, Portugal, 1997; Chicago, USA, 2000.

the Person-Centered and Experiential (PCE) conference. Since the advent of the World Association for Person-Centered and Experiential Psychotherapy and Counseling (WAPCEPC) in 2000, the tribes have had an organisational meeting point where information exchange, challenging debate, support, project development and international representation can take place.

'Challenging debate' is still high on the agenda. Issues of definition still loom large as the tribes debate the criteria which should determine whether a therapeutic approach falls within the broad definition of the term 'client-centred' (or broader still, 'person-centred'). The debate continues to return to two core issues, namely directivity/non-directivity and the necessity and sufficiency of the therapeutic conditions. Historically the debate parameters have been set by the position of the classical non-directive client-centred therapists, and my personal view is that this continues to be the case. I also can find very little evidence that Rogers himself moved very far if at all from these basic principles during his life. However, one of the aims of this book is for the reader to come to their own view and find their own position. You will, therefore, find these issues emerging in each chapter of this book according to the understanding of each author.

New ideas emerge

As the tribes of the person-centred nation continue to develop their identities, genuine new theory has been developed. For some it was facilitated by the cross-fertilisation of ideas between the tribes; for others by taking ideas from psychology, theology or philosophy. Some of these new ideas do claim a space in this book since they may be the germ of a new tribe.

It is clearly beyond the brief of this book to detail the developments listed below. Most diploma-level trainings should have a sufficiently good library to take your reading further on the majority of these topics. They should be considered 'leading edge' ideas, but not in the sense that they are tentative or undeveloped. Most have passed their period of gestation and have now been absorbed into the best contemporary person-centred literature. They are leading edge in the sense that, in terms of understanding theory, they should be tackled after the basics have been thoroughly understood.

• Pre-Therapy

Pre-Therapy was developed by Garry Prouty for nearly ten years before he published his first publication in 1976. Since then, this

In 2003, the conference became the Person-Centered and Experiential (PCE) conference sponsored for the first time by the new World Association for Person-Centered and Experiential Psychotherapy and Counseling (WAPCEPC), and was held in Egmond-aan-Zee, The Netherlands.

In the introduction to this book you will find 'person-centred' approaches and methods which lay greater or lesser claim to being a 'tribe'. The criteria for inclusion in this book as a tribe seemed quite simple at the time and can be found on page i. This book hopes to encourage and give support to fledgling practitioners in the UK to demand training and literature in approaches which in mainland Europe are taken for granted.

Nick Baker takes a different view and as evidence of new theory points to Rogers' work with Jim Brown and Rogers' 1975 'Empathy: An unappreciated way of being' (reprinted as Chapter 7 in *A Way of Being*, published in 1980). See Nick's Chapter 4, pp. 75–7 and pp. 87–91, this volume

The best introduction to Prouty's work is Prouty, G., Van Werde, D. and Pörtner, M. (2002). *Pre-Therapy: Reaching contact-impaired clients*. Ross-on-Wye: PCCS Books.
A Brief summary can be found in Mearns, D. (2003). *Developing Person-Centred Counselling*. 2nd edition. London: Sage.

Mearns, D. (1999). 'Person-centred therapy with configurations of the self.' *Counselling, 10* (2): 125–30.
For the most accessible general introduction to theory and practice for person-centred practitioners, see Mearns, D. Chapters 6 and 7, in Mearns, D. and Thorne, B. (2000). *Person-Centred Therapy Today: New frontiers in theory and practice.* London: Sage, pp. 101–43.
Cooper, M. (1999). 'If you can't be Jekyll be Hyde: an existential-phenomenological exploration of lived-plurality.' In J. Rowan and M. Cooper (eds.) *The Plural Self.* London: Sage, pp. 51–70.

Mearns, D. and Thorne, B. (2000). 'Advancing person-centred theory.' In D. Mearns and B. Thorne, *Person-Centred Therapy Today: New frontiers in theory and practice.* London: Sage, pp. 172–95.

Mearns, D. (1996). 'Working at relational depth with clients in person-centred therapy.' *Counselling, 7* (4): 306–11.

Schmid, P. F. (2001a). 'Authenticity: the person as his or her own author: Dialogical and ethical perspectives on therapy as an encounter relationship. And Beyond.' In G. Wyatt (ed.) *Rogers' Therapeutic Conditions. Volume 1: Congruence.* Ross-on-Wye: PCCS Books, pp. 213–28.
Schmid, 2001b at bottom of page.
Schmid, 2001c and 2002 on facing page.

The most accessible location for this aspect of Margaret Warner's work is Warner, M.S. (2000). 'Person-Centred Therapy at the difficult edge: a developmentally based model of fragile and dissociated process.' In Mearns. D. and Thorne B. (2000). *Person-Centred Therapy Today: New frontiers in theory and practice.* London: Sage, pp. 144–71.

Schmid, P. F. (2001b). 'Comprehension: The art of not-knowing. Dialogical and ethical perspectives on empathy as dialogue in personal and person-centred relationships.' In S. Haugh and T. Merry (eds.) *Rogers' Therapeutic Conditions. Volume 2: Empathy.* Ross-on-Wye: PCCS Books, pp. 53–71.

method of making psychological contact with 'contact-impaired' clients has been used with remarkable success in North America and throughout mainland Europe.

• Pluralistic self
There have been various attempts to develop Rogers' self-theory for many years. One strand of ideas includes the possible plurality of the self-structure. The most accessible general introduction to theory and practice for person-centred practitioners is Dave Mearns' notion of 'configurations of self' (Mearns, 1999; Mearns and Thorne, 2000) with an influential contribution also from Mick Cooper (Cooper, 1999).

• More than the actualising tendency
Mearns and Thorne (2000) again draw together the concerns of many theorists and practitioners to restate the pro-social aspects of the actualising tendency. They advance the idea that the actualising tendency, usually portrayed as singularly concerned with enhancement of the *individual*, must be balanced by a positive, socially mediated motivational drive.

• A dialogical approach
A dialogical approach to therapy is one that emphasises or even rests completely on dialogue, that is, the co-created relationship between the helper and person helped. This is different from the 'traditional' phenomenological approach of CCT/PCA wherein we look at the separate experiences of the therapist and client. A dialogical approach is concerned with the 'between'. Dave Mearns' work on 'relational depth' (Mearns, 1996) reflects emerging dialogical influences and Peter Schmid (2001a, b and c; 2002) has so far been most prolific in this area.

• Fragile and dissociated process
Since the early 1990s, Margaret Warner has developed person-centred theory and practice for clients with difficult processes. Other, more diagnostic, therapeutic approaches might refer to such clients as having borderline personality disorder or suffering dissociation and depersonalisation. Margaret Warner (Warner, 2000) has developed not only genuine new theory, but also sensitive practice and a respectful vocabulary for describing clients' experiences.

• Person-Centred Therapy as a fundamentally ethical activity
Related to his writing on Person-Centred Therapy as a dialogical approach, Austrian scholar Peter Schmid also positions Person-

Centred Therapy as an ethical activity at the heart of ancient European philosophy. He describes Person-Centred Therapy as a fundamentally ethical way of conducting oneself as a human being, rather than a set of qualities limited to specifically therapeutic relationships. Increasingly published in English, his work can be found in a variety of places, probably most accessibly in Schmid 2001a, b and c; 2002.

Across the Atlantic, American psychologist Barry Grant published what has become, for some, a seminal paper in the understanding of the ethical base of non-directive Client-Centred Therapy (Grant, 1990/2002). His paper outlined the difference between *using* non-directivity (and indeed other CCT 'conditions') as instruments or tools rather than holding them as qualities and values as a person. This strand of thinking has developed in the work of some North American practitioners (Grant, 2003) to become an 'ethics-only' approach to therapy.

• Spirituality and the PCA

For many years, practitioners and writers struggled to establish human spiritual experience as valid territory for psychotherapy, regardless of therapeutic orientation. In the PCA tradition, Brian Thorne was, and still is, a pioneer in encouraging practitioners to include spiritual experience and practice in their repertoire of therapeutic possibilities. Collections of his essays and chapters (Thorne, 1991; 1998; 2002) continue to be sources of inspiration for practitioners, not least because of the challenging nature of Thorne's message.

In closing this first chapter I want to remind readers that this book is an introduction. On page xii I say that it is parochial — it is presented with UK practitioners and students in mind. Move around the world and the terminology and definitions will also shift. That is one reason why we repeatedly encourage students to read widely. The remainder of this book is the starting point for the reading that will broaden your understanding of what it can mean to be person-centred.

Schmid, 2001a and b on facing page.

Schmid, P. F. (2001c). 'Acknowledgement: The art of responding. Dialogical and ethical perspectives on the challenge of unconditional personal relationships in therapy and beyond.' In J. Bozarth and P. Wilkins (eds.) *Rogers' Therapeutic Conditions. Volume 3: Unconditional Positive Regard*. Ross-on-Wye: PCCS Books, pp. 49–64.

Schmid, P. F. (2002). 'Presence: Im-media-te co-experiencing and co-responding. Phenomenological, dialogical and ethical perspectives on contact and perception in person-centred therapy and beyond.' In G. Wyatt and P. Sanders (eds.) *Rogers' Therapeutic Conditions. Volume 4: Contact and Perception*. Ross-on-Wye: PCCS Books, pp. 182–203.

Grant, B. (1990). 'Principled and Instrumental Non-Directiveness in Person-Centered and Client-Centered Therapy.' *Person-Centred Review, 5*: pp. 77–88. Reprinted in D. J. Cain (2002)(ed.) *Classics in the Person-Centred Approach*. Ross-on-Wye: PCCS Books, pp. 371–7.

Grant, B. (2003). 'Client-Centered Therapy: ethics, knowledge and perfection.' Presentation at the PCE Conference, Egmond-aan-Zee, July 2003.

Thorne, B. (1991). *Person-Centred Counselling: Therapeutic and spiritual dimensions*. London: Whurr.

Thorne, B. (1998). *Person-Centred Counselling and Christian Spirituality*. London: Whurr.

Thorne, B. (2002). *The Mystical Power of Person-Centred Therapy*. London: Whurr.

classical client-centred therapy

tony merry

2

Introduction

Client-Centred (or Person-Centred) Therapy developed from the original work of Carl Rogers, an American psychotherapist, researcher and academic, and his colleagues from about 1940 onwards. It offered a radical way of working with people that departed sharply from the Freudian and cognitive-behavioural approaches that were dominant in psychology at that time. With its emphasis on the qualities of the relationship between client and therapist, and its rejection of diagnostic assessment and labelling, it remains as radical today as it was in the 1940s. Currently, Person-Centred Therapy is one of the most widely used approaches to helping relationships in the UK and Europe, though not always the best understood.

Person-Centred Therapy has developed through a number of evolutionary phases and has been known by different terms at different times. These are, firstly, 'non-directive therapy', then 'Client-Centred Therapy' and finally, 'Person-Centred Therapy'. The name changes are significant in that they illustrate some shifts of emphasis over the last 60 years or so.

According to Barrett-Lennard (1998), the 'non-directive phase', from about 1940 to 1950, emphasised the development of a non-judgemental atmosphere in the therapy relationship in which the accent was on the skills of the counsellor to promote the therapy process.

From the 1950s to the early 1960s (the 'client-centred phase') the emphasis was on counsellor attitudes rather than skills, and on reflecting the client's feelings. The idea of the counsellor as a person involved subjectively in the therapy relationship began to take shape.

From the 1960s to the present day (the 'person-centred phase'), the emphasis shifted again, this time towards counsellor attitudes, values and relationship qualities.

For additional information on the development of Person-Centred Therapy, see Pete Sanders, Chapter 1 and Nick Baker, Chapter 4, pp. 67–8 this volume.

For a full discussion of the history and development of the PCA, see **Barrett-Lennard, G. T. (1998)**. *Carl Rogers' Helping System: Journey and Substance.* London: Sage.
See also, Raskin, N. (1996). 'Person-Centred Psychotherapy: Twenty Historical Steps.' In W. Dryden (ed.) *Developments in Psychotherapy: Historical Perspectives.* London: Sage.

However, throughout this period, some basic philosophical and theoretical ideas have remained fairly constant, though new perspectives and understandings have emerged over the years. The sections that follow explore these ideas, and build up a comprehensive picture of the theory and practice of Person-Centred Therapy in its original or 'classical' form.

The person and 'human nature'

For more discussion on 'human nature' and the PCA, see Merry, T. (2002). *Learning and Being in Person-Centred Counselling.* 2nd edition. Ross-on-Wye: PCCS Books, pp. 16–26.

Rogers took an optimistic view of human nature. He described 'the person' as forward-moving, constructive, realistic and trustworthy, in contrast to those who favoured such terms as hostile, antisocial, destructive, or evil. This positive, constructive view of the person is a recurring feature of Rogers' thinking, but he was not naïve about the existence of destructive, antisocial or other negative aspects of human behaviour. He did not, however, regard such negative aspects as inherent, or somehow a basic component of the human condition.

The term 'human nature', though an imprecise concept open to a variety of interpretations, is used in person-centred psychology to denote certain characteristics of persons that Rogers thought to be universal. He viewed individuals as constantly in the process of developing and, in Rogers' term, 'becoming'. He regarded people as being motivated by a tendency for growth and enhancement, and that they are constructive, trustworthy, responsive, creative and adaptive, or capable of becoming so.

Though Rogers is usually associated with his work with individuals, his concern was with the person in relation to others and to society at large, as well as with the individual's 'inner world'. His theory of personality, for example, suggests how individuals build up pictures of themselves (their self-concepts) through early (and subsequent) relationships with others. In individual terms, what is 'real' to any person is that which exists within their internal frame of reference, or inner subjective world. This reality forms the basis for the way a person behaves in the world and responds to events and experiences. This 'phenomenological' approach holds that the best way to understand a person's behaviour and feelings is to understand how that person perceives and interprets the surrounding world. For Rogers, then, the most important area of psychological study was the individual's subjective experience, because this experience informs and underpins all behaviour.

Rogers described his trust in human nature in the following terms,

. . . the basic nature of the human being, when functioning freely, is constructive and trustworthy . . . When we are able to free the individual from defensiveness, so that he is open to the wide range of his own needs, as well as the wide range of environmental and social demands, his reactions may be trusted to be positive, forward moving, constructive . . . His total behavior . . . as he moves toward being open to all his experience, will be more balanced and realistic, behavior which is appropriate to the survival and enhancement of a highly social animal. (Rogers, 1961, p. 194)

Rogers, C.R. (1961). *On Becoming a Person: A therapist's view of psychotherapy.* London: Constable.

The theory of actualisation

The key to understanding Rogers' view of the person is his formulation of the theory of 'actualisation'. This theory suggests that organisms (including humans) tend to develop positively and constructively in environments that support such development, but hostile or destructive environments, on the other hand, tend to inhibit development of constructive potential. The theory of actualisation, then, is a biologically-based theory that describes the interaction between an individual organism and its environment. It is not a 'moral theory', and doesn't ascribe values to particular kinds of behaviour or kinds of people.

'Actualisation' is one of the basic theoretical constructs in person-centred psychology. The tendency for an individual to fulfil his or her potential is regarded as the sole motivation for human behaviour and development.

To Rogers 'the environment', which includes the social environment with its complex human relationships, plays a central part in influencing how individual persons develop, form self-concepts, acquire self-esteem and so on. The process of actualisation is not regarded, in human beings, as a conscious 'activity' in which the individual makes choices between alternatives, but as a process in which the total organism is involved at both conscious and non-conscious levels. 'Consciousness' or 'self-awareness' is regarded as a uniquely human characteristic which enables a wide range of choices to be made, with the person's behaviour, values and attitudes open to change and reformulation in the light of learning and experience.

In human beings, actualisation occurs in a physical, biological, social and psychological context, and this constitutes the environment in which the person lives. An interaction between genetic predisposition, the environment and individual experience shapes the specific ways in which actualisation is expressed.

Behaviour is seen as 'goal directed' in that it represents attempts by the person to maintain and enhance him- or herself in response to whatever environmental conditions are being experienced. The theory of actualisation proposes that there is a 'growth tendency' which, in an ideal or perfect environment, would result in each individual fulfilling all of his or her constructive, personal and pro-social potentials. Such an environment would, from the moment of a person's birth, be experienced as nurturing, safe and accepting of individual differences. In these circumstances, human capacities for constructive relationships, the understanding of others, and creative action, for example, would be expressed. It is important to note that not all potentialities of individuals, such as the potential to commit violent acts towards others, are regarded as aspects of the directional nature of the actualising tendency. When such behaviour does occur, the concept of actualisation directs our attention to the environmental conditions that have distorted or corrupted the pro-social direction of the actualising process for an explanation.

However, the environment is never ideal or consistently constructive. There are always constraints to be confronted, many of which are likely to obstruct a person's capacity for growth towards the theoretical ideal of being fully functioning. These constraints might include poor physical conditions, but crucially they include unsatisfactory relationships with others ranging from emotional neglect, the lack of love and nurturing, to various degrees of abuse and deprivation. Nevertheless, each person interacts with his or her environment, including those aspects of the environment that tend to inhibit growth, in an effort to develop as fully as possible in whatever circumstances prevail. If, for example, the developing person experiences relationships with others that are only hostile or aggressive in some way, then the person's need for nurturing and emotional warmth will remain unmet. This is likely to have destructive or inhibiting effects on the person's emotional or psychological development, and these effects are likely to manifest themselves throughout the person's lifetime. Even so, the actualising tendency is still present, no matter how unsuitable the environment in which the individual person finds herself. The only way to destroy the actualising tendency completely is to destroy the organism itself.

Until about the mid-1970s, environmental factors were viewed, in the main, as negatively distorting the process of actualisation. It was as if the individual was in a constant battle to overcome the negative constraints of the social world in order to become free of all conditioning and thus achieve some ideal state of being a fully-functioning person. In more recent times, this view has shifted significantly, so that some environmental influences are seen as necessary in order to preserve and maintain a degree of order and stability in the social world. Mearns and Thorne (2000), for instance, regard some tension between the actualising tendency and the need to maintain the viability of a person's 'life space' as exerting appropriate checks and balances. For example, the urge towards creativity and experimentation in life may, at times, be

---

Humans have both constructive and destructive potentials. In an environment in which positive regard is lacking, the actualisation of destructive potential is more likely. Destructive potential includes destructive behaviours towards self or others.

Mearns, D. and Thorne, B. (2000). *Person-Centred Therapy Today: New frontiers in theory and practice.* London: Sage.

self-enhancing but at others may be potentially destructive if not balanced with a realistic appraisal of the demands of other aspects of the person's life. Mearns and Thorne remark,

Ibid.

> The forces of social mediation form a coherent and functional part of our existence as human beings, allowing us expression of the actualising tendency but exerting an imperative which cautions against the endangering of the social life space. (*ibid.* pp. 182–3)

Some aspects of behaviour that may be interpreted by others as 'negative' or 'self-destructive', when viewed phenomenologically (that is, from within the individuals own frame of reference), can be regarded as manifestations of the actualising tendency's capacity to defend the person against further threat. For example, a person's apparent inability to form or sustain close, intimate relationships with others and to opt instead for a series of unfulfilling casual relationships seems to challenge the notion of actualisation always working towards the individual's enhancement. When viewed from within the person's inner subjective world, however, this behaviour is understandable if previous attempts at intimacy have resulted in significant emotional hurt. In this case, 'actualisation' is towards self-defence because emotional and physical survival take precedence over self-enhancement. This does not mean, however, that the self-destructive behaviour is not open to change, as we shall see in later sections.

The actualising tendency is, then, a universal characteristic of living things, but its detailed expression in human beings is always unique to the individual. It is the motivation for all individual action whether or not the circumstances at any one moment are favourable or unfavourable for growth and development. In unfavourable conditions the expression of the actualising tendency may become distorted, but even so the tendency remains as constructive as the environment allows. In Rogers' words, the human being 'has one basic tendency and striving — to actualize, maintain and enhance the experiencing organism' (Rogers, 1951, p. 487).

Rogers, C.R. (1951). *Client-Centred Therapy.* Boston: Houghton Mifflin.

Self and self-actualisation

The general process of actualisation results in the differentiation of some experience into an 'I' or 'me', in other words, a self or self-concept. Rogers viewed this 'self' as fluid and changing, though at any one time it has certain consistent characteristics. Thus, the self is a particular part of the person's total experiencing

to end 31

(this total experiencing is sometimes referred to as 'organismic experiencing'). The person as a whole, as an aspect of his or her growth, fulfils the potential to differentiate as a separate person with a specific identity. The process of *self-actualisation* appears after the development of a self-structure, and it is this process (self-actualisation) that maintains and develops that self-structure.

The constructs of self and self-actualisation are very significant in Rogers' theory of the development of the person, and how the person may become disturbed. In favourable conditions, the formation of a self-concept, and the actualisation of the self, results in the person being open to experience with a self-concept that is in harmony with the person's organismic experiencing. On the other hand, unfavourable conditions may result in the actualisation of a self that is in conflict with organismic experience. It is this conflict that results in psychological disturbance. For example, a child may have the experience that a particular situation is frightening, and he or she reacts accordingly by showing fear and crying, in other words, the child's organismic experience is one of being afraid. In favourable circumstances, the child's fear would be responded to by an adult with understanding and reassurance. The child would continue to be held in positive regard and the fear accepted, both by the child and the adult, as a natural and spontaneous response to a perceived threat. The child's developing sense of him- or herself and actual experience would be in harmony and no conflict would result. On the other hand, if the child's fear were responded to without understanding and in a way that tended to negate the experience of fear, the experience would be overridden and denied or distorted by the child's emerging self. The organismic experience (I am afraid) would be denied by the self (I am not afraid, or fear is not an acceptable part of me).

In this way, the process of self-actualisation (a sub-system of the general actualising tendency) will continue to express a self that contains conflicts between self-experience and organismic experience. Some experiences will be accepted into awareness because they are consistent with the self-concept, while others are denied to awareness, or distorted in some way because they conflict with the self-concept. The extent to which such conflicts accumulate through experiences similar to the example given above, determines the extent to which the person is disturbed.

Self-actualisation is best thought of as a sub-system of the general actualising tendency. These two concepts are often confused. The function of self-actualisation is to maintain and enhance the self-structure, rather than the organism as a whole.

Humans have constructive, pro-social potentials. They include nurturing and parenting abilities, abilities to create and sustain intimate relationships, and the ability empathically to understand the experiences of others.

Self theory

The 'self' is a central concept in the PCA. We can think of 'the self' as a consistent set of experiences and perceptions that we gradually differentiate into an 'I' or 'me'. As the self develops we begin to attach certain values to our experience and build up a picture of our 'selves' through our interactions with our environment, especially with others who have significance for us, like parents. The 'self' becomes the inner, experiencing person able to reflect consciously on experience, and act in the world in ways that are consistent with our experience of it.

Rogers' personality theory (Rogers, 1951) is organised into a set of 19 statements (he called them 'propositions') that account for the way an individual develops a sense of self, and which suggests the ways in which the person becomes either fully-functioning or not. He regarded each person as inhabiting a 'world' of which he or she is the centre. The individual is in a constant process of experiencing and perceiving the world and defining what is for them 'reality'. The actualising tendency (see above) provides the motivation for everything the person does, and every act reflects the tendency of the person to maintain and enhance him- or herself. Behaviour is, then, the goal-directed attempts by the person to satisfy needs as they are experienced.

Feeling and emotion accompany and influence this goal-directed behaviour, and the intensity of the emotion being experienced is related to the significance of the behaviour. For example, an emotion will be very strongly experienced if a powerful need is being frustrated or satisfied, and less strongly experienced if the need is not so great.

Rogers' 19 propositions also describe how the person positively values those experiences that tend to maintain and enhance the person, and negatively values those that do not. In other words, the self-structure consists both of experiences and the values attached to them. Some of the time, those values are experienced directly, but at other times experiences may become valued either positively or negatively because those values have been absorbed (or introjected) from others, often in a distorted fashion, as if they had been experienced directly.

This is key to understanding Rogers' theory of how people become emotionally disturbed. As experiences occur, the person may accurately perceive them and organise them into the self-structure, or the person may ignore them completely because they cannot perceive any relationship between the experience and the self-structure as it currently exists. Crucially, the person may distort

The 'self-structure' is the 'organised, fluid, but consistent conceptual pattern of perceptions of characteristics and relationships of the "I" or the "me", together with the values attached to those concepts.' **Rogers, C. R. (1951).** *Client-Centered Therapy.* Boston: Houghton Mifflin, p. 498.

See Rogers, C.R. (1951). *Client-Centred Therapy.* Boston: Houghton Mifflin. Also described in detail and more accessible language in Merry, T. (2002). *Learning and Being in Person-Centred Counselling.* 2nd edition. Ross-on-Wye: PCCS Books

Another way of putting it is to think of a sequence:

(i) At the beginning of life, the individual is fully congruent (able to admit all experience into awareness without distortion).

(ii) Later, the person meets disapproval, rejection or other threat and experiences anxiety.

(iii) The formation of the self-concept becomes conditioned by these negative experiences, and the person internalises negative judgements about him- or herself.

(iv) This conditioned self-concept becomes reinforced by further experiences, and the person becomes alienated from their 'true self'.

(v) The person is 'incongruent'.

The terms used in this chapter are defined and discussed in Tudor, K. and Merry, T. (2002). *Dictionary of Person-Centred Psychology.* London: Whurr.

or deny the experience because it is inconsistent with the existing self-structure and may threaten to undermine that structure if the experience is incorporated accurately. The example we gave above, where a child does not allow himself to experience fear because to do so would be inconsistent with a self-structure that is unable to admit fear into awareness, is an example of this kind of denial. Alternatively, this child may distort the experience of fear into a feeling of guilt, for example, if guilt were an acceptable component of the self-structure at that time.

Psychological maladjustment, then, results when a person denies or distorts experience and does not absorb it accurately into the self-structure. On the other hand, adjustment exists when the self is able to allow all experience into awareness without any distortion. Any experience that is inconsistent with the current self-structure may be perceived as a threat, and the more threat is perceived the more rigid the self-structure becomes to defend itself against the experience. If the individual finds him- or herself in a relationship where there is little or no threat of negative judgement, the person is in a better position to allow hitherto denied or distorted experience more fully and accurately into awareness. When this happens, the person begins to reorganise her self-concept so that the introjected and distorted values that have been attached to experience become replaced by the person's own values. The person becomes more trusting of their own experience, and less vulnerable to the values and judgements of others. Ultimately, he ceases to behave in the world in ways he has learned are acceptable to others, denying and devaluing his experience, and begins to behave more authentically and with greater confidence and trust in his own internal valuing process.

The 'locus of evaluation'

Rogers thought that when people were making judgements about issues and people, they were guided either by the values they had previously introjected from others, or by their own valuing process. Where people relied heavily on the values of others, Rogers described them as experiencing an 'external locus of evaluation', and when they were able to be more reliant on their own 'organismic valuing process', he described them as having an 'internal locus of evaluation'. This is important because Rogers believed a characteristic of the healthy or fully-functioning person to be a trust in the validity of one's own values and judgements.

Conditions of worth and the self-concept

The term Rogers chose for introjected values was 'conditions of worth'. He argued that we are brought into the world with two related needs. The first of these is the need to develop positive self-regard through the formation of a constructive self-concept. The second need is to experience unconditional positive regard from those in our environment on whom we depend for survival. It is through experience and feedback from the environment that we develop a self-concept, and where this feedback is positive and constructive, our self-concept will enable us positively to value our self-worth. In other words, where our experience, feelings and behaviour are accepted, understood and valued positively by those on whom we depend, our needs for positive self-regard and for positive regard from others are met.

However, because the need to experience positive regard from others is so great (in an individual's perception it is a survival need), we will sometimes accept the values and judgements of others even when those values and judgements contradict our own experience. In the child's perception of the world, thinking, feeling and behaving in ways that continue to attract positive regard becomes more important than accepting and valuing personal experience. We will absorb (introject) the judgements and evaluations of others into our self-concept as if they were our own.

As we gradually build up and refine our self-concept we are unaware of which elements are the result of direct experience and which are introjected from others. The self becomes composed of a mixture of personal values and values derived from others. Whenever people of significance to us value some aspects of us as more deserving of positive regard than others, we begin to avoid or seek-out certain self-experiences in terms of how worthy they are of self-regard. This process of positively valuing only those experiences that contribute to positive self-regard, and rejecting or avoiding those that do not are the result of us acquiring conditions of worth. If we were only ever to experience unconditional positive regard from others, then no conditions of worth would develop. Self-regard would be unconditional, and the need for positive regard from others and positive self-regard would never conflict with our internal (or 'organismic') valuing system.

However, it is unlikely that we would only ever experience unconditional positive regard, and it is therefore inevitable that we develop some conditions of worth. This makes us vulnerable to perceiving and making sense out of our experiences somewhat selectively. We allow into our awareness those experiences that are consistent with our self-concept, and deny or distort those that are inconsistent with it. This can become something of a circular process. We tend to regard experiences that are inconsistent or incongruent with our self-concept as threatening, and we tend to protect ourselves from such experiences by distorting or denying them. In this way, we reinforce the incongruence between experience and self, and we become even more defensive and less open to experience.

Mearns, D. (1999). 'Person-centred therapy with configurations of the self.' *Counselling, 10* (2): 125–30.
Mearns, D. and Thorne, B. (2000). *Person-Centred Therapy Today.* London: Sage.

Recently, Mearns (1999) and Mearns and Thorne (2000) have advanced a modification of Rogers' theory of self that is still consistent with general person-centred theory. They suggest that the self can take on different configurations of the elements present within it in response to the varying situations of a person's life. Feelings, thoughts and behaviour change as the person adapts to and responds to the environment, but 'the self' remains consistent no matter what circumstances are encountered. In this way, while a person may think, feel and behave in a particular way in one set of circumstances, her feelings, thoughts and actions might be very different in another set. Certain configurations might exist as an adaptation to the introjection of particular conditions of worth. A person may, for example, regard herself as 'bad' or 'worthless' when it comes to being a mother, but 'good' or 'of value' when it comes to being a school teacher. Each configuration serves a purpose in maintaining the person's self-concept in different circumstances or in response to different experiences, but Mearns and Thorne are careful to point out that this does not amount to a 'splitting' of the personality or any kind of 'dissociative state', because the person's fundamental values and level of self-esteem remain constant.

Counselling and psychotherapy

The PCA is unique in the emphasis it places on the qualities of the relationship between client and counsellor.

Rogers did not make a distinction between 'counselling' and 'psychotherapy', seeing them as essentially the same activity, an attitude that persists among person-centred practitioners today. Whatever label is used, person-centred counselling is a form of therapy in which the relationship between client and counsellor is the most significant factor in promoting change and development. Whilst this therapeutic relationship is accepted as important in most forms of counselling, the person-centred approach is unique in viewing the relationship itself as therapeutic aside from anything that may be said or done within it. In other words, the formation and maintenance of a strong therapeutic relationship is not seen as a preparation for the implementation of strategies or techniques. Rogers' view was that psychological or emotional healing was promoted within a relationship in which the client experienced being accepted, valued and understood. The motivation for healing is supplied by the person's tendency to actualise constructively in an environment that facilitated such development.

Rogers was led to this view as a result of his clinical experience and of his research into the factors that promoted change within therapy and those that militated against it. In 1957, Rogers first published his now most famous scientific paper in which he outlined 'the necessary and sufficient conditions of therapeutic personality change'. He identified and described six of these necessary and sufficient conditions in the following way:

1. Two persons are in psychological contact.
2. The first, whom we shall term the client, is in a state of incongruence, being vulnerable or anxious.
3. The second person, whom we shall term the counsellor, is congruent or integrated in the relationship.
4. The counsellor experiences unconditional positive regard for the client.
5. The counsellor experiences an empathic understanding of the client's internal frame of reference and endeavours to communicate this experience to the client.
6. The communication to the client of the counsellor's empathic understanding and unconditional positive regard is to a minimal degree achieved.

> **Rogers, C. R.** (1957). 'The necessary and sufficient conditions of therapeutic personality change.' *Journal of Consulting Psychology,* 21: 95–103. This is one of the most widely known papers in the counselling world. It is reprinted in H. Kirschenbaum and V.L. Henderson (eds.) (1990). *The Carl Rogers Reader.* London: Constable, pp. 219–35.

> There are six 'necessary and sufficient conditions', but three of them have become known as 'the core conditions'.

No other conditions are necessary. If these six conditions exist, and continue over a period of time, this is sufficient. The process of constructive personality change will follow.

This theory of therapeutic relationships has become known as the 'conditions model', and three of the six conditions have been identified as most important, or at least have received most attention, becoming known as 'the core conditions'. However, recently more attention has been given to conditions one and six. The first condition, for example, is that 'Two persons are in psychological contact', and this seems so obviously a condition for therapeutic change to take place that until recently it was largely ignored or simply taken as read. In his original 1957 paper, Rogers regarded the first condition as a simple one, and that it should, perhaps, be termed an assumption or precondition.

> *Ibid.*

Prouty, G., Van Werde, D. and Pörtner, M. (2002). *Pre-Therapy: Reaching contact-impaired clients.* Ross-on-Wye: PCCS Books.
Pete Sanders takes a more detailed look at Pre-Therapy in the introduction to this volume, pp. xii and xiv–xvi.

Mearns, D. and Thorne, B. (1999). *Person-Centred Counselling in Action.* 2nd edition. London: Sage.
Merry, T (2002). *Learning and Being in Person-Centred Counselling.* 2nd edition. Ross-on-Wye: PCCS Books.
Tolan, J. (2003). *Skills in Person-Centred Counselling and Psychotherapy.* London: Sage.
Wyatt, G. and Sanders, P. (2002). (eds.) *Rogers' Therapeutic Conditions: Evolution, theory and practice. Volume 4. Contact and Perception.* Ross-on-Wye: PCCS Books.

Two things are worth noting here. First, Garry Prouty's development of 'Pre-Therapy' (e.g. Prouty, Van Werde and Pörtner, 2002) evolved from his work with clients for whom any form of contact seemed deeply impaired. Prouty has developed ways in which contact can be made with those whose degree of psychological impairment seems to make contact impossible. Such clients include those with some psychotic experiences, or those in deep shock or in catatonic states. 'Pre-Therapy' is not, strictly speaking, 'Person-Centred Therapy', but it is a major development of the principles of the PCA and their application to this group of clients.

Second, condition six is concerned with ways in which counsellors communicate their attitudes, and the ways in which clients perceive and experience them, and much has been written about the skilled ways by which counsellors can communicate empathy and positive regard effectively and sensitively (see, for example, Mearns and Thorne, 1999; Merry, 2002; Tolan, 2003). Wyatt and Sanders (2002) have recently compiled a collection of papers that deal both with 'contact' and the way in which Rogers' therapeutic attitudes are perceived and experienced by clients.

Most familiar to trainees and practitioners alike of the Person-Centred Approach, are 'the core conditions'. These are, firstly, that the therapist is congruent in the relationship, secondly that the therapist is experiencing unconditional positive regard toward the client, and thirdly the therapist experiences an empathic understanding of the client's internal frame of reference. It should be remembered that these three 'core conditions' are only meaningful in the context of all the conditions taken together and that they do not, therefore, constitute Rogers' therapy theory in the absence of the other conditions.

Because the core conditions are so important in Person-Centred Therapy theory, what follows is a brief description of each of them.

Empathic understanding

Empathic understanding involves an active process of reaching out to another person. It means trying to capture something of the feeling and meaning of a person's experience. It is not 'just listening'. This involves a process of 'being with' another person, that is, attempting to 'step into the other person's shoes' and 'see the world through the other person's eyes', laying aside one's own perceptions, values, meanings and perspectives as far as possible. The term 'internal frame of reference' is a useful one here. It refers to the need for the counsellor to understand the experiences of the client from the client's point of view, rather than by comparing a client's experiences with our own and assuming some degree of shared meaning.

It is useful to distinguish empathy from sympathy. A sympathetic response to another person's distress, welcome and human though that often is, is not necessarily accompanied by any significant degree of understanding. It is this component, *understanding*, that begins to differentiate an empathic response from a sympathetic one. Rogers described empathy as a 'way of being', and this distinguishes it from a skill that can be modelled and taught in a structured or methodical way as a particular kind of communication process. A helpful way to conceptualise empathic understanding is to think of it as an internal experience of the counsellor, followed by the sensitive and skilful communication of that experience to the client. We can then regard empathy as a process in which the client's feelings, thoughts and other experiences are received by the counsellor who then checks or tests his or her understanding in an intentional and purposeful way. This enables the client to experience being heard and, to some degree, understood, and to correct any misunderstanding or incomplete understanding, allowing the process to continue.

A further aspect of empathy should be emphasised here — the *as if* quality of empathic understanding. This refers to the idea that one can enter the frame of reference of another person to the extent that events, feelings, etc. can be experienced, to some extent, *as if* those events, etc. were one's own, but without losing the *as if* quality. The empathic counsellor maintains his or her separate identity, 'resonates' with the client's experience and engages with the client as a person, but does not become overwhelmed by any strong feelings that may be expressed.

The following is an example of the unfolding process of empathic understanding. The full transcript of this session between the therapist (Carl Rogers) and the client (Ms G) can be found in Merry (1995):

Merry, T, (1995). *An Invitation to Person-Centred Psychology.* London: Whurr.

Ms G: I . . . er . . . For a long time I've felt like there, there
            is this thing in me and I don't know what it is . . .
            and . . . sometimes when I hear other people talking
            I . . . and it's not so much the words that they're
            using but the feelings that I can sense in them . . . of

There are many transcripts of counselling interviews between Rogers and his clients available. See Tudor, K. and Merry, T. (2002). *Dictionary of Person-Centred Psychology.* London: Whurr. Here, you will find a good list of such transcripts and where they can be found. Some transcripts are published in Rogers' books, such as *On Becoming a Person.* Another excellent source is Farber, B. Brink, D. and Raskin, P. (eds.) (1996). *The Psychotherapy of Carl Rogers.* New York: The Guilford Press.

	. . . um . . . I feel heavy and I know that their feelings are touching the same kind of feelings in me.
Carl:	They're touching that secret part of you that you don't quite know what it is.
Ms G:	Mm a lot of the time that is hurt or pain and sometimes it's anger as well.
Carl:	But you feel that whatever this is that is sort of frightening within, is of negative feelings of pain and hurt and possibly anger.
Ms G:	[*nods*] And if I get in touch with them that they will overwhelm me and there's a fear of getting lost in them somehow and of not being able to find my way back to the joy that I can feel.
Carl:	That if you ever let yourself really live in or feel those feelings, maybe you'd never find your way back to pleasantness and happiness and joy.
Ms G:	'Cos I feel like I *can't* let go of things like hurt and I can't let go of things like resentment . . . I *want* to, want to let go of those things, but I don't know how, how to do that, so I don't want to explore them, I feel that if I explore them they will always be with me and I've kind of learnt to experience joy . . . but having said that to you I'm questioning whether that joy is real.
Carl:	Makes you wonder whether maybe the joy would be more real if you were able to explore some of those frightening feelings.

This is empathic because Rogers is attending very closely to Ms G's internal world with its mixture of thoughts and feelings that she can't as yet express completely. Rogers does not attempt to guide or direct his client, or give advice or make suggestions about what Ms G should do or focus her attention on. Instead, Rogers concentrates on careful listening to what Ms G expresses and the way she expresses it, and he checks with her the extent of his understanding of her world as she is currently experiencing it.

'Empathic reflection' of the kind illustrated above has often been misunderstood as a 'technique' or 'strategy'. It is neither of these things. Empathic understanding is primarily an attitude or, in Rogers' terms, 'a way of being'. It is not simply a sophisticated form of 'active listening', but a genuine dedication, on the part of the counsellor, to understanding the internal, subjective world of another person without the value judgements that normally accompany such an activity. Empathic understanding is not employed in order to achieve any particular effect or outcome, including encouraging clients to focus on selected aspects of experience, to bring issues or problems to the client's attention, or help a client towards insight or 'personal growth'. Paradoxically, however, any of these (and others) may be outcomes of the client's experience of being understood with empathy and without judgement. Rogers' objection to the term 'reflection of feelings' was based on his dislike of empathy being misrepresented as the 'technique' of reflection, but Shlien saw real advantages in the use of the term as it transformed a 'philosophy' into constructive action.

This is a subtle and often overlooked point, which may become clearer on reading the brief discussion of 'the non-directive attitude' later in this chapter. The client-centred counsellor is not trying to produce a particular effect, or achieve a set of specific therapeutic goals, other than the creation of a relationship in which the client's internal resources become released for the purposes of bringing about psychological change. This is not, however, a haphazard process or one left to chance. The empathic non-directive attitude of the counsellor contributes to the building of a relationship in which the actualising tendency of the client becomes available to reorganise the client's internal world to one which is less defended and more open to experience without the same defences that have hitherto prevailed. 'Skills' and 'techniques' in classical Client-Centred Therapy are confined to the skilled ways in which counsellors communicate their non-judgemental empathic understanding.

John Shlien wrote to Carl Rogers: 'It [reflection] is an instrument of artistic virtuosity in the hands of a sincere, intelligent, empathic listener. It made possible the development of client-centered therapy, when the philosophy alone could not have. Underserved denigration of the technique leads to fatuous alternatives in the name of "congrence."' Cited in Rogers, C.R. (1986). *'Reflection of Feelings.' Person-Centered Review, 1* (4): 375–7. Reprinted in H. Kirschenbaum and V.L. Henderson (eds.) (1990). *The Carl Rogers Reader.* London: Constable, pp. 127–9.

Congruence

'Congruence', 'authenticity' or, sometimes, 'realness' are all terms that describe the counsellor's capacity to enter into the therapy relationship as a self-aware person whose feelings are available to them, and who can express feeling honestly and openly should it be appropriate. We can distinguish between congruence as it applies to the internal, psychological state of the counsellor, and as it applies to the counsellor's communication and other behaviour during the therapy hour. In the first case, congruence describes a state in which feelings are not denied or distorted in awareness (they are accurately symbolised), and in the second case it refers to the therapist's behaviour being consistent with those feelings.

For example, a congruent counsellor who is afraid of, or intimidated by a client would be able to admit those feelings to him- or herself

• Congruence refers to the internal, psychological state of the person who can admit all experience into awareness without distortion or denial. In other words, it means being aware of feelings, emotions and sensations without 'blocking them off'.
• Congruence also refers to outward communication matching our inner feelings.
• Congruence is not the same as 'self-disclosure'.

and would acknowledge them internally. The counsellor may decide that directly communicating those feelings to the client would be the most honest and appropriate thing to do, especially if the feelings interfered with the counsellor's capacity to remain empathic. On the other hand, the counsellor may decide to discuss and explore those feelings elsewhere (perhaps in supervision), before communicating them to the client. (The counsellor may also decide that it would not be appropriate to communicate them.) The counsellor would be fulfilling the congruence condition in so far as the feelings were not being denied or distorted. If the counsellor's behaviour were to become inauthentic, perhaps as a result of trying to cover up the feeling, then the counsellor's behaviour would become incongruent to this extent. It can be a matter of fine judgement in deciding whether or not to disclose a feeling to a client, and may depend on a number of factors, including the client's present state of vulnerability or anxiety, the current strength of the therapy relationship and the counsellor's experience.

Total congruence in both its 'internal' meaning and its 'communication' meaning is undoubtedly only a theoretical ideal. Rogers believed that the extent to which a counsellor was able to experience congruence determined, in some measure, the extent to which the client experienced the relationship as therapeutic.

It is important to emphasise that, just as with empathy, congruence is not a skill or technique, but refers to a fundamental value or attitude that contributes to the counsellor's total 'way of being' in the world and with clients in therapy. Congruence implies a commitment to the development of authenticity and self-awareness, with those qualities being integrated expressions of the counsellor's values and attitudes in relation to clients.

Unconditional positive regard (UPR)

UPR refers to the generally non-judgemental, accepting attitude of the counsellor. It does not imply any approval on the part of the counsellor for destructive behaviour of the client, but an acceptance of its existence and that its roots are located within the client's psychological history. It is neither necessary nor desirable for the counsellor to be engaged in making moralistic evaluations of the client.

Perhaps the most contentious of the three core conditions (because of its apparent impossibility to achieve), unconditional positive regard refers to the consistent acceptance, by the counsellor, of a client's experience. An important characteristic is the lack of *conditions* of acceptance, i.e. no sense of 'I feel positive towards you on condition that you behave in ways I find acceptable'. It involves an acceptance for both 'positive' and 'negative' aspects of a person, and can also be expressed as non-possessive caring for a person as a separate individual. Rogers (1957, reprinted in Kirschenbaum and Henderson, 1990) thought that the term itself might be a little unfortunate as it had an absolute, 'all-or-nothing' ring to it, and remarked that,

> It is probably evident . . . that completely unconditional positive
> regard would never exist except in theory . . . I believe the
> most accurate statement is that the effective therapist
> experiences unconditional positive regard for the client during
> many moments of his contact with him, yet from time to time
> he experiences only a conditional positive regard — and
> perhaps at times a negative regard, though this is not likely in
> effective therapy. It is in this sense that unconditional positive
> regard exists as a matter of degree in any relationship. (Footnote,
> p. 225, in Kirschenbaum and Henderson, 1990)

Again, as with empathy and congruence, UPR cannot be
considered as a skill or one of a counsellor's repertoire of
techniques. It is part of a person's system of values and is an
integrated aspect of that person, not something that can be adopted
temporarily and, perhaps, inauthentically in order to fulfil the core
conditions. It is also unlikely that UPR is directly expressed by
the counsellor with any frequency, and does not usually take the
form of 'supportive', 'encouraging' or 'approving' statements
made by the counsellor to the client (though such statements may,
from time to time, be made). UPR is more likely to be conveyed
through the counsellor's close, empathic and non-judgemental
following of the client's experiencing as he or she expresses it.

Bozarth (2001) views unconditional positive regard, 'as the
curative factor for the pathological development of personality',
and asserts that,

> This has to be true given Rogers' conceptualisation of personal
> dysfunctions being predicated upon the introjection of
> conditional positive regard by significant others and by society.
> Conditional regard is countered by the unconditional positive
> regard of the therapist. (p. 16)

This position is echoed by Wilkins (2000/2001) whose view is
that, 'if any condition is more important than another, it is the
communication of unconditional positive regard' (p. 46). Similarly,
I have previously attempted to restate Person-Centred Therapy
theory giving particular prominence to the communication of
unconditional positive regard through close empathic attending
to the client as a person (Merry, 2002, p. 67).

Finally, it is important to recognise that Rogers did not say that a
therapist had fully to experience empathic understanding,
congruence and unconditional positive regard in order for therapy

Rogers, C. R. (1957). 'The necessary and
sufficient conditions of therapeutic
personality change.' *Journal of Consulting
Psychology*, 21: 95–103. Reprinted in H.
Kirschenbaum and V.L. Henderson (eds.)
(1990). *The Carl Rogers Reader.* London:
Constable, pp. 219–35.

Bozarth, J.D. (2001). ' Client-Centred
Unconditional Positive Regard: A
historical perspective.' In J.D. Bozarth
and P. Wilkins (eds.) *Rogers' Therapeutic
Conditions: Evolution, Theory and Practice.
Volume 3. Unconditional Positive Regard.*
Ross-on-Wye: PCCS Books, pp. 5–18.

Wilkins, P. (2000/2001). 'Unconditional
Positive Regard Reconsidered.' British
Journal of Guidance and Counselling 28
(1): 23–36. Reprinted in J.D. Bozarth
and P. Wilkins (eds.)(2001) *Rogers'
Therapeutic Conditions: Evolution, Theory
and practice. Volume 3. Unconditional
Positive Regard.* Ross-on-Wye: PCCS
Books, pp. 35–48.

Merry, T (2002). *Learning and Being in
Person-Centred Counselling.* 2nd edition.
Ross-on-Wye: PCCS Books.

to be effective. It is closer to the spirit of Rogers' words to suggest that it is the extent to which the therapist is able to experience these things that determines the extent to which the relationship is experienced as constructive by the client. In other words, therapy can proceed even if the therapist experiences the core conditions only partially at times, and even not at all at others, provided the overall experience of the relationship by the client is one of significant empathy, authenticity and non-judgemental respect.

The six conditions work together

Whilst it can be useful to separate the six conditions, particularly the core conditions, in order to understand their meaning, it should be emphasised that they form a coherent whole, or *gestalt,* of interdependent elements. In terms of the counsellor's observable behaviour, it is likely that the communication of empathic understanding will appear to be the counsellor's main activity. However, it is probable that deep empathic understanding cannot be experienced by a counsellor who is to some significant extent incongruent or lacking in positive regard. The 'conditions' constitute the counsellor's total 'way of being' with the client, and it is this way of being that establishes the psychological environment in which the client's actualising process will tend to be expressed in positive and constructive ways.

Empathy, congruence and UPR are experiences of the counsellor, not strategies or techniques. They amount to a description of the counsellor's 'way of being' with clients.

Unlike many other approaches to counselling and psychotherapy, Person-Centred Therapy has not developed a set of associated techniques, strategies or methods, nor a system of diagnostic classification of psychological problems. This is not an oversight, and there are a number of good theoretical reasons why this should be the case.

First, 'the necessary and sufficient conditions' theory is a theory about the characteristics of constructive human relationships that can be extended beyond the therapy relationship to other aspects of human experience, not a 'how to do it' method. The theory requires counsellors to develop a particular set of values and attitudes towards others that are reflected consistently in the counsellor's behaviour. For example, the person-centred counsellor regards the change process as one involving the client's internal resources for growth and development, and that these resources become increasingly available in a psychological environment free of threat and rich in positive regard and empathic understanding. It is, then, not so much a question of what the counsellor *does*, but how he or she *is* in relation to clients.

Whilst there are no set techniques or strategies in person-centred counselling, the counsellor needs to be skilled in communicating empathic understanding.

Research (e.g. Brodley and Brody 1990; Merry, 1996) has shown that Rogers' behaviour in therapy characteristically consisted of him making empathic following responses for most of the time. He could be seen as dedicating himself to gaining as deep an understanding of his clients as was possible for him, and checking out or testing his understanding. The essentially non-judgemental and non-directive nature of his responses varied very little, if at all, from one client to another. There is no sense from reading Rogers' work, or that of other published person-centred practitioners, that they put into operation a set of predetermined skills, or that their underlying values varied with the kind of problem or issue the client was expressing.

Second, Rogers did not regard diagnostic categories as helpful (in fact he thought they were more likely to be damaging than of help), and certainly did not view them as useful in determining specific 'treatment plans'. All manifestations of psychological disturbance are regarded as having a single 'cause' — corruption or damage to the actualising tendency created by destructive or 'negative' experiences, resulting in the introjection of self-destructive conditions of worth.

The same remarks can also be directed towards the process of 'assessment'. It is usual for most therapeutic approaches to require the client's current state of emotional or psychological functioning to be assessed by the therapist prior to the initiation of therapy itself. Through this process, it is argued, therapy can be planned in advance to include those strategies and techniques most likely to 'fit' with the client's apparent 'treatment needs'. Assessment, in this case, is therefore an aspect of diagnosis and serves (in the view of the Person-Centred Approach) to shift attention away from the individual person of the client, to some theoretical label.

The theory that the six conditions are both necessary and sufficient is an area of some disagreement among the person-centred tribes discussed in this book. The contentious area is concerned with the sufficiency of the six conditions, with all variations of the approach in general agreement of their necessity. In the 'classical' position, the sufficiency of the six conditions is considered axiomatic. In this view, the therapist cannot both be attending empathically to the client's internal world and simultaneously engaged in making decisions about that experiencing or the manner of it with a view to intervening with any kind of technical instruction, suggestion, advice or other therapist-framed response. To put it most bluntly, any intervention that changes the client's

Brodley, B.T. and Brody, A.F. (1990). 'Understanding client-centered therapy through interviews conducted by Carl Rogers.' Paper presented to the panel: *Fifty years of client-centered therapy: recent research*. American Psychological Association Annual Conference, Boston, MA.

Merry, T. (1996). 'An analysis of ten demonstration interviews by Carl Rogers: Implications for the training of client-centred counsellors.' In R. Hutterer, G. Pawlowsky, P. Schmid and R. Stipsits (eds.) *Client-centred and experiential psychotherapy: A paradigm in motion*. Vienna: Peter Lang, pp. 273–83.

People have the right to their own psychological self-determination. In other words, each person has the right to establish their own identity, and to express their unique being in the world in ways that respect the right to self-determination of others.

In a reconciliation of person-centred practice with the demands of today's healthcare professions, Paul Wilkins has developed a different view. He presents it briefly in his book *Person-Centred Therapy in Focus*. London: Sage (2003), and more fully in Wilkins, P. and Gill, M. (2003). 'Assessment in Person-Centered Therapy' *Person-Centered and Experiential Psychotherapies, 2* (3): 172–87 where they conclude: 'Together, the necessary and sufficient conditions and the seven stages of process provide person-centered therapy with an assessment rationale for deciding the likelihood of establishing a successful therapeutic endeavor, for monitoring its progress and, to a lesser extent, for determining the nature of therapist behavior. Not only is this scheme legitimate in terms of person-centered theory, it is essential to good practice' (p. 186).

The person-centred counselling process is a non-invasive and non-directive one. Respect for a person's process of self-determination involves the creation of a relationship in which the resources for change reside within the client him- or herself. Respect is expressed primarily through the process of empathic, non-judgemental 'indwelling' in the subjective world of the client.

experiencing away from its current process towards one considered by the therapist to be of more benefit is considered counter-therapeutic, and a compromise of the essential non-directive nature of Person-Centred Therapy.

Person-Centred Therapy is best regarded as consisting of a coherent and consistent set of basic values and attitudes that a counsellor brings to her relationships with others. Implied in the 'conditions theory' is a deep respect for a person's uniqueness and individuality, together with a trust in the person's capacity for ongoing change and personal development. More explicitly stated in the theory are the values, attitudes and personal qualities of the counsellor that need to exist in order for the relationship to initiate and maintain the client's change process. A further characteristic of the relationship that is implied by the conditions theory is that it is a non-directive one, and this is such an important principle that it needs some further discussion.

Non-directivity: an implied characteristic of the person-centred relationship

Although Rogers did not use the term 'non-directive' in his original theory statement, he did use the term elsewhere, and Person-Centred Therapy was briefly known as 'non-directive therapy'.

'Non-directivity' refers to the general attitude that change is a naturally occurring process driven by the actualising tendency, and its content is uniquely determined by the needs of each individual. Rogers noted that the change process displayed its own direction in that it tended to be away from reliance on the evaluations and judgements of others towards increasing reliance on the individual's own valuing system (i.e. away from an external towards an internal locus of evaluation). Secondly, Rogers noted that, among other things, change involved a dissolving of conditions of worth so that the person became less inhibited by introjected values and attitudes and more free to respond to experience in novel and creative ways with less internal conflict.

Person-centred theory views these general developments as being outcomes of changes in the client's psychological environment provided by the Person-Centred Therapy relationship. In other words, the environmental factors (particularly including relationships with others) that led to the internalisation of conditions of worth and the development of an external locus of evaluation can be corrected for by the client's immersion in a more constructive environment. The absence of threat in this environment, together with the experiences of being understood empathically by a congruent counsellor who holds an attitude of unconditional positive regard, enables a client to allow more experience into awareness without the associated distortion and denial of internalised conditions of worth.

Person-centred theory regards this process as being unpredictable in its specifics, and likely to be idiosyncratic for each client. The principle of non-directivity is important because it enables each client's change process to unfold as more denied or distorted experience becomes accurately available to awareness. Since the content of this experience cannot be predicted, the counsellor cannot assume to know what direction the therapy should take, or what 'issues' may or may not prove to have significance for the client.

In a recent article, Merry and Brodley (2002) remark:

> The process of change in client-centered therapy is predictable only in very general terms. It is idiosyncratic and, in detail, unpredictable for each individual. It is this unpredictability, and the person-specific unique processes that it represents, that makes therapist attempts to direct the process both unnecessary and countertherapeutic. Directivity implies foreknowledge both of the destination and of the most efficient way of arriving there. Because each client's 'journey' is personal and idiosyncratic, direction needs to emerge from within the client, supported by the understanding relationship, rather than imposed by the therapist. (p. 72)

Merry, T. and Brodley, B. (2002). 'The Nondirective Attitude in Client-Centered Therapy: A Response to Kahn.' *Journal of Humanistic Psychology, 42* (2): 66–77.

The non-directive attitude minimises the possibility that the counsellor behaves, either knowingly or not, in ways that assume power over the client or expertise on the client's behalf. Grant (1990) distinguishes between 'instrumental' and 'principled' non-directiveness. 'Instrumental' non-directiveness he regards as a kind of technique, because it is adopted by the counsellor when the counsellor regards it as helpful to the client. Alternatively, Grant thinks of 'principled' non-directiveness as a moral choice, i.e. to respect clients as autonomous individuals. Principled non-directiveness is an expression both of respect for the client's own self-resources, and of the determination on the counsellor's part not to control the course of the therapy, but to follow the client's individual process as it emerges.

Grant, B. (1990). 'Principled and Instrumental Non-Directiveness in Person-Centered and Client-Centered Therapy,' *Person-Centred Review, 5*: 77–88. Reprinted in D. J. Cain (2002).(ed.) *Classics in the Person-Centred Approach.* Ross-on-Wye: PCCS Books, pp. 371–7.

The principle of 'non-directivity' is the area that causes most difficulties for those coming new to the Person-Centred Approach, partly because it is such a commonly misunderstood term. It is also the issue that highlights many of the differences between Person-Centred Therapy and most (if not all) other approaches, including those discussed in this book. 'Non-directivity' does not mean the adoption of a laissez-faire attitude of non-involvement, or one of leaving the therapeutic process to the vagaries of chance. Rather, it is a principled and ethical stance taken towards the complex processes involved in human psychological growth and development, most of which are poorly or incompletely understood. Empathic following of an individual's idiosyncratic and unpredictable journey into the roots of their sense of 'self' requires an active, involved and non-judgemental concentration. The source of change is assumed as residing within the individual, and the imposition of externally located technical expertise is regarded as counter-productive in locating and activating the individual's self-healing resources.

Of course there are times within any therapeutic relationship where the client's resources seem unavailable or the process becomes stuck with little observable change taking place. The temptation in such circumstances is for the therapist to provide the direction, or to assume responsibility for, the client's process rather than for the therapist's own empathic resources and ability to remain immersed in the client's inner world. Such experiences of 'stuckness' are not confined to the classical Person-Centred Approach, but are common in all therapeutic traditions. In the 'classical position' these experiences are regarded as acceptable (if somewhat frustrating) realities of the process of personal development, and may often be essential components of it. The change process is commonly not a straight-line progression, but more usually one of moments of therapeutic movement and periods of retreat, consolidation and stasis. 'Classical' person-centred therapists regard these static moments as important parts of an ongoing process, and respect them as manifestations of a client's current limited capacity to confront personal issues. In such circumstances, the therapist is more likely to evaluate his or her ability to remain empathically attuned to the client and his or her experiencing, than to consider ways of directly intervening into the client's process.

The 'classical' position: an overview

The 'classical' position of Person-Centred or Client-Centred Therapy is derived from the original work of Carl Rogers and his colleagues in which emphasis was given, and continues to be given, to a number of central principles.

The theory of actualisation is regarded as the sole motivation for human behaviour, growth, change and development, and the theory of Person-Centred Therapy is based on this hypothesis. The theory postulates that the psychological conditions for the individual's actualising tendency to correct for psychological damage exist within a relationship of certain definable qualities. The theory describes these conditions as both necessary and, crucially, sufficient. In other words, provided these conditions exist and endure over time, then their presence is sufficient for change to occur. Even if other conditions also exist, their existence is unnecessary in theoretical terms. If the conditions do not exist, then the therapy relationship will not be a causal agent in promoting change.

The therapist's role is one of non-judgemental, empathic companion. He or she is dedicated to a close attention to the client as a person, and attempts to experience and communicate as deep an understanding of the client's experience and expression as possible. The therapist has also internalised and integrated a value system that allows for him or her to experience a non-judgemental (that, is unconditional) positive regard for the client as a person, and this attitude pervades and informs all communication with the client.

The therapist has also achieved a level of personal congruence or authenticity that enables her to be fully self-aware and open to her experience of herself, her client and the relationship between them. The therapist is, therefore, perceived and experienced by the client as genuine in her communication and genuine in her valuing and respecting of the client.

Finally, the therapist's behaviour towards the client, both verbal and non-verbal, communicates a deep trust in the client's internal processes and capacity for personal change. The therapist's non-directive attitude and behaviour results from the moral choice that a person's right to their own psychological self-determination is paramount, and that any attempt to direct the process of therapy, however well-intentioned, serves to undermine that right. The person-centred relationship is not 'instrumental' in that it does not constitute the 'context' of therapy, nor is it a preparation for techniques or strategies. The person-centred relationship is the therapy.

Research

In his introductory chapter, Pete Sanders noted that Carl Rogers and his colleagues at Ohio State and Chicago were the first to

See Chapter 1, pp. 3–8, this volume.

The research tradition of CCT has involved populations including college students, 'juvenile delinquents', hospitalized 'schizophrenics', mild to severe neurotics and a mixed variety of hospitalized patients. The Wisconsin project, for example, is fully referenced in the sidenote on page 8. The following is a very small selection of research from the past 60 years and I have listed the more recent references. The internet will be helpful in tracking them down.

• Truax, C.B. and Mitchell, K.M. (1971). 'Research on certain therapist interpersonal skills in relation to process and outcome.' In A.E. Bergin and S.L. Garfield (eds.) *Handbook of Psychotherapy and Personality Change.* New York: Wiley. (The Bergin and Garfield 'Handbook' is a good guide to what is considered to be 'accepted' research in the U.S. Now in it's 5th edition, it has a chapter by Robert Elliott and colleagues on experiential therapy (full reference in sidenote on page 81).)

• Lockhart, W.H. (1983). 'The Outcomes of Individual Client-Centred Counselling with Young Offenders in Secure Residential Care.' In J. Harbison (ed.) *Children of the Troubles — Children in Northern Ireland.* Belfast: Stranmills College Learning Resources Unit.

• Friedli, K., King, M., Lloyd, M. and Horder, J. (1997). 'Randomised controlled assessment of non-directive psychotherapy versus routine general practitioner care.' *Lancet, 350*: 1662–5.

• King, M. *et al.* (2000). 'Randomised controlled trial of non-directive counselling, cognitive behaviour therapy and usual general practitioner care in the management of depression as well as mixed anxiety and depression in primary care.' *Health Technology Assessment Vol. 4: No. 19.* Also published in the *British Medical Journal, 321,* (2000): 1383–8.

• Bozarth, J.D., Zimring, F.M. and Tausch, R. (2002). 'Client-centered therapy: Evolution of a revolution.' In D. Cain, and J. Seeman (eds.) *Handbook of Research and Practice in Humanistic Psychotherapies.* Washington D.C.: APA.

research psychotherapy sessions with the advent of new recording technology. They developed methodologies and measuring instruments, conducting small and large-scale studies from the early 1950s to the 1970s. Classical client-centred therapists were also at the front of developments in qualitative as well as quantitative research. That first flush of involvement has since subsided, and the classical position has been largely absent from quantitative research in recent years. This is partly due to the reluctance of classical practitioners to take part in measuring 'outcomes' in a standard way. Measuring devices seem too crude, invasive or simply miss the point. However, readers can see the evidence for the effectiveness of Rogers' therapeutic conditions in an implicitly nondirective relationship by looking at the studies listed on the left.

Resources

For an accessible introduction
Merry, T. (2002). *Learning and Being in Person-Centred Counselling.* 2nd edition. Ross-on-Wye: PCCS Books.

For a collection of the works of Carl Rogers
Kirschenbaum, H. and Henderson, V. L. (eds.) (1990). *The Carl Rogers Reader.* London: Constable.

For a presentation of new developments
Mearns, D. and Thorne, B. (2000). *Person-Centred Therapy Today: New frontiers in theory and practice.* London: Sage.

Organisations
There are no organisations dedicated exclusively to a classical approach to CCT; The British Association for the Person-Centred Approach (BAPCA) welcomes everyone with an interest in the PCA, whether their interest is in therapy or the wider applications of the approach.
• BM-BAPCA, London, WC1N 3XX.
    Membership enquiries, telephone 01989 770 948.

Journals
Person-Centred Practice. Published by BAPCA. Available to non-members by subscription: contact PCCS Books, Llangarron, Ross-on-Wye, HR9 6PT, or telephone 01989 770 707.

Websites
• British Association for the Person-Centred Approach: <http://www.bapca.org.uk>.

<table>
<tr><td>

focusing-oriented therapy

</td><td>

campbell purton 3

</td></tr>
</table>

Historical introduction

I begin with a sketch of the history of Focusing-oriented Psychotherapy. The history is important since some of it is not well known, and without it, it is hard to understand how members of this 'tribe' can possibly see their tradition as having a central place in the 'person-centred nation'.

Focusing-oriented Psychotherapy has developed from the work of the Austrian-American philosopher and psychotherapist Eugene Gendlin. Gendlin was a close colleague of Carl Rogers at the University of Chicago Counseling Center in the 1950s, and Rogers acknowledged the importance of Gendlin's influence in developing his ideas during that period (Rogers, 1958/61).

Gendlin's background is in philosophy, and about half of his publications are in that field, but the central philosophical theme which has concerned him relates very closely to what is involved in psychotherapy. It is the theme of how our immediate lived experiencing relates to the concepts we use to express and carry forward that experiencing. There is a rich, lived intricacy in our experiencing which can never adequately be put into explicit thought or words. Indeed, words and concepts can often dull our experiencing; it can become 'sicklied o'er with the pale cast of thought' (Hamlet, III: i, 85). Yet it is also true, as often happens in poetry, that words can focus and crystallise our experiencing, so that through them our experiencing actually becomes brighter and deeper, and more communicable to others.

Gendlin — at that time a philosophy PhD student — joined Rogers' group at the University of Chicago Counseling Center in 1953 because he saw that what Rogers and his colleagues were working with was just that process which interested him: the helping of people to fully engage with their own experiencing and to find ways of expressing or symbolising that experiencing. From his philosophical background Gendlin was also aware that experiencing can always be formulated in many *different* ways. The world is not 'just there', already divided neatly into objective

Rogers, C.R. (1958). 'A process conception of psychotherapy.' *American Psychologist, 18*:114–59. Reprinted in C.R. Rogers (1961). *On Becoming A Person.* London: Constable, pp. 125–62.

See Pete Sanders' brief account in Chapter 1, pp. 3–7, this volume, for more information on the Chicago Counseling Center.

categories; how we conceptualise the world depends a great deal on cultural factors, and on our own creative imagination. This point also fitted with what Rogers was doing in encouraging people to find their *own* way of seeing things, rather than trying to fit a client's experiencing into an accepted psychological theory.

At that time, Rogers was working on his process conception of psychotherapy, according to which therapeutic progress is a matter of movement 'from fixity to changingness, from rigid structure to flow, from stasis to process' (Rogers, 1958/61). This was also the period in which Rogers was stressing the necessity and sufficiency of the 'therapist conditions', especially empathy, acceptance and congruence (Rogers, 1957). However, Rogers tended to see 'the conditions' as aspects of a single condition. In an address to the American Academy of Psychotherapists (Rogers, 1956) he said 'I believe I can state this condition in one word . . . that the client experiences himself as being fully received'. And late in his life he remarked:

> I am inclined to think that in my writing perhaps I have stressed too much the three basic conditions (congruence, unconditional positive regard, and empathic understanding). Perhaps it is something around the edges of these conditions that is really the most important element of therapy — when my self is clearly, obviously present. (Rogers cited in Baldwin, 1987, p. 45)

Rogers' view was that given that the client feels received, the movement from rigid structure to flow will take place. In the early stages of therapy the client typically talks about external events, and does not communicate anything of their own experiencing. Rogers (1958/61) writes:

> The ways in which he has construed experience are set by his past, and are rigidly unaffected by the actualities of the present. He is (to use the term of Gendlin and Zimring) structure-bound in his manner of experiencing. (Rogers, 1961, p.133)

As the therapeutic process proceeds there is a loosening of the fixed structures, and feelings in the present moment are more freely expressed.

> There is a beginning tendency to realise that experiencing a feeling involves a direct referent . . . (p. 140). Gendlin has called my attention to this significant quality of experiencing as a referent. (p.150)

The 'direct referent' here is what Gendlin came later to call the 'felt sense'. Rogers gives the following illustrations:

Rogers, C.R. (1958). 'A process conception of psychotherapy.' *American Psychologist, 18*:114–59. Reprinted in C.R. Rogers (1961). *On Becoming A Person.* London: Constable, pp. 125–62.
Rogers, C.R. (1957). 'The necessary and sufficient conditions of therapeutic personality change.' *J. Consult. Psychol., 21*: 95–103. Reprinted in H. Kirschenbaum and V.L. Henderson (eds.) (1989). *The Carl Rogers Reader.* London: Constable, pp. 219–35.
Rogers, C.R. (1956). 'The essence of psychotherapy: moments of movement.' Paper given at the first meeting of the American Academy of Psychotherapists, New York, October 20.

Baldwin, M. (1987). 'Interview with Carl Rogers on the use of self in therapy.' In M. Baldwin and V. Satir (eds.) *The use of Self in Therapy.* New York: Haworth Press, pp. 45–52.

Rogers, C.R. (1958/61). 'A process conception of psychotherapy.' *American Psychologist, 18*:114–59. Reprinted in C.R. Rogers (1961). *On Becoming A Person.* London: Constable, pp. 125–62.

Nick Baker discusses the notion of the 'felt sense' further in Chapter 4, pp. 71–2. Most of what he says in his Chapter is consonant with the principles and procedures of focusing-oriented therapy.

Example: 'That kinda came out and I just don't understand it [*Long pause*] I'm trying to get hold of what that terror is.'

Example: Client is talking about an external event. Suddenly she gives a pained, stricken look. Therapist: 'What — what's hitting you now?' Client: 'I don't know. [*She cries.*] I must have been getting a little too close to something I didn't want to talk about, or something.'

Example: 'I feel stopped right now. Why is my mind blank right now? I feel as if I am hanging on to something, and I've been letting go of other things; and something in me is saying, "What more do I have to give up?"'

These examples, on page 140 of C.R. Rogers (1961). *On Becoming A Person*. London: Constable, pp. 125–62, are among many Rogers uses to illustrate different levels of process.

Thus by the late 1950s the theory which was emerging from Rogers' group was that when clients are 'received' by the therapist they gradually become more engaged with their own experiencing, become less 'structure-bound' and therefore more able creatively to resolve their difficulties. There were, however, some empirical results which were puzzling, if the crucial element in therapy was the receptive attitude of the therapist. Two members of Rogers' group, Kirtner and Cartwright, had obtained results which suggested that it was often possible to predict from the first few sessions whether a client was likely to be successful in therapy. It seemed that although the therapist conditions were important, much also depended on the personality of the client (Kirtner and Cartwright, 1958a), and on how the client related to their own experiencing (Kirtner and Cartwright, 1958b).

Kirtner, W.L. and Cartwright, D.S. (1958a). 'Success and failure in Client-Centered Therapy as a function of client personality variables.' *J. Consulting Psychology*, *22*: 259–64
Kirtner, W.L. and Cartwright, D.S. (1958b). 'Success and failure in Client-Centered Therapy as a function of initial in-therapy behavior.' *J. Consulting Psychology*, *22*: 329–33.
Rogers, C.R. and Russell, D.E. (2002). *Carl Rogers The Quiet Revolutionary: An Oral History*. Roseville, CA: Penmarin Books.

Recalling this period, Gendlin (in Rogers and Russell, 2002, p. xviii) remarks:

In 1956, when Kirtner distributed his study, the center staff was outraged. We could not believe that we worked with some clients in a way that was failure-predicted from the first few interviews. Surely there must be an error in the study, we declared. Only Rogers was calm. He told us, 'Facts are always friendly.' When I came to his office to argue about it, he said 'This study will help us with the next study.' As I was leaving and we stood in the doorway, he put his hand on my shoulder for emphasis and said 'Look, maybe *you* will be the one to discover how to go on from this.' He meant me only as an example, but I may have heard him on a deeper level.

It was clear that the theory needed to be further tested, something which was always very important for Rogers. What was required were tests which would assess

(a) the degree to which the therapist 'received' the client (i.e. the extent to which Rogers' 'core conditions' were present),
(b) the extent to which the client's experiencing became less structure-bound during the progress of therapy and
(c) the effectiveness of the therapy.

Scales were employed, or newly developed (such as Gendlin's scale for 'experiencing level') to measure these three variables, and a large-scale five-year project was initiated at the University of Wisconsin to test the theory with a client population of schizophrenics. Rogers maintained overall responsibility for the project, but handed over its direction to Gendlin.

The findings of the Wisconsin project were complex and not altogether what Rogers and Gendlin had expected. There was a significant correlation between a high level of the therapist conditions and high experiencing level, as the theory predicted there would be. There was also *some* evidence that the therapy resulted in constructive personality change. However, there was no evidence that high therapist conditions *caused* high experiencing levels. It was rather that some clients *began* at a higher experiencing level, that these clients did rather better in therapy, and that these clients' therapists exhibited relatively high levels of the core conditions. Rogers' response to these results was:

> The main thrust of these findings . . . appears clear: *The characteristics of the client or patient influenced the quality of the relationship which formed between him and his therapist* . . . The therapist's attitudes are clearly important, but the patient's characteristics appear to play a definite part in eliciting these qualities . . . All of this points to the conclusion that an early assessment of the relationship qualities and the process level of any given relationship is a good prognosticator of the probability that constructive personality change will occur. (Rogers, 1967, pp. 89–91; Rogers' emphasis)

In his summary of the findings of the Wisconsin project Rogers wrote:

> Some of our hypotheses were at least partially confirmed. Others were disproved. New evidence was unearthed which did not fit the theory from which we had started. Thus a re-thinking of the theoretical basis of our therapy became necessary. (*ibid.* pp. 74–5)

Pete Sanders discusses the Wisconsin project and its problems in more detail in Chapter 1, pp. 7–11, but does not give an account of the results. For a full account see the official write-up of the project: Rogers, C. R., Gendlin, E.T., Kiesler, D.J. and Truax, C.B. (1967). *The Therapeutic Relationship And Its Impact: A study of psychotherapy with schizophrenics.* Madison: University of Wisconsin Press.

Rogers, C.R. (1967). 'The findings in brief.' In C.R. Rogers, E.T. Gendlin, D.J. Kiesler and C.B. Truax, *The Therapeutic Relationship and its Impact: A Study of Psychotherapy with Schizophrenics.* Madison: University of Wisconsin Press, pp. 73–93.

Ibid.

The rethinking was that therapeutic effectiveness is not simply a matter of providing the therapeutic conditions. The conditions are important, but they arise *in the relationship* partly as a result of the *client's* level of experiencing.

Following the Wisconsin project both Rogers and Gendlin came to emphasise much more the importance of the therapist *engaging* with clients who are not initially very engaged in the relationship. Gendlin (1964b, pp. 170–2) wrote:

> The patient is ill, afraid and withdrawing. You know that but it is still painful — particularly painful not to be *able* to reach out to him for such a long period, when you want to . . . This, more than anything else, has moved us away from a concern with technique, a concern with being 'client-centered' or being any other particular way . . . We have shifted from talking about the optimal response behavior to much more basic and global factors: the attitudes of the therapist, the approach that as one person he takes towards the other person, how to make interaction happen where it isn't.

Gendlin, E.T. (1964b). 'Schizophrenia: Problems and methods of psychotherapy.' *Review of Existential Psychology and Psychiatry,* 4: 168–79.

Although Rogers did not work further on the crucial theoretical issues raised by the Wisconsin project, Gendlin did continue to work on the theory (Gendlin, 1964) and became increasingly concerned about the finding that if clients start therapy with a low experiencing level they are unlikely to make good progress. The logical response to this was to look at what the successful clients were doing, and to see whether the other clients could be helped to do this too. What the successful clients seemed to be doing was to *engage* with their own experiencing. That is, rather than talk mostly about external events or analyse their problems in an intellectual fashion, they would pause and turn their attention to what they were experiencing in the present. (Rogers' three examples above illustrate this.)

Gendlin, E.T. (1964). 'A theory of personality change.' In P. Worchel and D. Byrne (eds.) *Personality Change.* New York: John Wiley.

See Pete Sanders' account of the end of the Wisconsin project and Rogers' move to California in 1964, Chapter 1, pp. 11–13, this volume.

Gendlin wondered whether clients could be instructed on how to focus their attention on their experiencing, and further work suggested that this was indeed possible. Such instructions came to be known as 'focusing' instructions. However, such a procedure tends to change the character of the therapy session from one of client-centred receptivity to a teaching situation. Consequently, as Focusing-oriented Therapy has developed, the emphasis has been placed more on a gentle encouragement of attention to experiencing, rather than on explicit teaching.

The issue of encouragement, however gentle, can still raise concerns in connection with 'directivity' which I will address later.

Nick Baker notes that this is an area that person-centred experiential therapists would refer to as 'process identification' and 'process direction'.

Gendlin is best known for his book *Focusing* (Gendlin, 1978),

Gendlin, E.T. (1978). *Focusing.* New York: Everest House. (New British edition, London: Rider, 2003.)

which sets out the focusing instructions in a way that can be used by anyone, together with many suggestions on how to deal with difficulties which can arise in working with oneself in this way. The focusing procedure involves essentially bringing awareness into the body, noticing the concerns which are troubling one, getting a physically felt sense of each trouble, finding a way of articulating or expressing that felt sense in words or images, noticing where a word or image brings some release, and receiving what has come from that experiential shift. However, it is important to realise that this popular self-help work, with its explicit set of focusing instructions, was written in the spirit of 'giving therapy away', rather than as a guide to how therapists might work with clients. The book has sold nearly half a million copies and is still in print after 30 years. Many people have found it enormously helpful, but it is very much a spin-off from Gendlin's main work in the theory of psychotherapy, to which I now turn.

Human nature

Gendlin sees human nature as being essentially interactional. A child is born into a relationship with the world and can survive neither physically nor psychologically without interacting with the world. There is a level of interaction which we share with inanimate things: as physical beings we are the way we are through the interplay of physical forces which constitute and act upon us. Then there is the level we share with plants: our bodies are complex organic systems in which each element is what it is partly as a result of the impact of other elements, which are the way *they* are partly because of the way the first element is. In Gendlin's terminology a living organism is an 'interaffecting whole' which cannot be reduced to the sum of its parts. The interaffecting extends beyond the physical boundaries of the organism: organisms are what they are partly because of the way the environment is, and the environment is the way it is partly because of the way the organism is.

Then there is much that we share with sentient animals, in whom there is a new kind of interaction: an interaction between the animal and how it *registers* or perceives its environment. Unlike a plant, an animal reacts not exactly to its environment but to how the environment is *for it*. If the animal's temperature-regulation system is faulty, for example, it will behave in terms of the temperature *it registers* rather than in terms of the actual temperature. With sentience comes a whole new kind of interaction with the world. Finally, human beings have a mode of interaction with the world which involves our construing it in terms of concepts and general principles. This has both advantages and disadvantages. The advantages are that we can guide our lives by general principles which we can learn from others, without the need always to start from scratch by ourselves. For instance, we may know that it is not a good thing to drink salt water in order to quench our thirst, and this may make a difference to whether we survive when shipwrecked. All that which comes through language and tradition comes to us in terms of general truths or helpful principles, that is, the truths or principles of the culture which we are born into. But there is a catch, which is that where there are truths and helpful principles there can also be falsehoods and misleading principles. We can get caught in the general and fail to check whether the general principle really applies in our particular situation.

Gendlin emphasises that our situations are always more subtle and intricate than can be articulated in terms of general concepts. For example, suppose that a person is in a state which may correctly be described as 'angry'. That is an application of a general concept. Yet there is more to that person's experience: they *are* angry, but with an undercurrent of hurt, and not even exactly angry, but more full of resentment in connection with what was done to them, yet also angry with *themself* for letting it happen, and upset because they have let this happen *again* when they had only yesterday realised that this is what they always let happen . . . There is an intricacy in the lived experience which is not fully captured by the concept of anger.

For Gendlin, human life is an interplay between the rich, intricate sensed experience of our situations and the concepts which we employ to articulate those situations. It is an interaction between *this* — my immediate sensed experience now, and the forms or concepts in terms of which I express it. However, it is not as if my experience is sitting there, whole and complete, and just waiting to have the appropriate labels put on it. Immediate experience is not like that. It is something which prior to articulation has no fixed form; or we could say that the forms which are to come are there only implicitly. If we give our attention to our experiencing we can often sense something there which cannot yet be articulated adequately. (It can be articulated a *bit* just by saying 'I feel something there', and that is already to draw it a little into the realm of the explicit.) But *what* it is cannot yet be said. Gendlin often uses the example of a poet who is trying to get the final line for a poem. The poet tries out various possibilities, but as they do so they feel — physically feel — the not-rightness of these proposed endings. There is a physically felt sense that these endings are not right. They don't connect with that other felt sense of what the poem needs. In order to get a satisfactory ending (and it may never come), the poet has to stay with the felt sense of what is needed, and *wait* for what may come. When the right line does come there is a sense of release, perhaps a deeper breath — 'Ah! — that's it'. Now that the last line is there the poet may sense the need to *change* some of the earlier lines before the work is done. This last point shows vividly that one could not possibly get from the earlier lines to the last one by any process of logic.

In Gendlin's terminology the earlier lines *imply* the last line in a novel sense of 'imply'. It is not that the last line is determined by the earlier lines, but nor is it that any old last line would have done. There is an implication, but it is one that arises out of the felt sense of what has come before and of what is now needed. The example of the poet is just an illustration of what is involved in any aspect of our life which is not entirely governed by explicit principles. Much of our life *is* governed by such principles, and it would be foolish not to employ them when appropriate, but general principles, by their nature, are inadequate when we are faced with novel situations, or situations where we can all too clearly sense that none of the standard options are going to be satisfactory. In these situations we are stuck, and we have to let go of the general principles and familiar concepts for a while and dip down into the felt intricacy of the situation.

In that felt intricacy there is much that is implicit, and which may be of help to us. After all, we have built into our natures millions of years of evolution, as well as all that comes through our being born into a particular culture and family; also many years of experience with complex situations; also many imagined situations, situations about which we have read in novels or myths or biographies and so on. All this could not possibly be set out in an explicit way, but it is there in us, in an implicit interaffecting way which, if we will give it a chance, may give rise to a creative possibility. What emerges may not be *right*; we will have to see. How would it feel if I tried that? Liberating? Constricting? What is the felt sense of this new possibility that has come? What, actually, does this new thing amount to? Even if it would be absurd to do exactly *that*, I might be able to find some non-absurd thing which still preserves the spirit of what has come.

Gendlin's theory is developed in a 1997 work entitled *A Process Model* which has not yet been published, but which is available from the Focusing Institute in

In brief summary, Gendlin's view of human beings is that we are beings who are always moving between our own immediate individual experiencing and the *expression* of that experience in words, images, dance, music and so on, which allows our experiencing to be in communication with others' experiencing through its formulation in some way which is not just ours, but shareable. What we are able to share makes a difference to the cultural forms in which we live, just as much as the cultural forms make a difference to how we construe our experiencing. Human life is an experiential interaction process between what is private and individual and what is public and communal.

Theory of personality change

Strictly speaking, Gendlin does not have a theory of personality, but he does have a theory of personality *change*.

Theories of personality do not sit easily with the Person-Centred Approach. A theory of personality is a theory through which the therapist views the client, and if the therapist takes the theory seriously then they surely have some obligation to respond to the client in terms of what their theory tells them about people who are in the kind of situation the client is in. But it is central to the Person-Centred Approach that the therapist should respond to the client not in terms of the conceptual scheme which the *therapist* adheres to, but in terms of the scheme through which the *client* views their world. Applying a theory to a human being is quite different from applying a theory to something in the inanimate world. The inanimate thing does not have *its* view of its situation; in applying our scheme we are fitting it into our world, and in the case of inanimate things there can be no objection to that. (That it can be done at all is one aspect of the thing's being inanimate: it does not have a life of its own.) It is true that even the inanimate world will always be infinitely richer and more intricate than any scheme within which we try to frame it, but there is not the additional problem of its having its own view of things.

A person *is* a being with their own view. To understand a person we have to appreciate what *their* view is, and to help a person we have to respond in a way that is a response to *their* situation, that is, the situation as seen by them. It can then seem that *our* view, whether a personal one or one derived from a psychological theory, is simply irrelevant.

However, that is not quite right. It is often true that people *are* helped by psychological theories. Someone reads Freud, or Jung or Rogers and what they read throws a whole new light on their

New York, <www.focusing.org>. Briefer introductions to the theory can be found in 'Thinking beyond patterns: body, language and situations.' In B. den Ouden and M. Moen (eds.) (1992). *The Presence of Feeling in Thought.* New York: Peter Lang, pp. 25–151, also in Appendix B of his book *Let Your Body Interpret Your Dreams* (1986). Wilmette, Illinois: Chiron, and in the theory section of his paper 'The client's client: the edge of awareness', Gendlin, E.T. (1984). In R.L Levant and J.M Shlien (eds.) *Client-Centered Therapy and the Person-Centered Approach.* New York: Praeger.

In a sense Rogers *does* have a theory of personality, which he develops in 'A theory of personality and behavior', in Rogers, C.R. (1951). *Client-Centered Therapy.* Boston: Houghton Mifflin, pp. 481–533, and in 'A theory of therapy, personality and interpersonal relations as developed in the client-centered framework', in S. Koch (ed.) (1959). *Psychology: A Study of a Science, Vol. 3.* New York: McGraw-Hill, pp. 184–256, but it is primarily a theory of how people change, rather than of what they are.
There is little in Rogers which is analogous to Freud's personality structures (ego, id, superego) or Jung's archetypes.

Is it their situation or for others situation? [handwritten marginal note]

situation. Things which they hadn't thought of bringing together before now illuminate each other; things which previously looked much the same now are differentiated through the new concepts which the person has acquired. Their experiencing has changed, has been carried forward, by the new concepts. As I suggested at the beginning, words can dull our experiencing, but they can also enliven it. But *which* concepts will illuminate and carry forward a person's experiencing depends critically on who the person is. Reading Jung or Rogers can inspire one person and leave another quite cold. The concepts and personality theories which are important for a person are the ones which *help* that person.

This may seem an extreme form of pragmatism and relativism, but Gendlin's theory gives a novel twist to such terms. In Gendlin's scheme of things a person's experiencing is an implicit multiplicity of indefinite intricacy. In other words there are all sorts of things there, all interconnected, but not in explicit form. The implicit multiplicity has a forward-moving tendency which the person senses as something they need to be doing, or realising — but what exactly is it? Into this felt sense comes something explicit, an idea they have read about, or something which their therapist has said. This new thing interacts with the felt sense and draws something new out of it. Much that other people say to us in connection with our problems does not have any such experiential impact; the felt sense of 'something needed' simply stays as it was. But at other times a word or idea resonates with us and our experiencing changes. What our companion said carries us forward into new experiencing. If they had said something else then that too might have carried us forward. (A poem can be completed in more than one way.) But not just anything will carry us forward; in fact it is often the case that *nothing* seems to help. (The poem may not get completed.) It is not at all arbitrary which psychological theory will help a person, but nor can we say in advance what will help. The *client's experiencing* determines what the right concepts are for that client at that time. The right concepts are the ones which have the very specific impact of carrying forward what was implied in the client's experiencing. This is a matter of hard fact, and not at all relativistic or subjective.

Our experiencing can be carried forward by concepts taken from *any* field, especially if that field is something with which we are very familiar. For a football enthusiast ideas or images drawn from football can be much more helpful than those drawn from psychological theories. On the other hand, of course, psychological schemes such as those of Freud or Jung have been developed out of deep experience with human problems, so that ideas drawn from such schemes will *usually* have a better chance of resonating with most clients' experience than ideas drawn from schemes such as neurophysiology or astrophysics, or football.

So, Gendlin does not have *a* theory of personality; rather there are already many such theories, and no doubt more will be developed in the future. They are *all* relevant to the extent that they resonate with human experiencing, and each of them draws attention to things which may be less visible when looked at through the lenses of the others. For Gendlin the more theories with which we are familiar the better, because this increases the chances of something being elicited from our implicit awareness which may help the client.

Gendlin has a theory of personality *change* in the sense of having a philosophical account of how experiencing interacts with concepts. This account is to be found in his first book, *Experiencing and the Creation of Meaning* (1962/1997). Theories of personality are networks of concepts, and in a sense everyone has a theory of personality, that is, the conceptual scheme in terms of which they experience and think about their life and the lives of others. Everyday 'theories' of human nature, which are to a large extent embedded in language and culture, are often subtle and complex, often more sophisticated than those of the psychologists. When someone comes to a therapist it is often because their 'theory' — their way of seeing things — is unable to cope with the situation in which they find themself. But their 'theory' is not something purely cognitive; it is an aspect of their *life*. To change one's way of seeing things is to change as a person. Such personality change is what therapy is concerned with, and Gendlin's account of how concepts change through their interaction with experiencing is thus at the same time a theory of personality change.

Gendlin, E.T. (1962/97). *Experiencing and the Creation of Meaning.* Second edition. Evanston, Illinois: Northwestern University Press, 1997.

For Gendlin, psychological disturbances can be seen at the most general level as one or another kind of disturbance or block in the experiential interaction process. For instance, a person may withdraw from immediate experiencing into a world of abstractions. They then *analyse* their specific problems, but there is little personality change. Or someone relates effectively to practical issues in the external world, but avoids giving any attention to how external events strike them, how they feel about things, what things mean to them. In both these kinds of case the person's attention skips the phase of interaction with their

Gendlin's conception of psychological disturbance as blocked process can be seen as a more general form of Rogers' view that disturbance arises from conditions of worth. Introjection of conditions of worth is just one way in which the experiential process can be blocked. I mention other ways in the next paragraph.

immediate experiencing, jumping from one concept to another, or one event to another. Gendlin calls this 'process skipping'. Another sort of case is where we get caught in repetitive emotions. By contrast with the two previous cases we are, in this case, very much involved in our feelings, but are unable to stand back sufficiently to process them. There is, for example, just *this rage*, but we can't work with it, differentiate it, relate to it. Again the *interaction* process between experiencing and understanding is not there.

There are more specific factors which can interfere with the interaction process. For example, many people have an 'inner critic' who may disparage their giving attention to feelings because to do so is 'self-indulgent'. Or we may have *many* troubles facing us and cannot give attention to all of them at once. Or our experiencing may have been 'frozen' by traumatic events. Or we may have introjected other people's attitudes and be unable to distinguish our own experiencing from what has been introjected. This last difficulty is the one emphasised in classical Client-Centred Therapy, but I think it is unhelpful to try to reduce all kinds of psychological disturbance to this one (Purton, 2002).

Purton, C. (2002). 'Person-centred therapy without the core conditions.' *Counselling and Psychotherapy Journal*, 13: 6–9.

Theory of therapy

Gendlin's theory of therapy is grounded in his account of human nature as an interactional experiencing process which can become disturbed or blocked.

The most important aspect of the interactional process for human beings lies in our interactions with other people. When we are with another person we are different from the way we are on our own, even if the other person simply listens in silence. When we are troubled there is often the impulse simply to talk to another human being, and their mere presence can help, so long as they do not *block* the natural process of healing. With someone who listens and receives us in the way which Rogers described, our experiencing can unfold and carry us forward. We come to see things a bit differently, feel a bit less constricted or frightened. The presence of the other person helps us. However, if the other person interrupts us, misunderstands us, judges us, offers advice, draws comparisons with their own experiences, and so on, then very often we feel ourself shutting down, pulling back into ourself, and longing to be on our own so that we can at least be with the trouble as it is for us.

From Gendlin's perspective, the first two principles of therapy are that the therapist should *be there with the client,* and *not block the client's process.* That is already a great deal. Friends and relatives are seldom able to do this, partly because of not realising what is needed, and partly because their own personal involvement can make it difficult for them not to intervene in distracting ways. Rogers' 'core conditions' are implicit in this very special kind of 'being with'. The therapist needs to accept the client, in the sense of simply accepting in a friendly way what the client says. The therapist needs to track the client empathically so that the client can feel that what they are saying does make some sense. And the accepting and understanding need to be authentic: the client is unlikely to be helped if they pick up that the acceptance and understanding of the therapist are not genuine.

For clients whose interactional experiencing process is not significantly blocked, it may be sufficient simply for the therapist to be present with the client in this way. However, the therapeutic process is usually greatly helped through the therapist employing the reflective procedure which Rogers discovered. In making sure that he had understood the client, Rogers would reflect back to the client the essence of what they had said. For Rogers this was primarily a way of checking understanding, but he acknowledged later in his life that it also served a second 'mirroring' function (Rogers, 1986a, p. 376; 1986b, p. 202). When the client hears back what they have said, they typically correct it, or add to it, and when these corrections or additions are themselves reflected then the client moves that bit further into their experiencing. For example:

Rogers, C.R. (1986a). 'Reflection of feelings.' *Person-Centered Review, 1*: 375–7.
Rogers, C.R. (1986b). 'Client-centered therapy.' In I.L. Kutash and A. Wolf *Psychotherapist's Casebook.* San Francisco: Jossey-Bass.

C: I have a strange feeling about all this which I can't quite get . . . Sort of guilty . . .

T: It feels sort of guilty . . .

C: But there's something else . . . it's more like fear . . .

T: Like fear…

C: It's a fear of what people will say . . .

T: There's a fear of what people will say . . .

C: No, I don't really care what they say . . . [*Pause*] . . . It's more as if I'm afraid of really being me [*deep breath*] . . .

T: You're afraid of *being you.*

C: Yes, that's it . . . If I did it, I would *really* be me, and then I would be *seen,* and I couldn't pretend any more.

Here the client is naturally able to focus, and the therapist can simply reflect. In interchanges like this there is what Gendlin calls a 'self-propelled feeling process' — when what the client has said has been received, the client can move on a step further.

Aspects of their experiencing become explicit, and then still further aspects emerge. But the process is not simply one of acquiring deeper insight into oneself. Neither Rogers nor Gendlin think that insight is the primary aim of therapy. What happens in the therapeutic process is an actual shift in the way the person is. In the example above, when the client takes a deep breath after saying 'It's as if I'm really afraid of being me' they have *changed* a bit, and the change is felt and expressed in their body. Now things will be just that bit different for them.

Often the client needs some help in orienting towards their experiencing. Simple reflections of feeling may not help very much.

C: I was really angry, but also a bit scared.
T: You were both angry and scared.
C: He often makes me feel like that. I remember a time when he said to me (etc.).

The simple reflection of words such as 'angry', 'scared' and so on may not help the client to move into the felt sense of their situation, which is always less clear and more intricate than can be captured by any such terms. A good focusing-oriented response *points towards the felt sense* of the client's experiencing. A focusing-oriented response might be:

C: I was really angry, but also a bit scared.
T: You were feeling something there — there was anger, but also fear in it...
C: Yes, as if I was sort of paralysed . . . or . . .

The use of the word 'something' is often a helpful way to point towards the client's experiencing without fixing its form. Or the therapist may suggest a word which seems to them to catch the felt sense:

C: Yes, as if I was sort of paralysed . . . or . . .
T: You felt sort of frozen.
C: Yes *(a bit doubtfully)* . . . More like . . . paralysed . . .

Here, in spite of the client's 'Yes', the therapist's word has clearly resonated less well with the client's experiencing than the client's own word. But in spite of *that,* the therapist is helping the client through staying with them in their attempt to carry forward their experiencing.

A felt sense is *physically* felt. It is how the body is currently registering the situation. It can sometimes help the client to ask them what they are sensing in their body. For instance, 'When he said that, what did it make you feel inside?' Or 'You were really upset — what was that like? Sort of churned . . . or jittery . . . how was it?' People vary greatly in how much they are aware of their bodily responses to situations. We often respond on a largely cognitive level, or on the level of sheer emotion. But the more effective responses to situations usually come from a holistic sense of what is required. This sense, the physically felt sense of 'all that whole thing', is much richer than anything which can be expressed in concepts, and more subtle than a simple emotional response such as fear or anger. But just as we usually feel anger or fear there in the centre of our body, so we can sense in the body the more subtle, less clear, felt sense of the whole situation. If we can think and act from *that*, we will be more likely to be taking into account everything which we can take into account.

Above all, the therapist needs to encourage a sense of friendly interest in whatever comes. Of course what comes may be distasteful or painful, and then space needs to be made for *these* responses. 'You wanted to hurt her, but also there's a sense of not wanting it to be like that . . . of it being sort of wrong to have those feelings . . . '

The focusing-oriented therapist is, in all this, helping the client to sense where the stuck places are, and what might constitute some release or 'forward' movement. Only the client can find their way forward because only the client has a full sense of what and where the stuckness is. Only the client can sense the small steps which bring with them a little bit of relief, the steps which, in Gendlin's phrase, move 'in the direction of fresh air'. However, the therapist has an important function in helping the client to attend to and engage with what they are sensing; when we try to engage with our experiencing on our own we often get distracted and lose our way.

Since there are many ways in which the ongoing interaction process can be blocked there can be many ways of helping to free it up. I have so far mainly discussed how we might help someone engage more closely with what they are experiencing. But as I mentioned above, for some clients the difficulty is that they are *too* close to their experiencing, and need to establish a working distance from it. There is the sort of case where the client is overwhelmed by the sheer number of their problems. They could work on *this* one if they had a bit of peace, but there are also all the others clamouring for attention. Here the focusing procedure

Nick Baker observes that the person-centred experiential therapist sees the companionship offered by the therapist as of the highest significance.

Campbell Purton responds: to avoid misunderstanding, I would emphasise that the interaction with the therapist involves much more than this. The therapist's role is both to facilitate the client's interaction with their own experiencing through close listening and reflecting, *and* to provide an interpersonal interaction which can help to restore the client's ability to engage with their experiencing.

of 'Making a list' can help. The client is encouraged to *list* all their problems: 'We are not working on them right now, but just seeing what's there. There's that problem at work, and the trouble with your son, and . . . and . . .' It can help just to set the problems out like this and ask 'And apart from all *that*, is everything fine in your life?' This can give the client at least a few minutes respite from their problems. They can take a look at the problems from a distance, as it were, and decide which of them to work with first.

'Getting a distance' from one's problems is an important theme in Focusing-oriented Therapy. In Gendlin's theory, the person is conceptualised as being in some sense distinct from their experiencing. (It is characteristic of human beings that we can be aware of and can interact with our own experiencing.) We can say of some strong emotion, for example, 'That's there', and experience ourself as being aware of the emotion rather than being identified with it. It can help to say 'There's something frightened there' or 'You are noticing a scared bit of yourself — would it be all right for us to spend a bit of time with that scared bit? Would *it* like that?' If we can step back a bit from our emotions *then* we can begin to relate to them. Thus in Focusing-oriented Therapy we try to help the client find the 'right distance' from their feelings — not so distant that they can't be worked with, but not so close as to be overwhelming.

Focusing-oriented therapy is open to the possibility of using procedures developed in traditions other than the person-centred one, if they are helpful to the client. However, such procedures are always used *within* the overall relationship of trust and safety which the core conditions provide. The interpersonal relationship comes first, *then* the kind of client-centred reflecting which helps clients to relate to their experiencing, and *then where needed* other procedures which help to stimulate or free up the client's own experiential interaction process.

I referred above to such focusing procedures as 'making a list' or 'getting the right distance'. Procedures drawn from other approaches might include the Gestalt 'two-chair' and 'empty-chair' procedures, Laura Rice's 'evocative responding', role-playing a character from a dream, trying out an experimental 'action step' between sessions, and so on (Rice, 1970). Some of these procedures may be helpful for some clients. The focusing-oriented claim is that they will all be *more* helpful if they are done within a focusing-oriented framework, that is, if always the client and therapist check out what the impact of the procedure is on the

Gendlin discusses the two-chair procedure in Chapter 13 of Gendlin, E.T. (1996). *Focusing-oriented Psychotherapy.* London: Guilford Press. Dream work is discussed in Chapter 14 and 'action steps' in Chapter 17.

Rice, L.N. (1970). 'The Evocative Function of the Therapist.' In Wexler, D.A. and Rice L.N. (eds.) *Innovations in Client-Cenetred therapy.* New York: Wiley, pp. 289–311.

client's experiencing. Is the procedure carrying the client forward? If not, then the procedure is immediately dropped, and the therapist returns to a baseline of empathic following.

Non-directivity

Although Rogers' form of therapy was in the early days known as 'non-directive' therapy he later preferred the term 'client-centred'. This was perhaps because 'non-directivity' can suggest that there is no direction in Client-Centred Therapy, whereas for Rogers, there *is* a direction, but it is the client's direction (Cain, 1989, p. 125). Non-directivity also suggests that the therapist wishes to have no influence on the client. Yet that is not only undesirable; it is impossible. Whatever the therapist does (or doesn't do) will have an influence on the client, and the client would hardly come for therapy if they did not expect to be in some way affected by the what the therapist says or does.

'Client-centred' for Rogers was contrasted with 'theory-centred'. The client-centred therapist helps the client to determine their own goals, and their own preferred paths to those goals. This is in contrast with any form of therapy which starts from a theoretical conception of what the goals of human beings are, or should be. The client-centred therapist starts from the position that they *don't know* what the client's basic goals are. For example, they don't know whether the client wants to be a balanced integrated person, or prefers to develop certain capacities at the expense of all others; whether the client wants to adjust to the principles of society or challenge those principles; whether the client wants to fulfil their biological desires or 'rise above' them; whether the client wants to live in a rational, scientific kind of way, or to create of their life a work of art. Client-Centred Therapy doesn't have a theory of human nature beyond the principle that human beings have many and varied perspectives on what human nature is. The role of the therapist is not to direct the client in accordance with the therapist's view of human nature, but to help the client in formulating, and living by, their *own* view.

Directivity comes into Focusing-oriented Therapy only in so far as clients often encounter difficulties in formulating and living their own view of the world. The focusing-oriented therapist then tries to relate to the client in a way which will help the client to relate to their *own* experiencing. Thus Focusing-oriented Therapy could be said to be non-directive except in the sense of directing the client towards their own experiencing.

Richard Worsley asks: 'Is *empathy only* then to be discarded if it doesn't carry the client forward? What if empathy is crucial in the moment and process work would get in the way? Is that possible from a focusing point of view?'

Nick Baker says more about some of these procedures in Chapter 4, pp. 83–4.

Cain, D. (1989). 'The paradox of nondirectiveness in the person-centred approach.' *Person-Centered Review*, *4* (2): 123–31. Reprinted in D. Cain (ed.) (2002). *Classics in the Person-Centered Approach*. Ross-on-Wye: PCCS Books, pp. 365–70.

There is something of a paradox here. Both Rogers (e.g. in 'A therapist's view of the good life' in *On Becoming a Person*. (1961), pp. 183–96) and Gendlin have their views on what a 'good' human life amounts to. Gendlin addresses the paradox in 'Process ethics and the political question', in A.-T. Tymieniecka (1986) *The Moral Sense in the Communal Significance of Life*. Dordrecht: D. Reidel, pp. 265–75. See also Ch. 21 on 'Values' in his *Focusing-oriented Psychotherapy*. London: Guilford Press (1996).

Tony Merry notes, 'Carl Rogers (and CCT) had a lot to say about human nature in various publications (for summaries see Chapter 2, pp. 22–3, and Merry, T. (2002). *Learning and Being in Person-Centred Counselling*. Ross-on-Wye: PCCS Books.) In practice, a principled nondirective therapist has no view on human nature in terms of specific outcome.'

This is not very different from the position found in some 'more orthodox' person-centred thinking. For instance Mearns (1994, *Developing Person-Centred Counselling*. London: Sage, p. ix) writes that person-centred therapists are committed to the goal of helping a client 'to find and exercise more of his own personal power with regard to understanding and evaluating his actions'. He says it is nonsense to suggest that therapists should have no goals for the client other than the goals which the client has.

Grant, B. (1990). 'Principled and Instrumental Nondirectiveness in Person-Centered and Client-Centered Therapy.' *Person-Centered Review*, 5(1). Reprinted in D. Cain (ed.) *Classics in the Person-Centred Approach.* Ross-on-Wye: PCCS Books, pp. 371–7.

It is really more complicated than this, since in some traditions (often in the less orthodox wings of the tradition) what is 'right' is rather paradoxically held to involve the individual finding out for themselves what is right. Client-Centred Therapy can be seen as one of these 'paradoxical' traditions.

Barry Grant (1990) distinguishes between 'instrumental' and 'principled' non-directivity. A therapist shows 'instrumental' non-directivity if they respond non-directively except where they consider that a directive response will empower the client. By contrast, a therapist shows 'principled' non-directivity if they respond non-directively except where the *client* wants a different sort of response or the therapist spontaneously wants to do something different *in the moment*. The instrumental therapist has a general view of what is good for the client, and acts either directively or non-directively in terms of that view. The principled therapist objects to this on the grounds that Person-Centred Therapy should not impose on the client *any* view of what is good for them. Rather, the therapist should simply be there for the client in an open, spontaneous and respectful way.

It may seem that according to this distinction, Focusing-oriented Psychotherapy falls clearly in the instrumental category, since it holds the view that it is good for clients to engage with their own experiencing, and the focusing-oriented therapist tries to facilitate this. But I think one could equally well argue that the essence of Focusing-oriented Therapy lies in its respect for the client as the client struggles to find their own path. It is true that not *everyone* is concerned to 'find their own path'. For many people (historically, for most people) the point is rather to find the *right* path as determined by some valued tradition. But such people are unlikely to consult counsellors or psychotherapists. Instead they are likely to seek out someone within their tradition who can act as a personal or spiritual guide. People usually come to *counselling* when the resources of their tradition have failed them, or they have never belonged to any clear tradition. They come because they are in some way 'stuck' and unable to orient themselves with the traditional resources available to them.

It seems to me that the therapist should respect the client as someone who has chosen to seek therapy rather than some other form of help. The therapist should not only respect the client in the way that is right to respect *anyone*, but also respect the client's explicit or implicit request for a very special form of help: the form which is oriented toward helping the client find their own path. I think that many people who come to counselling today do have some sense that this is what counselling is about, and I think that if a client does not know this then the counsellor has a duty to inform them. But then, given that the client wants *this* sort of help, it is not true that the therapist is imposing their own view of what is good for the client. The therapist's assessment of when to be directive is not instrumental to a goal which the therapist has for the client; it is something that happens in the therapeutic relationship in accordance with the principle that the client wishes to find their own path. Helping people to find their own path, I suggest, is what counselling *is*. Focusing-oriented therapy merely makes this explicit.

The various procedures which a focusing-oriented therapist may use, such as reflection, making a list, or getting the right distance are all intended to help the client find their own path. The therapist is not committed to the view that 'finding one's own path' is always what is good for people; it is just that that is what *therapy* is, and the client has chosen to come for therapy.

In sum, then, Focusing-oriented Psychotherapy is 'client-centred' therapy. It involves relating to the client in a way which will help the client to find their own path, through engaging constructively with their own experiencing. It also provides a framework within which many forms of therapy can be practised. From a focusing-oriented perspective it is no longer a matter of the different 'schools' of therapy being in competition. One might expect that any of their ideas and procedures could be helpful, but only if the ideas and procedures are made secondary to the client's experiencing of them.

Research

If focusing-oriented theory is broadly correct then two important implications are:

(1) that the different concepts and procedures of the different therapy schools should not be strongly correlated with different therapeutic effectiveness. (The focusing-oriented position is that what is important is *not* the concepts or procedures themselves, but whether they are employed in a focusing-oriented way.)

(2) that what *is* therapeutically relevant should be (a) the capacity of the client to engage with their own experiencing and (b) the quality of the client-therapist relationship in providing the safety within which this capacity can be exercised.

Both these predictions are quite solidly supported by the research evidence. The more or less equal effectiveness of the different therapeutic approaches is one of the most consistent findings of psychotherapy research (Smith and Glass, 1977; Stiles, *et al.*, 1986; Lambert and Bergin, 1994; King, *et al.* 2000).

Smith, M.L. and Glass, G.V. (1977). 'Meta-analysis of psychotherapy outcome studies.' *American Psychologist, 32*: 752–60.

Stiles, W.B., Shapiro, D.A. and Elliott, R.K. (1986). 'Are all psychotherapies equivalent?' *American Psychologist, 31*: 165–80.

King, M. *et al.* (2000). 'Randomised controlled trial of non-directive counselling, cognitive-behaviour therapy and usual general practitioner care in the management of depression as well as mixed anxiety and depression in primary care.' *Health Technology Assessment, 4* (19).

Lambert, M.J. and Bergin, A.E. (1994). 'The effectiveness of psychotherapy.' In A.E. Bergin and S.L. Garfield, *Handbook of Psychotherapy and Behavior Change.* Fourth Edition. Chichester: John Wiley, pp. 143–89.

Orlinsky, D.E., Graw, K. and Parks, B.K.
(1994). 'Process and outcome in
psychotherapy — noch einmal.' In A.E.
Bergin and S.L. Garfield, *Handbook of
Psychotherapy and Behavior Change.*
Fourth edition. Chichester: John Wiley,
pp. 270–376.

Hendricks, M. (2002). 'Focusing-oriented/
experiential psychotherapy.' In D.J. Cain
and J. Seeman (eds.) *Humanistic
Psychotherapies: Handbook of Research and
Practice.* Washington: American
Psychological Association, pp. 221–51.
Brodley, B.T. (1988). 'Does early-in-
therapy experiencing level predict
outcome? A review of research.'
Discussion paper prepared for the Second
Annual Meeting of the Association for the
Development of the Person-Centered
Approach, New York, May 1988.

Clark, C.A. (1990). A comprehensive
process analysis of focusing events in
experiential therapy. Doctoral dissertation,
University of Toledo.

Sachse, R. (1990a). 'Concrete interventions
are crucial: The influence of the therapist's
processing proposals on the client's
intrapersonal exploration in client-centered
therapy.' In Lietaer, G., Rombauts, J. and
Van Balen, R. *Client-Centred and
Experiential Psychotherapy in the Nineties.*
Leuven: Leuven University Press, pp. 295–
308.
Sachse, R. (1990b). 'The influence of
therapist processing proposals on the
explication process of the client.' *Person-
Centered Review,* 5 (3): 321–44.
Hendricks, M. (2002). 'Focusing-oriented/
experiential psychotherapy.' In D.J. Cain
and J. Seeman (eds.) *Humanistic
Psychotherapies: Handbook of Research and
Practice.* Washington: American
Psychological Association, pp. 221–51.

There is also strong evidence that what is important is not the theoretical orientation of the therapist but (a) certain characteristics of the client and (b) the quality of the client-therapist relationship. Orlinsky, Graw and Parks (1994), in an extensive review of process research based on a literature search from 1985 to 1992, conclude that it is not so much *what* clients talk about but *how they talk about it* which is significantly related to outcome (p. 296), that client self-relatedness (in Gendlin's terms, 'experiencing level') is very significant (p. 339), and that the quality of the therapeutic relationship is almost always important (p. 308).

Client-Centred Therapy was the earliest form of therapy to be subject to empirical research and although interest in such research waned in the years following the Wisconsin project, there has recently been some renewed interest. (No doubt partly because of the increasing demands for 'evidence-based practice',) So far as Focusing-oriented Therapy is concerned Marion Hendricks (2002) has provided a review in which she cites 26 studies which suggest that higher experiencing levels correlate with successful outcome in therapy, though some of the earlier studies, it should be said, are open to criticism (Brodley, 1988).

There is more to psychotherapy research than outcome studies. Claudia Clark (1990) investigated what takes place when clients engage in focusing in the course of experiential therapy. Amongst her findings are the suggestion that focusing may be of value to unassertive clients where their inability to assert themselves comes from their difficulty in knowing what their experience is, and that focusing is interrupted not so much by strong emotion but by the intrusion of 'inner critics'. Rainer Sachse (1990a, 1990b; Hendricks, 2002) has a series of studies on the effects of therapist responses on the 'depth' of client experiencing. His conclusions are that if the therapist responds at an experiencing level which is 'shallower' than that of the client's previous response, the client's next response will itself be shallower. Conversely, if the therapist responds at a deeper level, the client's subsequent response tends to be deeper. He also showed that the therapists of more successful clients tend to make more 'deepening responses' than the therapists of less successful clients. Other studies are detailed in Hendricks (2002).

Resources

Focusing-oriented therapy
Gendlin, E.T. (1996). *Focusing-oriented Psychotherapy*. London: Guilford Press.

Purton, C. (2004). *Person-Centred Therapy: The Focusing-Oriented Approach*. Basingstoke: Palgrave Macmillan.

Focusing as a self-help procedure
Gendlin, E.T. (1978). *Focusing*. New York: Everest House. (New British edition, London: Rider, 2003.)

Cornell, A.W. and McGavin, B. (2002). *The Focusing Student's and Companion's Manual*. Berkeley, CA: Calluna Press. (Available through *The Focusing Connection*, below.)

Other useful perspectives
Campbell, P. and McMahon, E. (1997). *Bio-Spirituality: Focusing as a Way to Grow*. Chicago: Loyola Press.

Hinterkopf, E. (1998). *Integrating Spirituality in Counseling: A Manual for Using the Experiential Focusing Method*. Alexandria, VA: American Counseling Association.

Websites
The most important website is that of the Focusing Institute: <www.focusing.org>.

Video recordings of focusing sessions by Gendlin and others are available from the Focusing Institute.

Journals
The Focusing Folio, published by the Focusing Institute, 34 East Lane, Spring Valley, NY 10977, New York. Phone/fax 914 362 5222. email: <info@focusing.org>.

The Focusing Connection, published by Focusing Resources (Ann Weiser Cornell). 2625 Alcatraz Ave, PMB #202, Berkeley, CA 94705 USA. Phone 5190 666 9948. Fax 510 666 9938. email: <awcornell@aol.com>.

experiential person-centred therapy

nick baker 4

If my heart could do my thinking
And my head begins to feel
I would look upon the world anew
And know what's truly real
I Forgot That Love Existed: Van Morrison

We are living in interesting times. There has been a resurgence of interest in both 'classical' Person-Centred Therapy and experiential approaches, but as one who finds himself working in ways labelled 'experiential', what I notice is that descriptions which originated with experiential writers such as, 'edge of awareness', 'experiential track', 'felt meaning' and 'felt sense', are now on everyone's lips. They are becoming common currency. At a British Association for Counselling and Psychotherapy (BACP) meeting for representatives of BACP Accredited courses, Tim Bond talked about the 'felt sense' behind the new Ethical Framework, and did not seem to feel he had to explain it. Yet at the same time, experiential work is viewed in a somewhat confused way. For example, at The British Association for the Person-Centred Approach (BAPCA) conference at Durham in autumn 2002, experiential work was presented in the form of Focusing-Oriented Psychotherapy. Whilst I feel very warmly towards this approach (after all, it comes from the same place as the four phrases above), I discovered during my conversations with Mary Hendricks and Campbell Purton, that my way of working is not fully accounted for in the Focusing approach. There are several streams in the experiential approach which I will briefly identify and outline, and I will also endeavour to identify what I feel are some defining strands which appear in all experiential work.

What is experiential person-centred counselling?

In his chapter 'The Development of Client-Centered Therapy' (1970), Hart advanced the view that there were three periods in the development of the Approach. His table is reproduced overleaf.

Dialogues: BAPCA Conference held Durham University, September 19–21 2002. Recordings of the main sessions may still be available from BAPCA; details from <www.bapca.org.uk>.

Hart, J.T. (1970). 'The Development of Client-Centered Therapy', in J.T. Hart and T.M. Tomlinson, (eds) *New Directions in Client-Centered Therapy. Boston*: Houghton Mifflin, pp. 3–21.

Hart's time scale was up to 1970 when he was writing the piece. It is interesting to speculate whether, if he were writing this today, there would be *no* end date for the third phase of development (see next page).

Periods in the Development of Client-Centered Psychotherapy (Hart, 1970). Reproduced by permission.

	Functions of the therapist	Personality Changes
Period I 1940–1950 **Nondirective Psychotherapy**	Creation of a permissive, noninterpretative atmosphere; *acceptance* and *clarification*.	Gradual achievement of *insight* into one's self and one's situation
Period II 1950–1957 **Reflective Psychotherapy**	*Reflection* of feelings, avoiding threat in the relationship.	Development of congruence of self-concept and the phenomenal field.
Period III 1957–1970 **Experiential Psychotherapy**	Wide range of behaviors to express basic attitudes. Focus on the client's experiencing. Expression of the therapist's experiencing.	Growth in the process continuum of inter- and intra-personal living by learning to use direct experiencing.

Rogers, C.R. (1957). 'The necessary and sufficient conditions of therapeutic personality change.' *Journal of Consulting Psychology*, reprinted in H. Kirschenbaum and V.L. Henderson (eds.) *The Carl Rogers Reader.* London: Constable, pp. 219–35.

Rogers, C.R. (1959). 'A theory of therapy, personality and interpersonal relationships, as developed in the client-centred framework.' In S. Koch (ed.) *Psychology: A Study of a Science, 3. Formulations of the Person and the Social Context.* New York: McGraw-Hill. Reprinted in Kirschenbaum, H. and Henderson, V. L. (eds.) (1990). *The Carl Rogers Reader.* London: Constable, pp. 236–62.

Rogers, C.R. (1961). 'A Process Conception of Psychotherapy', in C.R. Rogers, *On Becoming A Person.* London: Constable, pp. 125–62.

Hart, J.T. (1970). 'The Development of Client-Centered Therapy.' In J.T. Hart and T.M. Tomlinson (eds.) *New Directions in Client-Centered Therapy.* Boston: Houghton Mifflin.

Prouty, G. (1999). 'Carl Rogers and Experiential Therapies: A Dissonance?' *Person-Centred Practice, 7* (1): 4–11.

The concept of *experiencing* is fundamental to person-centred work. I think it is conventional person-centred wisdom that as a result of having a therapeutic relationship characterised by what we have come to refer to as the six conditions (Rogers, 1957), our belief would be that clients would be able to live more fluidly, more spontaneously, more autonomously, and more in ways informed by their organismic valuing process. The more integrated *all* of our experiencing is into our awareness, and therefore available to us as a referent for action is a theme throughout all the classic texts of Rogers (1957, 1959, 1961). Some confusion may spring from, as Hart notes (1970), the fact that 'experiencing' refers to both the *act of experiencing* (to which all person-centred practitioners hold dear) and the *theory of experiencing* which carries with it ways of being which separate out experiential therapists from their classical colleagues.

As Prouty (1999) argues; to be in touch with our experiencing spontaneously of both our inner world and of the world of which we are part, and to have it as a trustworthy source of information on which to rely for our feelings and actions, is a state much to be desired. In much of Rogers' writings, this is the 'evidence' of the personal psychological integration that comes from successful therapy. Through our therapy we have become more 'whole', relying less on the opinion of others' and more on our own internal organismic valuing. We trust our own experience. However, as

Gendlin pointed out earlier (Gendlin, 1962), this is seeing experience as *content*. By being more reliably open to our experience of ourselves and of our responses to the world around us, we are fulfilling a definition of being a more 'fully functioning person'. Prouty, in the same article (Prouty, 1999), goes on to make the point that experiential writers talk about accessing the experiential process as being the 'right royal road' to personal integration, *not* its measure. And the key here is the word '*process*'. So, what exactly is meant by this split between content and process in terms of experience?

Gendlin, E. T. (1962). *Experiencing and the Creation of Meaning*. New York: Free Press.

Prouty, G. (1999). 'Carl Rogers and Experiential Therapies: A Dissonance?' *Person-Centred Practice 7* (1): 4-11.

Experience is what we all have. It is the general name for all that happens between us and the world, and what happens inside of ourselves. However, for Gendlin (1962) this was not enough. There was something else happening. He called it 'felt experiencing'. Any sharing of experience is a symbolised activity. We use words to communicate what we feel, but Gendlin argued there was a 'partly unformed stream of feeling that we have every moment' (p. 3) which exists in a pre-symbolised (i.e. not yet put into words) way within us. How often do we hear people say, and ourselves as well, that we just cannot find the words to say what we feel or mean. We have a sense of some aspect of our lives deep within us, and yet we cannot find an adequate form of expression. For Gendlin, we have within us a deep intuitive sense of this something, that we ignore at our cost. He writes:

Gendlin, E. T. (1962). *Experiencing and the Creation of Meaning*. New York: Free Press.

> A moment's experiencing contains implicitly so many meanings that no amount of words can exhaust it. (*ibid*. p. 34)

Ibid.

He is not advocating that we dismiss the content aspect of experience, that is our verbal, symbolised sense of what has happened, and what is happening, to us. What matters is this other aspect does not get overlooked. Yet there is a powerful 'Catch 22' implication. How can we access this pre-verbal sense of experiencing something without using words? This introduces an approach which will appear frequently in all later experiential writers and practitioners: the idea of *direct referencing*.

He argues that personal meaning is created in the interaction between experiencing something and finding ways to symbolise that experiencing. 'Feeling without symbolisation is blind; symbolisation without feeling is empty' (*ibid.* p. 5). So we need to directly refer to the raw unprocessed non-verbalised experiencing that is within us, which has the following characteristics:

Ibid.

- even though it is not existing in words *it is there in a concrete way within our bodies*

- even though we may not choose to access it *it is always there*
- even though it may not be verbal *we can always ask it questions*
- even though it may not be openly labelled as something specific *it is always implicit in how we are in any given situation*

Put simply: the felt sense exists and we can attend to it or not. To summarise, experiential work is based on the following triad of ideas:

- it is concrete
- it is bodily felt
- it is a process

Thus we can engage with our experiential stream and by so doing let there be a move from our direct experiencing being implicit to it being explicit and consequently able to enrich our expression of our feelings with the life blood of direct experience.

It may help if I describe the import of experiential responses. An effective experiential therapist response will:

- attend to the words used by the client, but will also be concerned with the non-verbal aspects of their communication.
- demonstrate that the client has been as fully heard as possible by the therapist.
- invite the client to turn inwards so the client can be more directly in touch with their inner sensing (this can be achieved by a response along the lines of, 'What does it feel like when you say . . . ?').
- be concerned to help the client connect with their implicit felt meanings and, in so doing, help them find words which will more clearly give voice to their personal meanings.
- take the form of a series of steps or stages as the client, with the therapist's full attention, can edge nearer and nearer to their deeply felt and truer sense of how they are actually involved with this issue or feeling or emotion.

The experiential therapist will be operating in ways which carry the following values.

The client is the most reliable source of information and wisdom about how they are (even when they say they have no idea) and so close attention to everything they say is a fundamental aspect of the work. The same reasoning lies behind the commitment to continual checking to maintain close, empathic contact with the client.

The relationship will be open and democratic, as the therapist is committed to the client being the expert on all that they say and feel. Having an understanding of how people in general function does not imply knowledge about any one individual. As a consequence, process comments (that is, tentatively offered comments on what the therapist sees as the client talks) are offered by the therapist in the spirit of a co-operative venture and are always invitational.

Experiential therapeutic work is concerned with clients becoming closer to their experientially defined inner core (that is, their continually flowing, non-verbal stream of experiencing in the moment) and, by so doing, help them regain more control of their lives. Different writers and practitioners use different language, but all believe in clients regaining their 'agential' status over their lives.

The therapist needs also to pay appropriate attention to their own experiencing as a full participant in the relationship. The focus of therapy is always the client and their reconnection with their inner felt meanings, but, bounded by that, the experiential approach consistently underscores that the work is about two people being with each other as ordinary human beings who know how hard it is to live.

All person-centred practitioners accept the idea that people are creative imaginative beings who want to make their lives personally meaningful. People do that, for the most part, even when, in retrospect, we find we have gone up a cul-de-sac. The 'classical' view, I believe, would argue that the role of the therapist is to remove the all-too-familiar obstacles of a judging, dismissive environment to allow the agentic push of the actualising tendency to flow from the client. The experiential therapist would argue that we need to engage with the agentic aspect in a more positive and invitational way which seeks to aid the client to not just *discover* aspects of themselves, but *create* themselves anew in a more experientially-based way.

What is the 'felt sense'?

Prouty makes the valuable point in distinguishing between the 'felt sense' and the 'felt meaning'. He argues (1994) that the 'felt sense' is unclear and fuzzy, but when fully attended to in the manner of reflective responding and inner referring can become more clearly delineated and symbolised as a 'felt meaning'.

Prouty, G. (1994). *Theoretical Evolutions in Person-Centered/Experiential Therapy: Applications to schizophrenic and retarded psychoses.* Westport, CT: Praeger.

The felt sense is hugely significant in experiential work and a discussion of it opens up to other assumptions and beliefs about human functioning that give life to the experiential approach. The felt sense is:

• Something which exists within all of us. It can be physically experienced and it also has, at the same time, an emotional quality. So the prospect of my going to the dentist is something I feel in my twisting stomach physically, but it is also a feeling somehow deeper within me (but also in the trunk of my body).

- It is related to something in our lives. It is not some hypothetical, abstract concept. It is part of how I relate to the world. It is the source of my personal meaning.

- It is implicit, that is it is not understood symbolically by even ourselves (by this I mean we as yet don't have the words to fully communicate it).

- When we are open to receiving it from within ourselves and when we can find the words or images or actions that most fully 'fit', that is that contains the all-of-it, then we can name it, and when we do that we emotionally and physically feel better. Even if the felt sense is about something we find upsetting.

- We have experienced a shift within us as it is more fully symbolised within our awareness, and we are ready for the next felt sensing.

- Our experiencing is a crucial aspect of us which requires our fullest, closest and regular attention. But it is only part of us. To be in touch with our experiencing does not take up all of our attention. We can live *and* simultaneously be in touch with our experiencing. As we shall explore later, this view is a significant point of difference between experiential writers and classical person-centred proponents, especially in terms of what is the role of the therapist in relation to the client's felt sense.

When did this approach begin?

Pete Sanders discusses the Wisconsin project and its problems in more detail in Chapter 1, p. 11, and for a full account see the 'official' write-up of the project: **Rogers, C.R., Gendlin, E.T., Kiesler, D.J. and Truax, C.B. (1967).** *The Therapeutic Relationship And Its Impact: A study of psychotherapy with schizophrenics.* Madison: University of Wisconsin Press.

Thorne, B. (1992). *Carl Rogers.* London: Sage.

Lietaer, G. (1990). 'The Client-Centred Approach after the Wisconsin Project: A personal view on its evolution.' In G. Lietaer, J. Rombauts and R. Van Balen (eds.) *Client-centred and Experiential Psychotherapy in the Nineties.* Leuven: Leuven University Press, pp. 19–45.

As indicated above, it was around the late 1950s that these ideas surfaced. In fact, I believe one of the factors that has led to experiential work having a somewhat 'bad press' within the person-centred world or at the very least not being fully discussed until recently, is the occasion of its birth. It found a voice in the research project that Rogers and his co-workers undertook in the late 1950s which has become known as the 'Wisconsin project' (Rogers, Gendlin, Kiesler and Truax, 1967). Rogers wanted to test out his therapeutic approach in what he felt would be a most rigorous setting — the back wards of a State Psychiatric Institution.

This piece of work is rarely discussed because, as Thorne states, it was a piece of research work 'deeply flawed' (Thorne, 1992), and Lietaer records the end of the Wisconsin project as a 'crucial moment' in the decline in scholarly activity amongst person-centred theorists and practitioners (Lietaer, 1990). So it is not surprising that any theoretical developments emerging from the work would have an uphill job to be acknowledged. And that is such a pity, because what did come from the project was a series of insights and understandings which inform *all* our work as person-centred practitioners, most notably, the increasing therapeutic significance of therapist congruence.

I have tried to identify several different approaches all of which put themselves under the general heading of experiential person-centred work. Let me begin with the work of Eugene Gendlin. I want to acknowledge there are other writers, most notably Hendricks (1986), Purton (2002) and Iberg (2002) who have also made important contributions to this area of work.

Gendlin and his colleagues

Gendlin is, perhaps, most well known for his work on Focusing, but I want to explore some of his other writings, most of which were written during what Prouty (1994) has called Gendlin's 'person-centred phase', a period running from the early 1960s until the 1970s. I have identified a series of articles (Gendlin, 1967, 1970, 1974, 1990) which make some crucial points regarding the experiential dimension in person-centred work, but which have not had the recognition they deserve. I want now to identify the key points that Gendlin underlines in these articles.

(1) He cannot make clear enough that the key is *listening*. In 1974 he wrote that it was not accurate enough to characterise client-centred work as 'say back what the person said'. Rather, it was all about staying in touch with the person's directly-felt concrete experiential datum. So therapist and client both attend to the client's *experiential track*, that is they both stay with what is alive for the client and do not offer explanations or interpretations.

(2) The therapist needs to keep checking, to make sure that what was being said between therapist and client is an accurate account of the client's experiencing.

(3) He argued that experiential work was really at home with client-centred work because of the pivotal significance of listening, but could operate in different therapeutic settings.

(4) The work was all about two people being together in a particular way. In 1990 he wrote 'the essence of working with another person is to be present as a living being' (Gendlin, 1990).

Hendricks, M.N. (1986). 'Experiencing Level as a Therapeutic Variable.' *Person-Centred Review, 1* (2). Reprinted in Cain D. (ed.) *Classics in the Person-Centred Approach.* Ross-on-Wye: PCCS Books, pp. 71–81.

Purton, C. (2002). 'Focusing on Focusing.' In Watson J.C., Goldman, R.N. and Warner, M.S. (eds.) *Client-Centered and Experiential Psychotherapy in the 21ˢᵗ Century; Advances in theory, research and practice.* Ross-on-Wye: PCCS Books, pp. 89–98.

Iberg, J. (2002). 'Psychometric Development of Measures of In-session Focusing Activity', pp. 221–46. *ibid.*

Prouty, G. (1994). *Theoretical Evolutions in Person-Centered/Experiential Therapy: Applications to Schizophrenic and Retarded Psychoses.* Westport: Praeger.

Gendlin, E.T. (1967). 'Subverbal Communication and Therapist Expressivity: Trends in Client-Centered Therapy with Schizophrenics.' In C.R. Rogers, and B. Stevens (eds.) *Person To Person: The Problem of Being Human.* New York: Souvenir Press, pp. 119–28.

Gendlin, E. T. (1970). 'A theory of personality change.' In J.T. Hart, and T.M. Tomlinson (eds.) *New Directions in Client-Centered Therapy.* Boston: Houghton Mifflin, pp. 129–73.

Gendlin, E.T. (1974). 'Client-centered and experiential psychotherapy.' In D. Wexler and L.N. Rice (eds.) *Innovations in Client-Centered Therapy.* New York: John Wiley and Sons, pp. 211–46.

Gendlin, E.T. (1990). 'The small steps of the therapy process: How they come and how to help them come.' In G. Lietaer, J. Rombauts and R. Van Balen (eds.) *Client-Centered and Experiential Psychotherapy in the Nineties.* Leuven: Leuven University Press, pp. 205–24.

Gendlin, E. T. (1970). 'A Theory of Personality Change.' In J.T. Hart, and T.M. Tomlinson (eds.) *New Directions in Client-Centered Therapy.* Boston: Houghton Mifflin, pp. 129–73.

Gendlin, E. T. (1984). 'The Client's Client: The Edge of Awareness.' In R.F. Levant and J.M. Shlien (eds.) *Client-Centered Therapy and the Person-Centered Approach: New Directions in Theory, Research, and Practice.* New York: Praeger, pp. 76–107.

There may be echoes of Rogers' 'integrative statement' (Jerold Bozarth's term for Rogers 'necessary and sufficient conditions' paper) of 1957 here, perhaps?

Gendlin, E.T. (1967). 'Subverbal Communication and Therapist Expressivity: Trends in Client-Centered Therapy with Schizophrenics.' In C.R. Rogers, and B. Stevens (eds.) *Person To Person: The Problem of Being Human.* New York: Souvenir Press, pp. 119-28.

See Natiello, P. (2001). *The Person-Centred Approach : A Passionate Presence.* Ross-on-Wye: PCCS Books, pp. 25–38 for a powerful account of this.

Perhaps similar to the Pre-Therapy approach of Prouty and his colleagues, see Prouty, G., Van Werde, D., and Pörtner, M. *Pre-Therapy: Reaching Contact Impaired Clients.* Ross-on-Wye:PCCS Books.

In 1970, Gendlin expressed in a poetic way that the therapist needed to live 'personally towards the client' (Gendlin, 1970).

(5) Clients' self-understanding and acceptance comes most often in small steps. Through careful, close work an aspect of the felt sense leaves the edge of awareness or 'border zone' of fuzziness and becomes explicit and recognisable. The term 'edge of awareness' (Gendlin, 1984) is a way of capturing that sense of a feeling or thought that seems just at the corner of our 'internal vision'. If we rush to symbolise with a word, we usually miss its essence. We need to sit with it more patiently. Having a companion can be a real asset here and through their persistent attention to a part of ourselves with which we may have a growing impatience, we, as client, can learn to honour this inner source of wisdom. When the unclear sense has been held in a representation that truly fits with the personal meaning — it can move from the shadowy area at the edge of our awareness to take its place more centrally. This leads on to being ready to look at the next piece of the puzzle moving up to the surface.

(6) Clients may undertake these steps on their own, but for Gendlin the relationship is key. He argues that it is deeply disrespectful if the therapist is a careless or inattentive companion and works insensitively so that the client feels alone and unaccompanied. We need help to hear ourselves.

(7) Throughout all this work, but perhaps most notably in his piece on therapist expressivity (Gendlin, 1967), he describes a much more visible role for the therapist. This commitment to the therapist having a more interactive engagement with the client seems directly linked to the experience of working with clients in the Wisconsin project. Put simply, the therapists were working with clients labelled schizophrenic, who were often to a degree disconnected both from others and from their own inner worlds. The therapist had nowhere to go but back inside themselves to see if, by attending to their own experiencing within the relationship, they could find a point of contact. The use of self by the therapist and the belief in the healing potential that lies within the relationship is, of course, familiar terrain. What is special about this approach is the *active* involvement of the therapist and the belief that by being *pro-active ,* the therapist will connect with the client and help them re-connect with themselves Gendlin (*ibid.,* pp. 122–4) identifies three aspects to this proactive involvement: firstly , the therapist goes inside themselves and locates what is truly happening for them at that moment in the

relationship. It is then presented to the client in an owned way and not imposed on the client, and finally the client's own expressions are offered back accurately and with clarity. Gendlin was not alone in this realisation, as will be evident from my discussion later about the work Rogers himself undertook with Jim Brown as part of the project. It is here that a more active sense of therapist congruence was formed.

This approach carries within it the clear idea that we are, to use Rennie's term, *reflexive*, i.e. we can 'look' at the different aspects of how we actually are, and how we are functioning. Thus, we can be aware of our felt sense and talk about it and even talk to it! It is part of us, but only part of us.

Gendlin's contribution to person-centred work is deep and durable. According to an interview with Lietaer, referred to by Prouty (1994), Gendlin thought his work on the *Process Scale* — also known as the 'seven stages of therapeutic process' (Rogers, 1961) — was his most significant contribution. There are some interesting concerns being expressed about the scale (Keemar *et al.*, 2004) which deserve some attention. These authors note that Rogers' dilemma is that he is endeavouring to describe a *process* by a series of *stages or steps* and no matter how frequently he cautions restraint within the reader not to see the divisions in a rigid way, there are still seven stages described. However, no one can fail to see that the Process Scale is undoubtedly experiential in its direction and its thrust. In the discussion of the stages of process, Rogers uses the phrases 'direct referent' and 'inner referent', and in the discussion of the seventh stage states:

> the self becomes increasingly simply the subjective and reflexive awareness of experiencing. (*ibid.* p. 153)

The hard work of the whole therapist team in the Wisconsin project clearly made congruence a more alive issue. The struggle to be more apparent and real in the relationship, to clearly demonstrate commitment to the client through sensitive but meaningful contact, is visible in Rogers' writings and demonstration work from then onwards. In addition, we need also to look at the clear acknowledgement Rogers makes to the ideas of Gendlin and his colleagues in his 1975 reformulation of empathy (Rogers, 1980) which is almost marinated in the experiential approach. In it Rogers talks of:

1. empathy being a 'process'
2. 'changing felt meanings'
3. 'frequently checking with the person as to the accuracy of

In the same article, he introduces the idea of *subverbal interaction*, by which he means responding in ways which help restore the link between *what* is said by the client with the source of the words-the client's experiencing. The therapist responds to the words by 'pointing' their response at the felt meanings, rather than simply at the words themselves.

Rennie, D. L. (1998). *Person-Centred Counselling: An experiential approach.* London: Sage, pp. 2–6.

Prouty, G. (1994). *Theoretical Evolutions in Person-Centered/Experiential Therapy: Applications to Schizophrenic and Retarded Psychoses.* Westport: Praeger.
Rogers, C.R. (1961). 'A Process Conception of Psychotherapy.' In C.R. Rogers, *On Becoming A Person.* London: Constable, pp. 125–62.
Keemar, K., Embleton-Tudor, L., Valentine, J., Worrall, M. and Tudor, K. (2004). *The Person-Centred Approach: A contemporary introduction.* Basingstoke: Palgrave.

The **Process Scale** (see 'A Process Conception of Psychotherapy.' In Rogers, C.R. (1961). *On Becoming A Person.* London Constable, pp.125–59) records the impact of therapy in terms of noting the move from a rigid sense of self, cut off from organismic experiencing to full immersion in the experiential flow: a journey from fixity to flowingness

Rogers, C.R. (1980). *A Way of Being.* Boston: Houghton Mifflin.

your (the therapist's) sensings'

4. being a confident 'companion'

5. 'by pointing to the possible meanings in the flow of another's experiencing, you help the other to focus on this useful type of referent, to experience the meanings more fully, and to move forward in the experiencing' (p. 142).

Rogers, C.R. (1959). 'A theory of therapy, personality and interpersonal relationships, as developed in the client-centered framework.' In S. Koch (ed.) *Psychology: A Study of a Science, 3. Formulations of the Person and the Social Context.* New York: McGraw-Hill. Reprinted in Kirschenbaum, H. and Henderson, V. L. (eds.) (1990). *The Carl Rogers Reader.* London: Constable, pp. 236–62.

If we compare this with his previous description of empathy (Rogers, 1959) we can see how deeply imbued with experiential ideas is this later piece. This belief that here is clear evidence that experiential work *as we are discussing here* is alive and well, will be further supported when we look at some of Rogers' actual work. Let me try and further illustrate some of these ideas in the following example.

We have within us a somatic sense of how we are relating to all aspects of our world. It is not verbal nor can it be described as being emotions. It is below that. It is a viscerally held sense of how we are, and usually held in the trunk of the body. For example when I am about to visit the dentist, I have a range of symbolised (i.e., verbally held in my awareness) responses. I know, that whilst I don't enjoy these visits, it is sensible to undergo regular checks on my teeth and gums. I know also I have put a bit of money away for such visits.

I also have another set of responses, which are not expressed in words. Rather, they are bodily sensations that sit in my belly. As I have explored these sensations already, I can now put them into words., but if I 'go back' a little I can evoke a jumble of feelings and felt senses which include the following elements:

• There will be pain, and nerve pain for me is excruciating.
• I want to be, and think I should be, brave.
• I do not want to go.
• Will my breath be smelly for the dentist?
• I feel like an eight-year-old as my memories of visiting the dentist are full of recalled pain. When I was young, the dentist was a family friend. What would he tell my mother?
• I need to set a good example to others.
• I am not sure I am looking after my teeth properly, and now some young 'oick' of a dentist is going to tell me off!

Unaddressed, this jumble stays powerfully inside me but impacts on me at the mere mention of a visit to the dentist. Before they were addressed, I would be hot and sweaty at the prospect of going to the dentist, usually bad-tempered with everyone around me and ill at ease with myself. When they are addressed, I can turn to each element and look at it and find the words that fit that particular aspect of it. When it is named; it is heard, when it is heard; it loses its power as it kind of 'shrinks down' to the size of the words. I am more free. That does not mean all of the aspects of the jumble have gone, but they are more manageable, and yes, some have gone!

The key, as has been stated already, is to pay proper and full attention to me inside. What is happening to me ? Can I tease out a part of it with some clarity? Can I then stay alongside it long enough and in an open and accepting enough way for it to dare to be heard? Gendlin (1996) describes this way of listening to the client as a series of steps which are as follows:

Gendlin, E. T. (1996). *Focusing-Oriented Psychotherapy: A Manual of the Experiential Method.* New York: The Guilford Press.

- We have within us a 'felt sense' of something. It is a multi-layered thing 'which is the wholistic, implicit bodily sense of a complex situation' (p. 58). It cannot yet be expressed in words. It is at our 'border zone' between the unconscious and the conscious, or as Gendlin referred to it earlier (1984) it is at the 'edge of our awareness'.

Gendlin, E. T. (1984). 'The Client's Client: The Edge of Awareness.' In R.F. Levant and J.M. Shlien (eds.) *Client-Centered Therapy and the Person-Centered Approach: New Directions in Theory, Research, and Practice.* New York: Praeger, pp. 76–107.

- We need to turn inward and be open to the whole of this 'felt sense' in a patient and accepting way. Our experiencing is carrying the significance of our response to whatever is troubling us but initially in an unclear way.
- In listening, a word or phrase will come and with the aid of the therapist we can see if it fits or resonates with that part of the felt sense. If it does, we will experience an actual bodily 'shift' within us. That thing which was unclear and implicit is now clear and explicit. It is owned and is part of us. It is in our awareness and, as it can be named, its power is lessened.
- We can continue the process, and address another aspect of this felt sense.

The key is that the therapist listens, and keeps checking with the client, and the client in turn checks with their experiential flow within. This is what is meant by the phrase 'direct referent'. The 'felt sense' is a direct referent, and therapist and client conjointly need to pay full attention to this bodily held wisdom which is no less wise for not being verbal.

Gendlin himself does not duck the fact that this Focusing-oriented way of working is instructional and therefore, in the argot of person-centredness, gets caught up in the controversy about directivity. Yes, he would own, this way of working *is* directive — but more of this discussion later on.

Rennie and his experiential approach

Rennie's ideas are elaborated in his book *Person-Centred Counselling: An Experiential Approach* (1998). He uses familiar experiential language but also introduces some ideas of his own. In the first chapter, he clearly positions himself as being on the experientialist wing of the approach and a long way from the classical or 'literalist' element. The latter is a term he borrows from Shlien (1970). He also makes clear that he is not a focuser, and nor is he as technical in his approach as Greenberg (see below for a discussion of the views of Greenberg and his colleagues). So, what is Rennie's approach all about? There are some important defining elements as I see them:

- Whilst having a weather eye on the need for 'efficiency' (1998, p. v), Rennie is committed to working with the client in ways which help them be more in charge of their lives and to consequently live more fully.
- For him, the key is that clients become more 'agential' in their lives, and that can be best achieved in the company of a self-aware, active and confident therapist.
- Much of the work is organised around the concept of 'reflexivity'.
- Rennie differentiates between (i) the story as told by the client, (ii) how they tell it, and (iii) what is happening for them as they tell it.
- The therapist's job is to be attentive to the client; to pay full attention to what is said; but also to how it is said and increasingly, as a result of getting to know the client, to explore the personal meanings of what they are doing and saying. This may well mean spending time to look at what is happening between the client and themselves. He calls this 'metacommunication'.

Rennie knows he is moving into controversial terrain when he talks of the therapist having at times the role of the expert. The 'expertness' comes from an understanding of the fact that how we feel about ourselves or the life stories we tell will evidence itself in a myriad of ways which are non-verbal as well as to do with the narrative. Throughout this work, he argues that the therapist is always bounded by the client's experiential track. The client is clearly in charge. Interestingly, he argues this principle can itself have a powerful formative role for the client as she gets hold of what being an agent in their own lives can mean. Thus, the methods used by the approach are consonant with the theory.

Rennie, D. L. (1998). *Person-Centred Counselling: An experiential approach.* London: Sage.

Shlien, J. M. (1970). 'The literal-intuitive axis and other thoughts.' In J.T. Hart, and T.M. Tomlinson (eds.) *New Directions in Client-Centered Therapy.* Boston: Houghton Mifflin. Reprinted in J.M. Shlien (2003). *To Lead an Honorable Life.* Ross-on-Wye: PCCS Books, pp. 83–92.

Rennie, D. L. (1998). *Person-Centred Counselling: An experiential approach.* London: Sage.

By 'agential', he means creating our life, not simply having it defined by others and accepting it passively. See also the sidenote on page 71 this chapter.

By 'reflexivity' he means that at the same time as doing something or having feelings about some aspect of our lives, we are capable of being aware of ourselves, of what we are doing and of what we are feeling. This is a sort of 'self-awareness in action' and is similar to Focusing in this respect.

For Rennie, the work of the therapist is to discover 'the client's path to meaning' (*ibid.* p. 44). Whilst this involves empathic and respectful listening, he argues the attentive therapist needs also to pay regard to the vividness of the client's language, noting the imagery that arises from the client and also, if we are careful, to make use of the metaphors and images that arise in us as we listen. Let me illustrate that with an awareness that came to me in some counselling I had years ago. In discussing aspects of my life, it dawned on me and my counsellor that all of my images and language was martial or warlike in some way. I was always 'battling', always 'fighting wars of attrition', 'seeking allies', 'thinking strategically'. My language was not deliberately being selected by me. It just came from me. It was not in my awareness. To pay attention to me and not my language would have missed a great source of information about how I was seeing the world.

Ibid.

Of course, all counselling has a place to look at how a client presents themselves, but what Rennie is doing is really underlining that this is not only a significant source of information, but that *not* to pay attention is *dis*respectful.

Rennie's discussion of '*process identification*' and, more controversially, '*process direction*' need our attention. Rennie defines a client's process as:

> the activities in which clients engage as they work with their experience from moment-to-moment. (*ibid.* p. 72)

Ibid.

The identification comes when the counsellor draws the client's attention to what they are doing. And in drawing attention to the manner in which the client is presenting themselves, we are inviting the client to be aware of their felt sensing at that precise moment. And that can bring relief, in ways that Focusers know all about. When I, as a client, realised that out of my awareness I was choosing to talk as though at war, I had a flood of a sort of physical relief throughout me. It made sense. Not an intellectual sense, but a visceral sense that seemed so true. Yet in the moment of this realisation I instantaneously had room for more choices. My war could continue, or I could sue for peace.

All interpersonal work, including, of course, therapy, has regard for the disparity between what we say and how we say it. In arguments we can say the words, 'I'm sorry' but if our actions or the way we deliver the apology pulls away from the actual words we may as well try to dowse a fire by the addition of petrol. In counselling, the idea of 'emotional leakage' is well understood.

My client says they are feeling fine, but as they say it their lips go thin and they cross their legs at great speed. How they are non-verbally seem to be at variance with their words. We can control our mouths more effectively than we can control our bodies. Rennie is saying 'use all of your immediate, and with time, historical understanding of your client'.

He also makes the point (which is also held by other experiential writers, notably Greenberg — see below) about clients being agents of their lives. This is particularly pertinent with clients who are feeling depressed, but I feel it applies to all of us when clients. To work with clients in ways that enable them to 'stand outside of themselves' and see how they are in their relationships is reminding them that they have in fact more choices available than they imagine and that they have, in fact, 'chosen' to act in a certain way even though, as likely as not, they will not experience having choice. They are being, even in a minimal way, agential in their lives.

This raises the recurrent theme which lurks just below the surface of all discussions about experiential work. *Is this directive?* I am going to delay discussion of this until a bit later, but, at this juncture, it needs some time to be at least kept company with as we look at process direction. Rennie states that it is:

> ... the act of process direction that most clearly separates this experiential person-centred approach from the literal approach. (*ibid.* p. 81)

Rennie, D. L. (1998). *Person-Centred Counselling: An experiential approach.* London: Sage.

He goes on to say this is when the counsellor 'takes charge', as they 'assume the role of expert — an expert on process' (*ibid.* p. 81). Yet these words are harsher than the act they describe (although you may say an iron fist in a velvet glove is still a fist, and fists can hurt). The kind of examples Rennie gives are along the lines of the counsellor, who, after bringing to the client's awareness some fracturing between how they are being and what they are saying, then invites the client to *stay* with this apparent disparity, or maybe attend to the tightening of the lips and the speedy leg-crossing as they are saying they feel fine. And all or any of this is invitational: nothing is or can be enforced. The key that, for Rennie, keeps this way of working not only ethical but person-centred, is that the client is always in charge. This ownership is not just tacitly acknowledged, but actively and openly so. Throughout, Rennie talks of the need for counsellor transparency and for a constant commitment to looking at, discussing, evaluating the nature, quality and efficacy of the working relationship with the client. This is what Rennie calls 'metacommunication' — talking about what we are doing.

Process experiential approach: The work of Greenberg, Rice and Elliott

I want to concentrate on their 1993 book, *Facilitating Emotional Change: The Moment-by-Moment Process* (1993) as a means of looking at their contribution to the experiential approach. Of all of the experiential writers, I feel these authors are perhaps the most overlooked, at least until Richard Worsley's book (2002) on process was published. Worsley himself makes the point very clearly that this trio of therapists is outside the Person-Centred Approach and indeed they can be presented as being 'not one of us' for the following reasons:

- They identify particular therapist techniques for certain dysfunctional client behaviours.
- They do not recognise the actualising tendency as the foundation block of their therapeutic work.
- They do not use the language of the Person-Centred Approach, and have no place for a self-concept as a unitary psychological element as Rogers describes it.
- They acknowledge Rogers' ideas as only one of several formative influences (Gestalt Therapy being perhaps of equal weight as a defining influence).

And yet their work is certainly experiential in its approach and the authors themselves, whilst using language which may be strange, and therefore challenging, to person-centred practitioners, see themselves as not being aliens. Let me offer you my simplified account of their approach as outlined in this book. The basic assumption behind the approach is that:

> each client needs to access and change their self-in-the-world cognitive/affective schemes that are interfering with adaptive, satisfying and growth enhancing functioning. (Greenberg, *et. al.,* p. 141)

Or, put another way:

- Our emotions are adaptive devices, known as 'emotion schemes', designed to help us monitor our inner and outer lives. Emotion schemes are how we construct who we are and how we make sense of the world.
- They are organised sets of thoughts, beliefs, feelings and memories which are about us in relationship with others and are also about getting our needs met. The schemes develop with us and are formed in response to our experiences of life. Those formed early on having greater durability. These early schemes are concerned with hugely

The term 'experiential psychotherapy' has practically been defined by the work of these theorists. Now recognised as a major approach since its inclusion in Lambert, M.J., Bergin, A.E. and Garfield, S.L. (2003). (Eds.) *Handbook of Psychotherapy and Behavior Change 5th Edn.* New York: Wiley.

A recent key text is Greenberg, Watson and Lietaer, 1998, full reference below.

Greenberg, L.S., Rice, L.N. and Elliott, R. (1993). *Facilitating Emotional Change: The moment-by-moment process.* New York: Guilford Press.

Worsley, R. (2002). *Process Work in Person-Centred Therapy: Phenomenological and Existential Perspectives.* Basingstoke: Palgrave.

Increasingly, nowadays, clearly accepted person-centred authorities such as Dave Mearns (Mearns, D. (2002). 'Further Theoretical Propositions in Regard to Self Theory within Person-Centered Therapy.' *Person-Centered and Experiential Psychotherapies 1* (1 & 2): 14–27), are beginning to question the appropriateness of the self as a unitary concept, and are seeking to move to a more dialogic position whereby our sense of who we are is a result of a continual interchange between our inner experiencing and the world around us. This is a clear and central concept in the experiential approach. See **Greenberg, L.S., Watson, J.C., Lietaer, G. (1998).** *The Handbook of Experiential Psychotherapy.* New York: Guilford Press.

Greenberg, L.S., Rice, L.N. and Elliott, R. (1993). *Facilitating Emotional Change: The moment-by-moment process.* New York: Guilford Press.

significant issues like feeling loved, suffering loss, experiencing anger and, perhaps, feeling threatened. These early schemes may move out of our awareness and may not be generally available to ourselves, but they are still in operation.

• Our inner worlds, with our needs and wants, are constantly changing, just as the world in which we live is changing. Our emotion schemes are open and flexible for the most part and are capable of readjusting to assimilate new internal and external information.

• Depending on what is happening for us, we may develop schemes which are clearly about us being acceptable and lovable. However, we may also develop schemes about us being unacceptable.

• This approach sees the client in information-processing terms, i.e. the concern of therapy is to look at the efficiency and efficacy of how we utilise the schemes in our lives.

• It is these emotion schemes and their relationship to how we process experience which are the concern of therapy.

I believe it is familiar terrain that is being covered here. Although there are clear differences, they are, in fact, further intensified when we explore how this approach describes the work of the therapist.

The view of the person is that they are barrelling along, processing themselves-in-the-world. They are acknowledging that new experiential material can come from inside themselves and from the world outside and that they have affective and cognitive mechanisms that constantly mediate between these two contributing aspects of their lives. As problems appear, this approach will see the problems as being either a result of poor symbolic processing of experiences (that is a current event is 'fitted in' to an existing emotion scheme) or that there is a dysfunctional imbalance between our thinking and our feeling. *Thinking* is how the approach views our controlled, conscious conceptual processing of information and *feeling* is the automatic processing of information about ourselves that happens out of our awareness. When there is a breakdown in our internal psychological systems (which are designed to keep us working in an optimum way) and there is not a proper dialogue between these two aspects, then we have psychological distress.

For example, if we are suddenly in a dangerous situation, our 'heads' may cognitively assess the situation and process both the external situation, and our internal capabilities and wishes, and decide we need to speedily depart. However, an out-of-our-awareness primordial emotion scheme may remind us that we cannot cope with crises (because of what we experienced many, many, years ago) and our 'heart' falls into panic (as we did many, many, years ago). If there is no pattern of internal dialogue between these two schemes we are likely not to do anything but fall into panic.

Greenberg *et al.* are very clear that the purpose of therapy is to restore within the client a sense of control and direction in their lives (they use the somewhat odd word, 'mastery'). This will be achieved by bringing all emotion schemes fully into awareness so they can be reconfigured and, where appropriate, revisit past events that have been processed in a maladaptive way and re-process them again within the supportive therapeutic relationship. The role of the therapist is to help the client to look at how they have handled that event and what sense of themselves they have taken from the event. Readers of Rice's earlier work (1970, 1984) on the evocative function of the therapist will recognise this idea of revisiting significant events as identified by the client as being troubling. The role of the therapist is to evoke aspects of the previous event to help the client re-examine its contribution to their current sense of themselves.

> The re-experiencing and reprocessing take place within a basically client-centred relationship in which the client is the expert of his or her own experience. (Greenberg *et al.*, 1993, p. 151)

The therapist will certainly direct the client's process at times, but they insist it will be the client who makes the discoveries. The therapist through what the authors call 'empathic attunement' will create a safe, accepting environment in which the client can examine their internal experiential processes to see if the sense they are making of their lives actually 'fits' with their inner world and a re-examination of the world in which they live. The therapist will:

- enter into the client's world, listening for what is 'poignant' (by which they mean telling or significant and tracking the client's experience as it unfolds),
- create a therapeutic relationship where the goals are clearly laid down by the client,
- seek to foster the client's growth and self-determination strategies and to listen out for what they call the 'growing edge' for the client (*ibid.* p. 114) which is very much their version of Gendlin's 'edge of awareness',
- help the client live more fully and in a more self-aware way. Thus, self-awareness is a desired outcome of the therapy.

Rice, L.N. (1970). 'The Evocative Function of the Therapist.' In D.A. Wexler and L.N. Rice (eds.) *Innovations in Client-Centered Therapy.* New York: Wiley, pp. 289–311.

Rice, L.N. (1984). 'Client Tasks in Client-Centered Therapy.' In R.F. Levant, and J.M. Shlien (eds.) *Client-Centered Therapy and the Person-Centered Approach: New Directions in Theory, Research and Practice.* New York: Praeger, pp. 182–202.

Greenberg, L.S., Rice, L.N. and Elliott, R. (1993). *Facilitating Emotional Change: The moment-by-moment process.* New York: Guilford Press.

Ibid.

There is a great deal of emphasis on being empathic, but as is their way, the authors deliberately describe all the nuances of empathic understanding:

- Empathic reflection (attending to the *all* of the experience and trying to divine what is most vivid, central or poignant).
- Following responses (encouraging responses which open up areas).
- Empathic exploration (this is empathy with a purpose, it being to stay at the 'edge of awareness').
- Exploratory questions (about encouraging the client to explore their experiencing further, such as 'what does that feel like?').
- Empathic conjecture (which is concerned to attend to current experiencing which seems not to have been symbolised).
- Process Directing (which might involve inviting the client to attend inwardly or to enact some aspect of themselves in the session).

There might also be some awareness homework set. This could involve the therapist suggesting some range of activities to be undertaken by the client between sessions. All of this is conducted by a therapist committed to being experientially present and responding fully and appropriately from themselves. The sessions may involve some experiential teaching. The therapist is fully and actively involved in the session, and will, as appropriate, suggest ways of working. Nothing will happen without the full collaboration of the client. So nothing is imposed, and the therapist is guided by a specific understanding of *this* client in particular and of people in general.

As has been indicated previously, this approach argues that certain identifiable problems require certain therapeutic responses. Thus the approach has its own diagnostic methods and categories. Consequently, for example, the authors argue that a 'two-chair dialogue' would be beneficial if the client feels internally divided about some issue. A slight variation of this (two-chair enactment) could be helpful if the client was having an internalised conversation characterised by internal arguing. The use of the 'empty-chair dialogue' would be appropriate for clients with unfinished business. Focusing (as per Gendlin) would work for clients with an unclear 'felt sense' and if a client was thrown by their disproportionate response to some memory or experience, then some 'systematic evocative unfolding' (revisiting past important events and reassessing their contribution to current emotion schemes) would fit. For clients with a debilitating sense of vulnerability, then the therapist would offer sustained empathic prizing.

Presented somewhat baldly in this manner, then the reader could easily move to being dismissive of the approach and not see it as part of the person-centred 'family'. Worsley does in fact adopt this stance (Worsley, 2002, pp. 202–5) but in a much more closely argued way. He does, however, have no argument with the place of 'process' in Person-Centred Therapy — but more of this later. I also feel that the use of such clearly delineated techniques and such precise problem identification does indeed put this approach at least on the outer limits of person-centred work, if not actually outside. I would not, though, want to ignore the hugely helpful attention which is paid to a client's process, both in life and in the therapeutic situation.

Worsley and process work

I want to look at Worsley's (2002) important contribution to the idea of process work in Person-Centred Therapy. For him, as with Gendlin, Greenberg *et al.*, Rennie, and Lietaer, *attending to process* is crucial. Worsley argues that it is not without its risks, as paying attention to *having* feelings can take you away from *being with* feelings. To respond to, say, a client weeping with a response which is seeking to explore what has evoked the tears may well be experienced as dismissive. However, to ignore process is equally risky. It may well be that the client has shown over previous sessions that weeping is often followed by direct expressions of anger, and to stay with the tears exclusively may dent a client's exploration of the full range of their emotional responding.

He argues that people are continually moving from *being in their feelings to looking at how they are handling them* at any one time. Part of the therapist's being empathic is that they are with the feelings when the client is and they can look at process when the client is reflexively thinking about how they 'always' or 'usually' handle a particular situation. What he is adamant about, and which differentiates him significantly from the other writers, is his clear statements

- That his way of working is consonant with the six conditions.
- That to attend to process is not to become the only expert on process work for that client. Clients are as expert on their own process as they are on all aspects of their lives. He writes:

Person-centred process work is a struggle to understand actively, not to interfere. What is added is the fact that the experience and meaning of the client are often exhibited by her body, her inner experiences which may be out of awareness. (*ibid.* p. 37)

Worsley, R. (2002). *Process Work in Person-Centred Therapy: Phenomenological and Existential Perspectives*. Basingstoke: Palgrave. Richard Worsley adds: 'I have, for a number of years, spent many weeks with second year diploma students looking at major aspects of the work of Rennie, Rice and Greenberg, and found thay they inform even the most literalist of students as well. They also offer others diverse ways of engaging critically and responsibly with clients.'

Ibid.

Although Richard Worsley has contributed a chapter to this book, in this volume he addresses the process of *integration*, rather than the *theory and practice of process work* (which he explores in detail in his book and I am briefly describing here).

Readers should note that Worsley's 2002 book *Process Work in Person-Centred Therapy* is breathtakingly wide-ranging. It looks at phenomenological and existential perspectives and dips into Gestalt and Transactional Analysis.

Ibid.

Worsley, R. (2002). *Process Work in Person-Centred Therapy*: Phenomenological *and Existential Perspectives.* Basingstoke: Palgrave.

Germain Lietaer is a professor at the Catholic University of Leuven in Belgium and has written and edited a wide range of authoritative and stimulating articles and books on person-centred and experiential theory and practice. The most readily available of his work are his chapters
• 'Unconditional Positive Regard: A controversial basic attitude in Client-Centered Therapy.' (1984). In R.F. Levant, and J.M. Shlien (eds.) *Client-Centred Therapy and the Person-Centred Approach.* New York: Praeger.
• 'The Client-centred approach after the Wisconsin Project: A personal view on its evolution.' (1990). In G. Lietaer, J. Rombauts, and R. Van Balen (eds.) *Client-Centered and Experiential Psychotherapy in the Nineties.* Leuven: Leuven University Press.
• 'From Non-Directive to Experiential: A paradigm unfolding.' (1998). In B. Thorne and E. Lambers, *Person-Centred Therapy: A European Perspective.* London: Sage.
• 'Being Genuine as a Therapist: Congruence and Transparency.' (2001). In G. Wyatt, *Congruence* (Vol 1 of the series *Rogers' Therapeutic Conditions: Evolution, Theory and Practice,* edited by G. Wyatt, Ross-on-Wye: PCCS Books)

For example, if the therapist does not have some expertise, what on earth is the point of counsellor education?

Lietaer, G. (2002a). 'The United Colors of Person-Centered and Experiential Psychotherapies.' *Person-Centered and Experiential Psychotherapies, 1* (1 & 2): 4–13.

A little later he writes: 'I strive to reflect (process) firmly enough to be hearable and softly enough so as to give the client a choice about hearing' (*ibid.* p. 43).

Thus Worsley's position is that we stay with feelings as much as possible, but we exclude a client's processing of experiences at our, and their, peril. As with all experientially-based authors and therapists, Worsley sees the role of the therapist as being active and involved. To enable clients to attend more fully and openly to their inner living does require the therapist to be a committed companion. Whilst the experiential therapist is not committed to a particular outcome, other than the client having greater self-understanding moving toward greater self-acceptance, they are committed to facilitating as full a working through of experiential material as the client feels able to undertake.

Lietaer: commitment and perseverance

Germain Lietaer has been writing about the experiential dimension for some 20 years, and whether he has been writing about specific aspects of theory or therapy (1984) or offering insightful overviews (1990,1998, 2002a, 2002b), what has been a common theme has been his steadfastness in presenting experiential work as both being distinctive and yet clearly within the person-centred fold.

Lietaer has consistently presented his ideas as being distinct from a classical Rogerian position. The work of the therapist is to help the client be more in touch with their experiential world, and to help make explicit what is implicit. Aware of the controversy he was courting, he never strayed from his firm belief that the aim of therapy was to stay true to the client's experiential track. He saw the work as being less about removing obstacles to the client changing, and more about acting as a facilitator to the client as they embraced the struggle to change. He later (2002a, 2002b) adopts the image of the 'midwife' (which is indeed a particular kind of companion) as indicating the therapist's relationship to change. He has not been scared to describe the therapist as an expert in process issues, and has always highlighted the constant checking with the client as to the direction of the therapeutic endeavour as being a powerful safeguard. The rationale for this checking is that the client has much bodily held wisdom about themselves, and their experiential world is *uniquely theirs*. If they can find their 'inner compass' (1998, p. 67) their journey will be personally meaningful because it will be *their* journey.
His latest offerings truly encapsulate the direction of his work,

and his commitment to staying in touch with all person-centred colleagues. His article, 'The United Colors of Person-Centred and Experiential Psychotherapies' (Lietaer, 2002a), covers much of the ground of his 'The Client-Centred/Experiential Paradigm in Psychotherapy: Development and Identity' (2002b), and it is on these that I wish to concentrate.

Germain Lietaer argues that for all person-centred practitioners, irrespective of how they label themselves, the focus *is* the client's inner world of experiencing. The job of the counsellor is to create the right conditions for this to happen. These involve respecting the client as having a greater role in structuring their lives than perhaps they have ascribed to themselves hitherto. The work of the therapist is to help the client reintegrate experiences and a sense of self, both of which are denied to full awareness. In so doing, the client can become the person they more truly are. Behind this aim is the belief that the client is trustworthy, and will want to lead a social, co-operative life since their achievement of their own goals actually involves being in relation with other people in ways which are mutually fulfilling. He does not deny differences between practitioners, but sees them as centring on *how* the therapist is in the relationship. This is important. He refers to Margaret Warner's writing (2000) and echoes that the differences are significant. He lists the characteristics of experiential person-centred exponents as:

- being fully present in the relationship,
- being process-directive,
- being committed to an active partnership with the client as they jointly explore the client's inner world of experiencing in a immediate, step-by-step way,
- being aware that the client is both *potentially* and *actually* agential in their stance towards themselves.

Lietaer clearly, but not aggressively, is saying that nothing stands still, not even person-centred theory. We all need to be monitoring our practice, exploring our ways of working, pushing forwards our understandings of how people are and how they change. It is in this light that he wants to talk only in terms of the client-centred/experiential paradigm and presents the primary defining elements of this paradigm as the following:

1. There is a focusing on the experiencing self.
2. There is moment-by-moment empathy.
3. There is a high level of therapist presence.
4. There is, between the two protagonists, an open dialogical stance.

Lietaer, G. (2002b). 'The Client-Centered /Experiential Paradigm in Psychotherapy: Development and identity.' In J.C. Watson, R.N. Goldman and M.S. Warner (eds.) *Client-Centered and Experiential Psychotherapy in the 21st Century; Advances in theory, research and practice*. Ross-on-Wye: PCCS Books, pp. 1–15.

Warner, M.S. (2000). 'Person-Centered Psychotherapy: One Nation, Many Tribes.' *Person-Centered Journal, 7* (1): 28–39.

confidence

5. There is a belief that the six conditions are *crucial* (as opposed to being both necessary and sufficient).

How is experiential client-centred work different from the classical approach?

An interesting place to commence this element of the discussion is to look at an aspect of the work undertaken by Rogers as part of the notorious Wisconsin project with 'a silent young man', who is in fact Jim Brown. As discussed previously, much of what has become known as the experiential aspect of person-centred work originated from this venture. This piece of work is, I feel, of great value, both in terms of this current discussion, but also as a free-standing piece of therapy. Something wonderful happens in the sessions (irrespective of which 'side' in the discussion/debate it favours). It is no wonder — and this is further evidence of its significance and durability — that in his last interview with Baldwin (Baldwin, 1987), Rogers goes back without hesitation to his work with the silent young man to illustrate his commitment to being ' fully present' with clients. It is in response to Jim Brown that Rogers declares that he wants the client to know that he (Rogers) cares for him; that he is not there as 'a stick'. This is illustrated in the following extract, where *T* is Rogers:

T: I see there are some cigarettes here in the drawer. Hm? Yeah, it is hot out.
[*Silence of 25 seconds*]

T: Do you look kind of angry this morning, or is that my imagination?
[*Client shakes his head slightly*] Not angry, huh?
[*Silence of 1 minute, 26 seconds*]

T: Feel like letting me in on whatever is going on?
[*Silence of 12 minutes, 52 seconds*]

T: [*softly*] I kind of feel like saying that 'If it would be of any help at all, I'd like to come in.' On the other hand if it's something you'd rather — if you just feel more like being within yourself, feeling whatever you're feeling within yourself, why that's O.K. too — I guess another thing I'm saying, really, in saying that is, 'I do care. I'm not just sitting here like a stick.'
[*Silence of 1minute, 11seconds*]

Baldwin, M. (1987). 'Interview with Carl Rogers on the Use of the Self in Therapy.' In M. Baldwin and V. Satir (eds.) *Journal of Psychotherapy and the Family*, 3, 1: 45–52.

T: And I guess your silence is saying to me that either you don't want to or can't come out right now, and that's O.K. So I won't pester you but I just want you to know, I'm here.

(Rogers *et al.*, 1967, p. 403)

In the important, but sometimes overlooked book, *The Psychotherapy of Carl Rogers* (Farber *et al.*, 1996) there is an intriguing discussion of Rogers' work with Jim Brown first by Jerold Bozarth, clearly a proponent of the 'classical position', and then by Leslie Greenberg, one of the proponents of the process experiential approach. The astonishing fact is that, whilst there is a clear sense of the two authors arguing their own 'corners' with great aplomb, and strenuously talking about their differences, each is using the same interviews and at times the very same specific exchanges between Rogers and Brown to illustrate hugely different points!

For Bozarth, Rogers responds to the client in ways consistent with the six conditions and with the belief that therapy is about removing the obstacles to the client accessing their actualising tendency more flowingly. Although Bozarth notes that at times Rogers 'appears occasionally to push for Jim to express his more intense feelings' (Bozarth in Farber *et al.*, 1996, p. 247), and further lends the client money and gives him a phone number, to Bozarth it all serves to demonstrate a real commitment to the personhood of the client. With regard to the extract quoted above, Bozarth regards this as 'a major personal expression' (p. 245) on Rogers' part. Bozarth echoes Rogers' statement that these two sessions illustrate moments of movement for the client.

For Greenberg, the two sessions provide illustrations of Rogers' having intentions other than the providing of the six conditions. The language of the six conditions, for Greenberg, does not:

fully explain the curative elements of the process that he [Rogers] and *other experientially oriented therapists* make possible. (Greenberg, 1996, p. 253, my italics)

He sees Rogers as (1) intentionally and selectively guiding the client towards deeper feelings, and (2) inducing the client to search experientially within himself. The evidence he cites concerns a passage during the first of the two transcribed sessions. As before, *T* is Rogers and Brown is referred to as *C*.

C: No. I just ain't no good to nobody, never was, and never will be.

T: Feeling that now, hm? That you're just no good to yourself,

Rogers, C. R., Gendlin, E.T., Kiesler, D.J. and Truax, C.B. (1967). *The Therapeutic Relationship And Its Impact: A study of psychotherapy with schizophrenics.* Madison: University of Wisconsin Press.

Farber, B.A., Brink, D.C. and Raskin, P.M. (eds.) (1996). *The Psychotherapy of Carl Rogers.* New York: Guilford Press.

Bozarth, J. D. (1996). 'A Silent Young Man, the case of Jim Brown — commentary 1.' In B.A. Farber, D.C. Brink and P.M. Raskin (eds.) *The Psychotherapy of Carl Rogers.* New York: Guilford Press, pp. 240–50.

Greenberg, L.S. (1996). 'A Silent Young Man the case of Jim Brown — commentary 2.' In B.A. Farber, D.C. Brink and P.M. Raskin (eds.) *The Psychotherapy of Carl Rogers.* New York: Guilford Press.

no good to anybody. Never will be any good to anybody. Just that you're completely worthless, huh? — Those really are lousy feelings. Just feel that you are no good at *all*, hm?

C: Yeah. [*muttering in low discouraged voice*] That's what this guy I went to town with just the other day told me.

T: This guy that you went to town with really told you that you were no good? Is that what you're saying? Did I get that right?

C: M-hm.

T: I guess the meaning of that, if I get it right, is that here's somebody that — meant something to you and what does he think of you? Why, he's told you that he thinks you're no good at all. And that just really knocks the props out from under you. [*Jim (Brown) weeps quietly.*] It just brings the tears.

[*Silence of 20 seconds*]

C: [*rather defiantly*] I don't care though.

T: You tell yourself you don't care at all, but somehow I guess some part of you cares because some part of you weeps over it.

[*Silence of 19 seconds*]

T: I guess some part of you just feels, 'Here I am hit with another blow, as if I hadn't had enough blows like this during my life when I feel that people don't like me. Here's someone I've begun to feel attached to and now *he* doesn't like me. And I'll say I don't care. I won't let it make any difference to me — But just the same the tears run down my cheeks.'
(*Ibid.* p. 404)

Greenberg, L.S. (1996). 'A Silent Young Man the case of Jim Brown — commentary 2.' In B.A. Farber, D.C. Brink and P.M. Raskin (eds.) *The Psychotherapy of Carl Rogers*. New York: Guilford Press..

Ibid.

Like Bozarth, Greenberg sees real movement coming from this work, but for him it happened, not because the client was in a relationship where he was allowed to be more fully himself, but because of the nature of the dialogic relationship that Rogers created with the client. He argues that it was the particular way of relating that activated, strengthened and brought to life the 'wanting-to-live-stance' within the client. And it is because of this dialogic impact that Greenberg writes 'the dialogue is privileged over the actualising tendency' (*ibid.* p. 256).

So here we have real difference. Is the concern of therapy to create a climate where there are no constraints upon the client and therefore they are able to reintegrate previously denied experiences into their way of being in the world, or is the concern to specifically assist clients through the relationship with the therapist to go inwards and reconnect with out-of-awareness experiencing?

Let me outline some other identified differences and then assess whether, as Brodley argues (Brodley, 1990), these two approaches are 'different kinds of therapy, not ones in an internally consistent continuum of development' (p. 104).

Brodley, B.T. (1990). 'Client-centered and experiential: Two different therapies.' In G. Lietaer, J. Rombauts and R. Van Balen (eds.) *Client-Centered and Experiential Therapies in the Nineties.* Leuven: Leuven University Press, pp. 87–107.

The six conditions

A belief in, and advocacy of, the six conditions is seen as the very essence of the work for classical client-centred practitioners. It is not surprising that experiential workers take a different stance. For Gendlin (1990) the client does not need to precisely *know* what the therapist is doing (i.e. the client does not need to perceive the empathic, accepting attitude of a congruent therapist) they just have to receive it (i.e. they need to *experience* it). For Greenberg *et al.*, (1993) the six conditions are just not efficient or effective enough. For Rennie (1998), the six conditions are certainly necessary, and *perhaps* they are sufficient. It is interesting to note that for Worsley, process work is clearly encompassed within the six conditions, because for him, clients are as 'expert' on their process as they are on the content of their lives. And how the client lives their lives, and how they are in their living (i.e. how they process), belongs to the client as much as does the actual content of their lives. The fact that we do not always live our lives as fully as we are able, and that how we function and communicate is not always in our awareness, does not rob us of our responsibilities. And finally, to note that for Lietaer, (2002) the six conditions are 'crucial'.

Gendlin, E.T. (1990). 'The small steps of the therapy process: How they come and how to help them come.' In G. Lietaer, J. Rombauts and R. Van Balen (eds.) *Client-Centred and Experiential Psychotherapy in the Nineties.* Leuven: Leuven University Press, pp. 205–24.

Greenberg, L.S., Rice, L.N. and Elliott, R. (1993). *Facilitating Emotional Change: The moment-by-moment process.* New York: Guilford Press.

Rennie, D. L. (1998). *Person-Centred Counselling: An experiential approach.* London: Sage.

The non-directive attitude

To practitioners outside of the experiential family, the non-directive issue is the 'Becher's Brook' where the experiential practitioners will fall. To direct the client is to break faith with all that defines person-centred work. The response of experiential writers is varied but certain themes can be detected in the numerous writings. Briefly, they are:

- **Experiential therapists are bounded by the client's 'experiential track'.** Experiential practitioners do not do anything *to* the client. Rather, there is a great deal of checking out understandings with the client which is in fact greatly facilitated by the operational/theoretical idea

Lietaer, G. (2002). 'The United Colors of Person-Centered and Experiential Psychotherapies.' *Person-Centered and Experiential Psychotherapies, 1* (1 & 2): 4–13.

of 'steps' as the client gets closer to their direct experiencing. Experiential workers are closely attuned to the client.

- **There is a perplexity about what the 'non-directive attitude' really means.** This may seem a heretical notion, but it is, I feel, significant that the term 'non-directive' has been transformed from being a way of behaving, to the current definitions which are all about lionising it as an attitude. See the papers by Grant (1990) and Brodley (2000).

Grant, B. (1990). 'Principled and Instrumental Nondirectiveness in Person-Centered and Client-Centered Therapy.' *Person-Centered Review, 5* (1). Reprinted in D. Cain (ed.) *Classics in the Person-Centered Approach.* Ross-on-Wye: PCCS Books, pp. 371–7.
Brodley, B.T. (2000). About the Nondirective Attitude. *Person-Centered Practice, 7* (2): 79–82.

Let me explore this a bit more. Grant (1990) makes the distinction between 'principled nondirectiveness' and 'instrumental nondirectiveness'. The former is characterised by an enactment of liberal values involving respect for the person and the subsequent removal of obstacles to allow them to develop as they wish. Under this approach, the therapist will have no agenda, in fact no intentions or wishes at all. To respond to a client in ways that would be classified as being 'instrumental' would involve the therapist having a set of behaviours with a clear goal in mind — that of facilitating growth. That is a scenario of the therapist wanting a particular outcome.

Prouty, G. (1999). 'Carl Rogers and Experiential Therapies: A Dissonance?' *Person-Centred Practice, 7* (1): 4–11.

Proponents of the classical position feel clear that their way of being is in accordance with the 'principled 'approach. Prouty (1999) argues the classical stance is concerned with the whole person, whereas the experiential practitioners, by their focus on the inner experiencing of the client, are being instrumental in their approach. They are, according to this paradigm, simply reducing the client to a 'process'.

My response to this is twofold. Firstly, the more I explore the 'principled' stance, the less clear it becomes and the less valuable it becomes as a therapeutic schema. I don't know what it means. Grant, in order to operationalise the schema, argues that as long as the intention of the therapist is true to this attitude, they may in fact behave in ways which seem to an outsider as being highly directive. They may, in response to a clear signal from the client, answer questions, give instructions, give advice or offer interpretations. Greenberg *et al.* (1993) and Rennie talk of interpretations, giving direction and asking questions. Yet these

Greenberg, L.S., Rice, L.N. and Elliott, R. (1993). *Facilitating Emotional Change: The moment-by-moment process.* New York: Guilford Press.

authors seek, almost beseechingly, to explain that this can co-exist within a relationship characterised as being person-centred, conscious that they are, at the very least, likely to be marginalised at the very edge of the approach.

Lietaer's stance is, echoing Hart's work in 1970, to argue that the world has moved on now and the whole issue of being 'non-directive' is at best passé if not redundant. In a recent article (2002a) he suggests that all experiential practitioners see themselves as person-centred (but not all person-centred therapists describe themselves as experiential). Further, he argues, that in his opinion, all client-centred/experientialist therapists see that the client's experiential world is absolutely central to the work. So in his view there is more in common than may appear. Yet it is, as Lietaer himself goes on to argue in the same article, the question of exactly *how* a therapist works with a client that does illustrate difference.

A brief look at Hart's work is on page 68.

Lietaer, G. (2002a). 'The United Colors of Person-Centred and Experiential Psychotherapies.' *Person-Centred and Experiential Psychotherapies, 1,* (1 & 2) 4–13.

Recently, there have been articles by Warner (2000), Sanders (2000) and Lietaer (2002b) which have sought to re-order or re-group client-centred work and experiential work in ways which allow a continuum approach to exist. The key is that experiential work is now clearly seen as being in the fold. This is not to require that there is to be no debate. On the contrary, the way forward which is in fact consonant with the approach, however it is precisely worded, is to talk with each other, explore, share and grow.

Warner, M.S. (2000). 'Person-centered Psychotherapy: One Nation, Many Tribes.' *Person-Centered Journal, 7* (1): 28–39.

Sanders, P. (2000). 'Mapping person-centred approaches to counselling and psychotherapy.' *Person-Centred Practice, 8* (2): 62–74. (This paper appears, adapted, as Appendix 1, this volume.)

Warner and Sanders are discussed in Wilkins, P. (2003). *Person-Centred Therapy in Focus.* London: Sage.

A tentative conclusion

I believe there are real differences between the experiential approach and the classical stance:

Lietaer, G. (2002b). 'The Client-Centred /Experiential Paradigm in Psychotherapy: Development and identity.' In Watson, J.C., Goldman, R.N. and Warner, M.S. (eds.) *Client-Centred and Experiential Psychotherapy in the 21st Century; Advances in theory, research and practice.* Ross-on-Wye: PCCS Books, pp. 1–15.

The first is to do with the role and place of a client's experiencing. The belief for classical practitioners is that by creating a relationship characterised by the therapist attitudes as indicated by the six conditions, a client's internal defences will become redundant, and the actualising tendency, long dormant, can come to the fore and the client will be able to access their organismic experiencing and live more fully and more spontaneously. For experientially-oriented practitioners there is the belief that they need to help the client access their inner wisdom in a more proactive way which involves paying close attention to how the client behaves and how they process their experiences. Moreover, they can nurture the client's re-emergence as a more fully together person, by themselves being appropriately present and committed. Their job is to help the client hear themselves more completely.

The second is to do with the role of the therapist. The classical position is about removal of obstacles which hinder the client's blossoming and thereby creating a relationship characterised by the six conditions. Further, the therapist's role is to *follow* the client as they explore their inner lives. For the experiential practitioner, there is a real need to actively connect with a client in a more challenging committed way. To work at the edge of awareness requires the therapist to not only follow, but sometimes be level with and, occasionally, be just a step ahead. This 'being ahead', though, is but an opportunity for open egalitarian sharing about what is happening within the relationship *and within each of the two participants*.

The third is to do with goals. Whilst the classical practitioner will have no goals whatsoever and would see having *any* goals, however laudable they may seem to an outside observer, as being dishonourable, experiential practitioners clearly do have goals. They want their clients to be more in touch with their inner experiencings and to honour their preverbal felt senses, given their huge significance. That, though, is not to imply they have a prescriptive role. They do not have a commitment to any specific outward behaviours coming from the therapy: but they most certainly have a commitment to the client being more connected to their experiential inner flow as that is the source of them leading a richer, fuller more actualised life.

However, the existence of difference, rightly, these days is seen as the occasion for dialogue. Let all person-centred practitioners keep talking — I believe we have more in common than we may realise.

Resources

The following books are, in my view, the essential introductions to this work. Listed in alphabetical order rather than order of importance, UK residents may have some difficulty locating a copy of Greenberg *et al.* The other two are published in the UK.

Training organisations with a good library may have a copy of Greenberg et al. and interlibrary loans might be able to locate a copy. Otherwise, readers might like to try a decent internet search engine to track down second-hand copies of difficult to obtain books.

Greenberg, L.S., Watson, J.C. and Lietaer, G. (eds.) (1998). *Handbook of Experiential Psychotherapy*. New York: Guildford Press.

Rennie, D.L. (1998). *Person-Centred Counselling: An Experiential Approach*. London: Sage.

Worsley, R. (2002). *Process Work in Person-Centred Therapy: Phenomenological and Existential Perspectives*. Basingstoke: Palgrave.

existential approaches to therapy

mick cooper 5

Introduction

Of all the therapeutic approaches discussed in this book, the existential approaches to therapy probably have the most complex relationship to classical Client-Centred Therapy. On the one hand, the two approaches emerged relatively independently: the client-centred approach on the west coast of America (for instance, Rogers, 1951) and the existential approaches primarily in Europe (for instance, Boss, 1963; Frankl, 1986). At the same time, however, there were numerous instances of communication and exchange between these two schools of thought. Rogers, for instance, dialogued with — and was influenced by — two of the foremost existential philosophers: Martin Buber and Paul Tillich (see Kirschenbaum and Henderson, 1990); corresponded and met with key existential therapists, such as Rollo May (see Kirschenbaum and Henderson, 1990) and R. D. Laing (see O'Hara, 1997); and even contributed a chapter to Rollo May's *Existential Psychology* (1969). Given, too, that existential philosophy preceded the emergence of Client-Centred Therapy by almost a century, it is almost certain that Rogers was influenced by the broader spectrum of existential thinking in numerous unspecified ways. Both existential philosophy (in its twentieth-century guise) and person-centred practice were also fundamentally grounded in Edmund Husserl's 'phenomenological' standpoint, which argues that human beings need to be understood in terms of their actual, lived-experiences. To complicate matters further, there is not one particular form of existential therapy that can be contrasted with the classical client-centred approach. Rather, there is a diverse range of independent-yet-interrelated existential therapies that vary enormously in their similarity to a classical client-centred practice.

The aim of this chapter, then, is not to present an overview of how 'existential therapy', as a whole, compares and contrasts with classical Client-Centred Therapy. Rather, it is to present something of the tapestry of existential ideas and practices, and examine how *each* of these compares and contrasts with a classical client-centred approach. Through this exploration, certain themes will emerge, and these will be drawn together in the conclusion. The chapter

Rogers, C. R. (1951). *Client-Centered Therapy*. Boston: Houghton Mifflin.

Boss, M. (1963). *Psychoanalysis and Daseinsanalysis*. New York: Basic Books, Inc.

Frankl, V. E. (1986). *The Doctor and the Soul: From Psychotherapy to Logotherapy*. (3rd ed.) (Trans. R. Winston and C. Winston.) New York: Vintage Books.

Kirschenbaum, H. and Henderson, V., (eds.) (1990). *The Carl Rogers Dialogues*. London: Constable.

O'Hara, M. (1997). 'Maureen O'Hara.' In B. Mullan (ed.) *R. D. Laing: Creative Destroyer*. London: Cassell.

May, R. (ed.) (1969) *Existential Psychology*. New York: Random House.

For a highly accessible introduction to phenomenology, see Spinelli, E. (1989). *The Interpreted World: An Introduction to Phenomenological Psychology*. London: Sage.
A more in-depth and comprehensive account can be found in Moran, D. (2000). *Introduction to phenomenology*. London: Routledge.

begins, then, with an exploration of how existential philosophers — the thinkers behind existential therapeutic practice — tend to view human being. It then goes on to look at five key existential approaches to therapy — Daseinsanalysis, Logotherapy, existential-humanistic therapy, the work of R. D. Laing, and the British school of existential analysis — all the time comparing and contrasting these practices with a classical client-centred approach.

The existential view of human being

Like existential therapy, existential philosophy is a diverse and heterogeneous set of ideas, within which there are numerous areas of conflict and disagreement. It is a philosophical approach that began to take shape in the middle-to-late nineteenth century through the writings of Søren Kierkegaard (1813–55) and Frederick Nietzsche (1844–1900), though its roots can be traced back to antiquity. Around the middle of the twentieth century, existential philosophy reached its peak, with numerous philosophers across continental Europe advocating an existential understanding of human being.

Key existential philosophers include: Martin Buber (1878–1965), Karl Jaspers (1883–1969), Paul Tillich (1886–1965), Gabriel Marcel (1889–1973), Martin Heidegger (1889–1976), Jean-Paul Sartre (1905–80), Maurice Merleau-Ponty (1907–61) and Albert Camus (1913–60).

John Macquarrie (1972) provides the best introduction to the development and themes of existential thinking, but unfortunately his book is no longer in print.

Existential philosophy is, perhaps, best understood as a *reaction* to systems of thought — whether scientific, philosophical or religious — that tend to de-humanise our understanding of human beings. Existential philosophers wanted to get away from theories of human being that saw people as causally-determined mechanisms, collections of bit-parts, or cogs within a larger wheel, and instead focus on the concrete, actual reality of human existence. In other words, they wanted to focus on what it is really like to live as a human being, and whilst they did not always agree on their descriptions, certain commonalities tended to emerge.

Existence as unique
First, virtually every existential philosopher emphasised the uniqueness of each human existence: that we are all individual, distinctive and irreplaceable. This contrasts somewhat with a scientific world-view, which tends to reduce human beings down to their common elements, like 'stimulus' and 'response' (Watson, 1925), or 'id', 'ego' and 'superego' (Freud, 1923).

Watson, J. B. (1925). *Behaviorism*. New York: Norton.

Freud, S. (1923). 'The ego and the id.' *The Standard Edition of the Complete Psychological Works of Sigmund Freud*. London: Hogarth Press, pp. 12–59.

This emphasis on the uniqueness of human beings is very similar to the classical client-centred approach, which tends to dispense with generalised theories of human behaviour, preferring instead to focus on the individuality and uniqueness of each being. It is worth noting, however, that classical client-centred theory — like existential philosophy, itself — continues to make certain generalisations about how people are. For instance, it assumes that each human being is motivated towards growth, and that each human being has a 'great' need for positive regard (see Tony Merry's chapter, p.29). Here, an existential perspective might want to question these assumptions: for instance, is it true that *all* human beings are motivated towards growth? Could it be that some individuals are predisposed towards self-destruction?

Existence as a process, not a 'thing'

Existential philosophers have also tended to argue that human existence is not a noun-like 'thing', but a verb-like 'process'. Existential writers, for instance, have referred to existence as a 'flux' (Merleau-Ponty, 1945/1962), an unfolding event (Guignon, 1993), a 'path' (Jaspers, 1986) or an 'upsurge' (Sartre, 1943/1958).

Merleau-Ponty, M. (1962). *The Phenomenology of Perception*. (Trans. C. Smith.) London: Routledge. (Original work published 1945.)
Jaspers, K. (1986). 'Boundary situations.' *Philosophy*. Chicago: University of Chicago Press.
Sartre, J.-P. (1958). *Being and Nothingness: An Essay on Phenomenological Ontology*. (Trans. H. Barnes.) London: Routledge. (Original work published 1943.)
Rogers, C. R. (1961). *On Becoming a Person: A Therapist's View of Therapy*. London: Constable.

This is almost identical to Rogers' (1961) view of the self as a 'process', as well as the emphasis within the experiential therapies on the human being as an *experiencing* organism (see, for instance, Campbell Purton's and Nick Baker's chapters). To a great extent, this is due to the fact that, as noted above, both twentieth century existentialism and Person-Centred Therapy are rooted in the phenomenological philosophy of Edmund Husserl, which argued that our experiences are the 'ultimate court of appeal' in our knowledge of ourselves and the world (Merleau-Ponty, 1962).

Merleau-Ponty, M. (1962). *The Phenomenology of Perception*. (Trans. C. Smith.) London: Routledge.

Existential philosophers and therapists, however, have tended to be even more adamant than person-centred practitioners that human existence needs to be understood in process terms, and that to talk about human being as a noun, at all, is to take something away from the humanity of our actual lives. For this reason, many existential therapists (for instance, Spinelli, 1994) are very wary about using terms like 'self' or 'parts of the self' to describe human existence; preferring, instead, terms like 'being-in-the-world' or 'lived-existence' which convey a more process-like sentiment.

Spinelli, E. (1994). *Demystifying Therapy*. London: Constable.

Existence as freely-choosing

At the heart of virtually all existential philosophies and therapeutic practices is a belief that human beings are fundamentally and ineradicably free. Sartre (1958), for instance, argues that even the prisoner in a jail is free, because he or she can still decide whether to try and escape or stay put. Furthermore, he tends to argue that everything we do and think is a choice — even what we feel (see Sartre, 1962).

Sartre, J.-P. (1958). *Being and Nothingness: An Essay on Phenomenological Ontology*. (Trans. H. Barnes.) London: Routledge. (Original work published 1943.)
Sartre, J.-P. (1962). *Sketch for a Theory of the Emotions*. (Trans. P. Mairet.) London: Methuen.

Rogers, C. R. (1961). *On Becoming a Person: A Therapist's View of Therapy.* London: Constable.
Rogers, C. R. (1977). *Carl Rogers on Personal Power.* London: Constable.
Rogers, C. R. and Freiberg, H. J. (1994). *Freedom to Learn.* 3rd ed. New York: Macmillan College.

Sartre, J.-P. (1958). *Being and Nothingness: An Essay on Phenomenological Ontology.* (Trans. H. Barnes.) London: Routledge. (Original work published 1943.)
Cooper, M. (2003). 'Between freedom and despair: Existential challenges and contributions to person-centered and experiential therapy.' *Person-Centered and Experiential Psychotherapies, 2(1)*: 43–56.

Kirschenbaum, H. and Henderson, V., (eds.) (1990). *The Carl Rogers Dialogues.* London: Constable.
Mullan, B. (1995). *Mad to be Normal: Conversations with R. D. Laing.* London: Free Association Books.

The term 'process' seems to be one of the most popular terms in the person-centred world, with phrases like 'I'm going through a major process, right now' commonly heard. But what does 'process' actually mean? Is our 'process' a choice? And, if not, does that mean it is determined to happen?

Heidegger, M. (1962). *Being and Time.* (Trans. J. Macquarrie and E. Robinson.) Oxford: Blackwell. (Original work published 1926.)

This is possibly one of the biggest contrasts between existential and person-centred views of human being. Rogers was very concerned to emphasise the human capacity for freedom (see, for instance, Rogers, 1961, 1977; Rogers and Freiberg, 1994), but he tends to present freedom as something that human beings can attain, rather than something that is intrinsic to our very being at every moment in time. Furthermore, within the client-centred field, there is a tendency to see growth as something that has a large, non-conscious, spontaneous element to it. Tony Merry writes in his chapter, for instance, that, 'The process of actualisation is not regarded, in human beings, as a conscious "activity" in which the individual makes choices between alternatives, but as a process in which the total organism is involved at both conscious and non-conscious levels' (p.23). By contrast, existential philosophers and therapists have tended to put a greater emphasis on conscious deliberation in the process of human development (see, for instance, Sartre, 1958). From an existential perspective, human development is like coming to a series of crossroads, each of which forces us to make decisions about the way we want to be (Cooper, 2003). So, for instance, if I and my partner are deciding whether or not to try for another child, the conscious decisions that we make will have a great impact on who we become in the future.

Furthermore, whilst an existential approach would not necessarily argue that such decisions are always consciously made, it would hold that our movement through life is a proactive one. From an existential perspective, then, there is no actualising force within us that drives us towards self-enhancement and self-maintenance. This is something that we actively have to choose to do. Similarly, in contrast to a classical client-centred perspective, there is no belief that we have innate tendency to move towards constructive and pro-social behaviours — rather, we must actively and deliberately choose good over evil (see Rogers' correspondence with May in Kirschenbaum and Henderson, 1990; and also Laing's comments on Rogers in Mullan, 1995). From an existential perspective, then, there are no inner drives or tendencies that cause us to be who we are and no 'process' we can trust. Rather, who we are is shaped by the choices that we make.

Existence as future- and meaning-orientated

Whilst existential philosophy and therapy is often associated with an emphasis on the 'here-and-now', existential philosophers have, in fact, tended to put a greater emphasis on the significance of the future (see, for instance, Heidegger, 1962). Here, it has been argued that human beings are inherently orientated towards particular goals, purposes, projects or meanings, and that this orientation has a great effect on how we think, feel and behave in the present; as well as how we might make sense of our past. Someone whose goal in life, for instance, is to earn as much money as possible, may consequently be very hard-working in the immediate present, and also think about their past in terms of the difficulties that they had to overcome — perhaps as a means of justifying their present workaholism. Such a view, then, turns on its head our normal way of understanding things, in which we assume that a past leads someone to behave in a particular way in the present, which then leads them to behave in a particular way in the future.

Such a view of human existence as goal-orientated is entirely compatible with a classical client-centred perspective; and, indeed, some person-centred authors have specifically highlighted the value of empathising with a client in terms of their orientation towards the future (for instance, Bohart, 2001). Within the classical client-centred view of human development, however, there does tend to be a tendency to account for psychological difficulties in terms of a person's early childhood experiences (see, for instance, Tony Merry's section on 'conditions of worth and the self-concept'), and this line of reasoning is something that many existential philosophers and therapists will be wary of adopting.

In contrast to some existential approaches, client-centred thinking also does not put any great emphasis on the human *need* for meaning; although it would not in any way deny that this may be central for some clients. Between the client-centred and some existential approaches, then, is something of a debate about whether the most fundamental human need is for *meaning* or for *actualisation*. From a client-centred perspective, for instance, one might argue that the need for meaning is one part of the wider need for actualisation. In other words, an individual strives to maintain and enhance themselves and, as part of this, they might try and find the meaning of the things that they do. By contrast, from an existential perspective, one might argue that the need for actualisation is actually only a sub-need of the need for meaning. In other words, human beings only 'need' to actualise themselves when they set this for themselves as a meaningful and worthwhile goal and, if they set for themselves another meaning or goal — such as to live a life of self-denial and asceticism — then this could over-ride the drive towards actualisation. Again, here, we can see elements of the debate touched on in the above section, about whether development is primarily a spontaneous, organismic process, or whether it is something more deliberate, conscious

Bohart, A. C. (2001). 'Emphasising the future in empathy responses.' In S. Haugh and T. Merry (eds.) *Rogers' Therapeutic Conditions: Evolution, theory and Practice. Volume 2: Empathy*. Ross-on-Wye: PCCS Books, pp. 99–111. (Original work published 1993).

and proactive, in which we set for ourselves meanings and goals, and then reach out in our behaviours towards them?

Within the existential approach itself, however, there is also substantial debate over the question of whether there are any actual, given meanings to life, or whether we have to create our own meanings. That is, is there some meaning or purpose to our lives that we can find or discover (as suggested by Buber, 1958; Marcel, 1949), or is it a case that we have to construct these for ourselves — like the Indian Fakir who throws a rope up in the air and then proceeds to climb it — and that these will never have any ultimate, solid or extrinsic value (as suggested by Camus, 1955; Sartre, 1958)? Again, a classical client-centred position would not necessarily take either of the sides in this debate, but the latter position — that life has no extrinsic value — presents some serious challenges to a classical client-centred perspective. Most significantly, it asks, 'So what?': 'So what if we actualise our potential?' 'What does it matter?' 'Is it not just one meaning that we have chosen for ourselves out of a plethora of possible purposes?'

Existence as limited
Existential philosophers and therapists, then, see human beings as fundamentally free, but it would be a mistake to assume that they think that people can do whatever they want. Rather, existentialists have been as concerned with the fundamental limitations that human existences face, such as the fact that we are going to die, the fact that we are born into a world that is not of our making, and the fact that we are surrounded by numerous economic, social, cultural, political and environmental givens.

Existential philosophers also talk about the 'paradoxes' or 'antimonies' of existence (for instance, Jaspers, 1932): these are contradictions or conflicts that cannot be overcome, however much we might try and 'work' through them. One such paradox, for instance, might be that the more that we try and be happy in our lives, the more we can often end up feeling frustrated and dissatisfied. Another such contradiction may be that the more we try and get people to like us, the more they can tend to push us away. Here, the point is that these contradictions cannot simply be 'worked through' in therapy, or by attaining a higher level of actualisation. Rather, such contradictions are intrinsic to life: they are the 'limits' to our existence which we run up against, and which cannot be overcome.

Buber, M. (1958). *I and Thou*. 2nd ed. (Trans. R. G. Smith.) Edinburgh: T. and T. Clark Ltd. (Original work published 1923.)

Marcel, G. (1949). *The Philosophy of Existence*. (Trans. M. Harai.) Freeport, NY: Books for Libraries Press.

Camus, A. (1955). *The Myth of Sisyphus*. (Trans. J. O'Brien.) London: Penguin. (Original work published 1942.)

Sartre, J.-P. (1958). *Being and Nothingness: An Essay on Phenomenological Ontology*. (Trans. H. Barnes.) London: Routledge. (Original work published 1943.)

Jaspers, K. (1932). 'Boundary situations.' *Philosophy*. Chicago: University of Chicago Press.

In contrast to this viewpoint, classical Client-Centred Therapy tends to put less emphasis on the limitations of human existence — apart from the surmountable limitation of conditional positive regard. With its more optimistic outlook, it tends to focus on what human beings can achieve, rather than on those things that are beyond our capacities. Indeed, Rogers explicitly states that such issues as death were no subjects to be dwelt upon (Swildens, 2002).

Paradoxically, then, existential thinking places more emphasis on both the freedoms and limitations of human existence than the classical client-centred approach. In metaphorical terms, its view of human existence is less like a sprouting seed, and more like a goldfish in a tank (Cooper, 2003): confined on all sides, but able to move freely within its boundaries. To take these metaphors further, whilst the sprouting seed, like the goldfish, is affected by its external environment (such as a lack of sunlight), in the right conditions it can grow to its fullest extent. By contrast, the goldfish can never move outside of its tank: never exceed its imprisonment and restrictions. Here, then, the external limitations are conceptualised as being more fixed and inescapable, and somewhat more indifferent to the organism's plight.

To illustrate this with a more familiar example: take the instance of a person-centred community meeting. Here, in my experience, there often seems to be an assumption that, if all the participants can express what they want, then as many needs as possible can be met. From an existential perspective, on the other hand, there is more of an acknowledgement that the limits of the situation — such as time boundaries — mean that there must inevitably be compromises, frustrations and feelings of disappointments. Indeed, from an existential standpoint, one of the paradoxes of this situation is that the more each person's needs are talked about, the more that certain people — such as those who 'want to get on with things' — will find that their needs are frustrated.

Existence as in-the-world

In this previous section, we have seen how, from an existential perspective, an individual's environment is seen as an ineradicable part of their existence, rather than something separate from them. In contrast to a classical client-centred perspective, it is not just something that either nourishes or fails to nourish the individual's internally-determined path in life, but something that is intrinsic to their very being. In this respect, Heidegger (1962) uses the term 'being-in-the-world' or 'da-sein' ('being-there') to describe human existence, to underline this fundamental connection

In my experience, such high expectations can lead person-centred practitioners and trainees to feel inadequate, or that they have failed, when they, or their clients, are still struggling with confusions, uncertainties and interpersonal tangles. Accepting these as givens of existence may help practitioners and clients to develop a greater degree of self-acceptance.

Swildens, H. (2002). 'Where did we come from and where are we going? The development of person-centered therapy.' *Person-Centered and Experiential Psychotherapies 1(1 & 2)*, 118–31.

Cooper, M. (2003). *Existential Therapies*. London: Sage.

Heidegger, M. (1962). *Being and Time*. (Trans. J. Macquarrie and E. Robinson.) Oxford: Blackwell. (Original work published 1926.)

Heidegger, M. (1966). *Discourse on Thinking.* (Trans. J. M. Anderson and E. H. Freund.) London: Harper Colophon Books. (Original work published 1959.)
Heidegger, M. (1996). 'Letter on humanism.' In L. Cahoone (ed). *From Modernism to Postmodernism: An Anthology.* Cambridge, MA: Blackwells Publishers Ltd (Original work published 1947.)
Merleau-Ponty, M. (1962). *The Phenomenology of Perception.* (Trans. C. Smith.) London: Routledge. (Original work published 1945.)
Boss, M. (1963). *Psychoanalysis and Daseinsanalysis.* New York: Basic Books, Inc.
Spinelli, E. (1994). *Demystifying Therapy.* London: Constable.

Heidegger, M. (1962). *Being and Time.* (Trans. J. Macquarrie and E. Robinson.) Oxford: Blackwell. (Original work published 1926.)
Buber, M. (1958). *I and Thou.* 2nd ed. (Trans. R. G. Smith.) Edinburgh: T. & T. Clark Ltd. (Original work published 1923.)
Merleau-Ponty, M. (1962). *The Phenomenology of Perception.* (Trans. C. Smith.) London: Routledge. (Original work published 1945.)

Recent authors have developed dialogical aspects of CCT in which the self can only exist in relation to others. (See Pete Sanders' Chapter, p. 18, this volume.) Also, Mearns, D. and Thorne, B. (2000). 'Advancing person-centred theory,' In *Person-Centred Therapy Today.* London: Sage, pp. 172–95. And Schmid, P. F. (2003). 'Knowledge or Acknowledgement? Psychotherapy as the 'art of not knowing': Prospects on further developments of a radical paradigm.' *Person-Centered and Experiential Psychotherapies 1* (1&2): 56–70.

between 'self' and world. Indeed, in his later writings (Heidegger, 1966, 1996), he described human beings as an 'opening' in which the 'Being' of the world can become manifest; or as a 'clearing' in the forest, in which the Being of beings can be seen for what it is. In other words, what he is saying is that the function of human beings is to 'witness' Being: to acknowledge that things exist, like a plant or a computer.

From the perspective of Heidegger (1962) and some of the later existential philosophers (such as Merleau-Ponty, 1962), then, existence is not something that is 'inside' of us, but something that is between us and the world. For this reason, many existential thinkers and practitioners (for instance, Boss, 1963, see section on Daseinsanalysis) are very wary of using terms like 'inner experiences' or 'inner feelings' to talk about human existence. Rather, they would use terms like 'lived-experiences' (Spinelli, 1994), which do not necessarily imply that the experiences are inside of the individual.

Existence as with-others
For Heidegger (1962) and some other twentieth century existential philosophers (for instance, Buber, 1958; Merleau-Ponty, 1962), being is not only in-the-world, but also 'with-others'. Heidegger argues this on the grounds that, whatever we do, we are always using tools and meanings that have emerged from a social environment. If, for instance, I push my daughter on the swing in the park, then our activity is orientated around a socially-constructed piece of equipment (the swing) for a project that has been defined by our social environment as pleasurable (playing). And when I tell her to stop trying to kick me every time she swings up to me, I am using the socially-constructed medium of language. And even the fact that I am going out to play in the park with her is part of the socially-constructed 'narrative' of what a father should do with his daughter on a Sunday morning. Even something as seemingly individual as this activity, then, can be seen as being infused with the social world in multiple ways.

Here, then, is another important point of theoretical divergence between a classical client-centred position and some existential perspectives. In the classical client-centred approach, human beings tend to be construed as separate, individual entities, who are in some way separable from others in their world. By contrast, in the existential perspective, human beings are conceived as ultimately inseparable from others: for even if they were abandoned on a desert island, it could be argued that they would still be using the socially-constructed medium of language to think with.

Another existential philosopher who has put a great emphasis on our intrinsic interrelatedness with others is Martin Buber (1958). This is the existential philosopher who is, perhaps, closest to a person-centred perspective than any other, and had a clear influence on the development of classical Client-Centred Therapy (see Anderson and Cissna, 1997). What Rogers takes from Buber, however, is not so much the idea that the I is always connected to another, but Buber's distinction between the humanising 'I-Thou' attitude to others, as opposed to the de-humanising 'I-It' attitude. For Buber, this I-Thou attitude is characterised by an acceptance of the other, an openness to the whole of who they are, and a willingness to take the risk of fully engaging with them with the totality of one's own being — a way of relating which has clear parallels with Rogers' (1957) conditions of acceptance, empathy and congruence. One slight difference with a non-directive client-centred approach, however, is that Buber puts more emphasis on the need for the I to bring his or her own 'otherness' into the relationship with an other. After all, argues Buber, if the I simply becomes a reflecting mirror to the Other, then there is no difference across which dialogue can take place.

Existence as embodied

In striving to see the person as a whole, some existential philosophers, most notably Maurice Merleau-Ponty (1962), have also challenged the idea that the mind can be separated from the body. For Merleau-Ponty, our bodies are not something that we *have*, but something that we *are*, and there is always a bodily-felt dimension to our lived-experiencing. Furthermore, from this perspective, our bodily-felt responses to the world are not irrational or inappropriate, but meaningful and intelligent reactions that need to be respected and attended to. In the words of Nietzsche: 'There is more wisdom in the body than in thy deepest learnings' (1967, p. 71).

Here, then, is a great similarity to Rogers' view that we should attend to — and trust — our emotions and feelings; and that it is important to try and overcome the mind-body divide (see Rogers, 1980) and conceptualise the organism as an organised whole. There are also great similarities here with Gendlin's (1996) work on felt-senses, and his view that our bodily-felt reactions tell us much about how we perceive and experience the world.

Buber, M. (1958). *I and Thou*. (2nd ed.) (Trans. R. G. Smith.) Edinburgh: T. and T. Clark Ltd. (Original work published 1923.)

Anderson, R. and Cissna, K. N. (1997). *The Martin Buber — Carl Rogers Dialogue: A New Transcript with Commentary*. Albany, NY: State University of New York Press. Even if you have read a previous transcription of this dialogue, it is worth reading this new transcript and analysis because it throws much new light on this famous exchange: in particular, the level of agreement between the two men and Buber's somewhat un-dialogic attitude to Rogers.

Rogers, C.R. (1957). 'The necessary and sufficient conditions of therapeutic personality change.' *J. Consult. Psychol.* 21: 95–103. Reprinted in H. Kirschenbaum and V.L. Henderson (eds.) (1989). *The Carl Rogers Reader.* London: Constable, pp. 219–35.

Merleau-Ponty, M. (1962). *The Phenomenology of Perception*. (Trans. C. Smith.) London: Routledge. (Original work published 1945.)

Nietzsche, F. (1967). *Thus Spake Zarathustra*. (Trans. T. Common.) London: George Allen and Unwin Ltd. (Original work published 1883.)

Rogers, C. R. (1980). *A Way of Being*. Boston: Houghton Mifflin. Gendlin, E. (1996). *Focusing-Oriented Psychotherapy: A Manual of the Experiential Method*. New York: The Guilford Press.

The tragedy of existence

Existential philosophy is well-known for its gloomy outlook on life, and this characterisation is not altogether inaccurate. By seeing human existence as a meaning-orientated flow of being that is free within limitations, it suggests that human beings will inherently experience many negative — as well as positive — emotions. From this perspective, for instance, we are likely to experience dread at our sense of nothingness and insubstantiality; anxiety in the face of having to choose between competing alternatives; guilt towards ourselves and others at having turned away from certain possibilities; hopelessness in the face of insurmountable limitations; and despair at the apparent meaninglessness of it all. Becker, a commentator on existential ideas, puts it this way:

> Anxiety is the result of the perception of the truth of one's condition. What does it mean to be a *self-conscious animal?* The idea is ludicrous, if it is not monstrous. It means to know that one is food for worms. This is the terror: to have emerged from nothing, to have a name, consciousness of self, deep inner feelings, an excruciating yearning for life and self-expression — and with all this yet to die. (Becker, p. 87)

From an existential standpoint, then, life has an unavoidably tragic element to it: that we come into the world eager and keen to make something of ourselves, discover that we will one day turn to dust, and realise that, in the short time available, there are so many possibilities that we must reject. From an existential standpoint, what we also realise as we grow is that life is not the benign and nurturing place we might have once hoped it would be. There are restrictions in every direction we turn, people who have little interest in our lives and our welfare, rules and regulations that carry on beyond us and regardless of us. Here, then, is a sadness about life, and it is not about conditions of worth or failures in the environment, but about the unavoidable limitations and paradoxes of existence. Such a sense of tragedy, then, contrasts somewhat with the more optimistic and hopeful client-centred perspective, which hypothesises that a 'good life' is attainable if we can experience the necessary and sufficient conditions (Rogers, 1961).

The choice between authenticity and inauthenticity

From an existential perspective, then, facing up to the reality of existence brings with it anxiety, guilt, despair, hopelessness and sadness. For this reason, it is argued, many of us will gladly turn away from the truth of our existence, and pretend our lives are other than they are. Like a person who does not want to open his

Becker, E. (1973). *The Denial of Death*. New York: Free Press Paperbacks.

Whilst some people, like myself, seem to find great resonance, and even comfort, in this openness to the tragic, others seem to find it relatively meaningless. My guess is that an affinity to existential ideas has much more to do with personal disposition — the 'Leonard Cohen-type' personality! — than anything else.

In the words of Robert Burns: 'many and sharp are the num'rous ills inwoven with our frame!' Burns, R. (1946). *Selected Poems*. London: Penguin.

Rogers, C. R. (1961). *On Becoming a Person: A Therapist's View of Therapy*. London: Constable.

or her bank statement because they know they are overdrawn, we hope that if we don't face up to life, then all the bad feelings will go away. So we don't acknowledge that we have choices in a particular situation; or we give ourselves a fixed and rigid identity — like 'an existential therapist' — so that we do not ever really have to think through the complexities and uncertainties of being a being-in-flux. Or, as Heidegger argues, we pretend that death will never really come to us: that it is something that happens to other people, and that somehow we will go on living for ever — or that our goals and projects will be carried forward by our children.

As with classical client-centred thinking, then, there is a belief within existential philosophy that human beings have the capacity to distort or deny certain self-experiences, or understandings of their own existence. There is a significant difference here, however, between the existential and classical client-centred views. From a classical client-centred perspective, it is argued that the tendency to deny or distort certain experiences arises out of our tendency to introject external values (Rogers, 1951), and particularly the values from others as to which of our experiences are worthy of positive regard (Rogers, 1959). Here, then, is a belief that denial and distortion arise from external sources and that, if individuals were left to their own devices, they would have little need to defend themselves against their own experiences. By contrast, from an existential perspective, denial and distortion are seen as arising from *within* the individual, as well as from the individual's encounter with other people. So, for instance, existential philosophers and therapists would argue that people may have a tendency to deny the fact that they are going to die (for instance, Yalom, 1980), and this is not principally to do with introjecting a belief from others that dying is wrong, or that they won't be positively regarded if they are on their death-bed. Rather, their denial of death comes about because of the sheer terror of the thought that their existence and projects will come to an end. This difference has substantial implications for therapeutic practice, and we will look at this later on in the chapter.

In many respects, however, person-centred and existential theories of authenticity and psychological difficulties are remarkably similar. For, in both approaches, whilst denial and distortion of experiences are seen as bringing temporary relief, it is argued that they ultimately cause more problems than they alleviate. From an existential perspective, our awareness of the reality of human existence — like denied self-experiences — does not go away.

Rogers, C. R. (1951). *Client-Centered Therapy*. Boston: Houghton Mifflin.
Rogers, C. R. (1959). 'A theory of therapy, personality and interpersonal relationships as developed in the client-centered framework.' In S. Koch (ed.) *Psychology: A Study of Science*. New York: McGraw-Hill, pp. 184–256.

Yalom, I. (1980). *Existential Psychotherapy*. New York: Basic Books.

Rather, it piles up, demanding to be heard, overwhelming us with feelings of anxiety and helplessness. And, by not facing up to this reality, it is argued that we cannot make the most of the possibilities we do have. We pretend to ourselves that we will go on living for ever, so we put off our lives 'for the future'; or we invite someone else to make our choices for us, and thereby end up feeling frustrated and victimised. So the existential approach, like the Person-Centred Approach, argues that, although acknowledging the truth of our existence can be difficult, it can also bring with it great vitality, passion and an unrivalled intensity of living. Indeed, whilst existentialism does emphasise the more discomforting aspects of life, it is ultimately part of an attempt to help people live life more fully and intensely.

In both the person-centred and existential approaches, then, psychological well-being comes from acknowledging the reality of our experiences and existence. Within the earlier existential writings, there was a tendency to focus on the resolve and courage required to do this: a willingness to 'stand naked in the storm of life' (Becker, 1973); and also the importance of separating oneself from the 'masses', who will always draw one down into the morass of everyday averageness (Heidegger, 1962; Nietzsche, 1967). In the later Heideggerian writings, however, there was more of an emphasis on adopting a meditative and reflective attitude, in which we could 'let Being be' rather than trying to manipulate and coerce existence through 'calculative', scientific thinking. Given the emphasis on being as 'in-the-world' or 'with-others', many existential writers have also argued that an acknowledgement of our true being requires an acknowledgement of our true connectivity with something outside of ourselves: whether other people, nature, or God (see, for instance, Buber, 1958; Kierkegaard, 1992; Marcel, 1949; Tillich, 2000). Here, then, are close connections with a classical client-centred approach, which would tend to see the move towards greater self-congruence as one that involves both courage, openness and a reaching out to others.

Therapeutic practices

Daseinsanalysis

One of the first 'schools' of existential therapy to emerge, and still to be found across mainland Europe today, is called Daseinsanalysis. It was founded by the Swiss psychiatrist, Ludwig Binswanger (1881–1966), in the early 1930s; and developed — particularly in terms of actual practice — by another Swiss

Becker, E. (1973). *The Denial of Death.* New York: Free Press Paperbacks.

Heidegger, M. (1962). *Being and Time.* (Trans. J. Macquarrie and E. Robinson.) Oxford: Blackwell. (Original work published 1926.)
Nietzsche, F. (1967). *Thus Spake Zarathustra.* (Trans. T. Common.) London: George Allen and Unwin Ltd. (Original work published 1883.)

Buber, M. (1958). *I and Thou.* (2nd ed.) (Trans. R. G. Smith.) Edinburgh: T. and T. Clark Ltd. (Original work published 1923.)
Kierkegaard, S. (1992). *Concluding Unscientific Postscript to Philosophical Fragments.* (Trans. H. V. Hong and E. H. Hong.) Princeton, NJ: Princeton University Press. (Original work published 1846.)
Marcel, G. (1949). *The Philosophy of Existence.* (Trans. M. Harai.) Freeport, NY: Books for Libraries Press.
Tillich, P. (2000). *The Courage to Be.* 2nd ed. New Haven: Yale University Press. (Original work published 1952.)

psychiatrist, Medard Boss (1903–90), in the middle of the twentieth century. Both Binswanger and Boss were devout followers of classical psychoanalytic practice, but both men abhorred the psychological principles underlying this practice, which they felt reduced human beings to a 'conceptual monstrosity' of parts, mechanisms and dynamics. The aim of Daseinsanalysis, then, was to reformulate the theory of psychoanalytic practice along more humanising lines; and, to do so, Binswanger and Boss turned to the teachings of the existential philosopher, Martin Heidegger.

This move to a Heideggerian framework meant that Daseins-analysis vigorously rejected many of the core concepts within psychoanalytic theory (Boss, 1963, 1979). First to go was the notion of the 'psyche': that human existence was some kind of self-enclosed, thing-like entity. Instead, Daseinsanalysis conceptualised human beingness as an 'openness' to the world — like Heidegger's (1996) clearing in the forest — in which person and environment were inextricably interconnected. With this also came a rejection of intrapsychic 'parts' — such as 'id', 'ego' and 'superego' (Freud, 1923) — and the idea that these parts could interact with each other like coloured balls on a pool table. Above all, Daseinsanalysts rejected the notion of an 'unconscious': the idea that the psyche contained a depository of hidden feelings and instincts which could cause the person to think, feel and act in certain ways. Rather, Daseinsanalysts talked about the way in which individuals could sometimes be 'closed' to aspects of their world. That is, that they might not allow themselves to experience what is beautiful in the world, or what is saddening, or what is chaotic.

From a Daseinsanalytic standpoint, then, psychological difficulties are not the result of intrapsychic conflicts (for instance, an ego that is dominated by its id), but a chronic closedness towards one's world (Boss, 1963, 1979). That is, the psychologically maladjusted individual is someone who does not allow themselves to experience the whole spectrum of possibilities in their world, but is like a torchlight that can only shine on a very limited range of surfaces, or like a clearing in a forest which is surrounded by 'KEEP OUT' signs. A depressed individual, then, might be understood as someone who is closed to what is joyful in the world, or a paranoid individual might be understood as someone who is closed to that which is trustworthy in others. By contrast, psychological well-being is understood as an openness to the world. From a Daseinsanalytic perspective, then, the

Boss, M. (1963). *Psychoanalysis and Daseinsanalysis*. New York: Basic Books, Inc.

Boss, M. (1979). *Existential Foundations of Medicine and Psychology*. (Trans. S. Conway and A. Cleaves.) Northvale, NJ: Jason Aronson Inc.

Heidegger, M. (1996). 'Letter on humanism.' In L. Cahoone (ed.) *From Modernism to Postmodernism: An Anthology*. Cambridge, MA: Blackwells Publishers Ltd. (Original work published 1947.)

Freud, S. (1923). 'The ego and the id.' *The Standard Edition of the Complete Psychological Works of Sigmund Freud*. London: Hogarth Press, pp. 12–59.

Boss, M. (1963). *Psychoanalysis and Daseinsanalysis*. New York: Basic Books, Inc.

Boss, M. (1979). *Existential Foundations of Medicine and Psychology*. (Trans. S. Conway and A. Cleaves.) Northvale, NJ: Jason Aronson Inc.

psychologically healthy individual is able to allow themselves to experience everything that the world presents to them — from the most joyful to the most deeply despairing — without distortion or denial.

This means that there are some striking similarities between the Daseinsanalytic view of psychological functioning and the classical client-centred one. As with Daseinsanalysis, classical Client-Centred Therapy, as we have seen, would argue that a psychologically healthy individual is one who is able to acknowledge, and engage with, the full spectrum of their experiences; whilst a psychological troubled individual is one who distorts or denies certain aspects of the self-experiential field. Indeed, Rogers (1961) actually defines 'an increasing openness to experience' as one of the characteristics of the 'good life', writing that, 'the individual is more open to his feelings of fear and discouragement and pain. He is also more open to his feelings of courage, and tenderness, and awe. He is free to live his feelings subjectively, as they exist in him, and also free to be aware of these feelings' (*ibid.* p. 188). Another similarity between these two approaches is that, as with the classical client-centred approach, Daseinsanalysts tend to hold that a chronic closedness to the world comes about through inadequate parenting, in which the client learns that certain ways of experiencing the world will lead to criticism and punishment (Boss, 1988).

What is subtly different about these two perspectives, however, is that the classical client-centred approach talks about openness or closedness *to one's own experiences*, whilst the Daseinsanalytic approach talks about an openness or closedness *to the world*. So, for instance, whilst a client-centred therapist might talk about an individual being closed to their feelings of vulnerability, a Daseinsanalyst might be more inclined to talk about an individual being closed 'to that which is frightening in the world'. This distinction is a subtle one, and may be just a matter of focus — with the client-centred approach focusing on the internal pole of an experience, and the Daseinsanalytic approach focusing on the external pole. It does offer client-centred therapists, however, a somewhat different way of thinking about their own, and their clients', experiences; and one that is less wedded to the notion of a self-enclosed, world-less 'self'.

In practical terms, too, there are many similarities between Daseinsanalysis and classical Client-Centred Therapy — despite the fact that Daseinsanalysts adopt many classical psycho-

Rogers, C. R. (1961). *On Becoming a Person: A Therapist's View of Therapy.* London: Constable.

Ibid.

Boss, M. (1988). 'Recent considerations in Daseinsanalysis.' *The Humanistic Psychologist, 16 (1)*: 58–73.

analytical practices, such as encouraging clients to free associate and recline on a couch (Boss, 1963, 1979; Condrau, 1998). The Daseinsanalytic rejection of unconscious mechanisms, for instance, means that Daseinsanalytic psycho-therapy is essentially a descriptive enterprise, in which the client is given the opportunity to explore any aspect of their lived-experience, free from interpretation or analysis by their therapist. Here, the role of the therapist is to provide a warm and facilitative environment, in which the client can come to articulate — and open themselves up to — all aspects of their lived-world. Furthermore, with a rejection of unconscious dynamics comes a rejection of the notion of 'transference', such that the Daseinsanalyst, like the client-centred therapist, strives to relate to their client in a genuine and authentic way. Indeed, Boss (1963) suggests that the mirror-like impassivity prescribed but not always enacted by Freud (Friedman, 1985) is, itself, an inadequate and restricted mode of relating, with the potential to close clients even further to their lived-worlds.

Boss, M. (1963). *Psychoanalysis and Daseinsanalysis*. New York: Basic Books, Inc.
Boss, M. (1979). *Existential Foundations of Medicine and Psychology*. (Trans. S. Conway and A. Cleaves.) Northvale, NJ: Jason Aronson Inc.
Condrau, G. (1998). *Martin Heidegger's Impact on Psychotherapy*. Dublin: Edition Mosaic.

Boss, M. (1963). *Psychoanalysis and Daseinsanalysis*. New York: Basic Books, Inc.
Friedman, M. (1985). *The Healing Dialogue in Psychotherapy*. New York: Jason Aronson, Inc.

In contrast to Client-Centred Therapy, however, Daseinsanalysis does put particular emphasis on the descriptive analysis of clients' dreams (Boss, 1977). To a great extent, this is a remnant of Daseinsanalysis's psychoanalytic roots, but it does offer client-centred therapists a particular interesting — and phenomenologically-sound — way of thinking about dreams. From a Daseinsanalytic perspective, dream images and narratives are not symbols of deeper, latent meanings; but an expression of what a client is open to or closed to in their lived-world. A client, for instance, who consistently dreams of being chased by monsters, would seem open to the terrifying and beastly, whilst closed to that which is supportive and safe. Daseinsanalytic dream work, then, consists of helping clients to describe their dreams in increasing levels of detail — through such questions as 'What?' 'Where?' and 'How?' (Condrau, 1998) — such that they can come to understand their spectra of world-openness and world-closedness more fully. According to Daseinsanalytic dream theory, however, a client's dreams not only reflect their levels of openness and closedness, but may also reveal, for the first time, new ways in which a client might experience their world. A highly paranoid client, for instance, might experience in his or her dreams — albeit very briefly — the love and care of a nurturing figure; or he or she may slowly approach such a figure, before backing away. Here, the role of the Daseinsanalyst is to help their client reflect on these new-found possibilities for experiencing their world; and also to affirm them in these experiences, such that they might feel more able to open themselves up to these possibilities in

Boss, M. (1977). *'I Dreamt Last Night...'* (Trans. S. Conway.) New York: John Wiley and Sons, Inc.

Condrau, G. (1998). *Martin Heidegger's Impact on Psychotherapy*. Dublin: Edition Mosaic.

waking life. A therapist might say, for instance, 'Isn't it great that you experienced someone who wanted to love and nurture you in your dreams — I wonder if you could allow yourself to experience this in your waking life too?'

Logotherapy

As discussed earlier, many existentialists believe that human beings are fundamentally orientated towards meanings and goals in their lives. Therapeutically, this assumption is nowhere more important that in the practice of 'Logotherapy', which strives to help clients discover such meanings and goals in their lives and to overcome feelings of meaninglessness and despair. Logotherapy was developed by the Viennese psychiatrist, Viktor Frankl (1905–97), in the early 1930s, and continues to be practised across mainland Europe and the American continent today. Logotherapy, as Frankl writes, may be more a supplement, than a substitute, for therapy, but its versatile nature means that it has been applied to a whole range of helping contexts, such as nursing (Starck, 1993) and social work (Guttman, 1996). Moreover, in recent years, there have been attempts to develop more comprehensive forms of Logotherapy practice, such as 'existential-analytical' therapy (Längle, 2001) and 'Meaning-centred Counselling' (Wong, 1998).

At the heart of logotherapy is a belief that every human being's most basic need is for meaning in his or her life (Frankl, 1986); and that, without such meanings, individuals will experience profound feelings of frustration, emptiness and/or despair. Moreover, it is argued that such feelings can develop into more serious 'existential neuroses', in which individuals may turn to such self-destructive behaviours as addictions, compulsions or phobias in an attempt to fill their existential void. The implication here is that many forms of psychological distress (though not all) are actually a consequence of a lack of meaning in people's lives. An individual who drinks heavily, for instance, might be understood as someone who cannot bear the feelings of pointlessness and futility that emerge when they are sober. And, of course, by remaining drunk, they may be not able to establish any valid meanings or goals in their lives, hence perpetuating a vicious cycle of futility, lethargy and despair.

Furthermore, in contrast to the views of the more nihilistic existentialists, such as Sartre (1958) and Camus (1955), Logotherapy does not hold that human beings *create* their own meanings, or that life is essentially meaningless. Rather, Frankl (1986), coming from a deeply religious background, believes that

---

'Logos' being the Greek term for 'meaning' (Frankl, V. E. (1984). *Man's Search for Meaning*. (revised and updated ed.) New York: Washington Square Press.)

Starck, P. L. (1993). 'Logotherapy: applications to nursing.' *Journal des Viktor-Frankl-Instituts 1*: 94–8.
Guttman, D. (1996). *Logotherapy for the Helping Professional: Meaningful Social Work*. New York: Springer Publishing Company.
Längle, A. (2001). 'Old age from an existential-analytical perspective.' *Psychological Reports, 89*: 211–15.
Wong, P. T. P. (1998). 'Meaning-centred counseling.' In P. T. Wong and P. Fry (eds.) *The Quest for Human Meaning: A Handbook of Theory, Research and Application*. Mahway, NJ: Lawrence Erlbaum Inc.
Frankl, V. E. (1986). *The Doctor and the Soul: From Psychotherapy to Logotherapy*. 3rd ed. (Trans. R. Winston and C. Winston.) New York: Vintage Books.

Sartre, J.-P. (1958). *Being and Nothingness: An Essay on Phenomenological Ontology*. (Trans. H. Barnes.) London: Routledge. (Original work published 1943.)
Camus, A. (1955). *The Myth of Sisyphus*. (Trans. J. O'Brien.) London: Penguin. (Original work published 1942.)
Frankl, V. E. (1986). *The Doctor and the Soul: From Psychotherapy to Logotherapy*. 3rd ed. (Trans. R. Winston and C. Winston.) New York: Vintage Books.

each of us have given meanings to our lives, and that each situation we encounter holds meanings and possibilities waiting to be fulfilled, whether through creative activity, an increased receptivity to our world, or through changing our attitudes. According to Frankl, then, meaning can be found in even the most appalling of environments, and there is no better example of this than in Frankl's own experiences of the Nazi death camps, in which he was still able to find meaning and purpose through helping others, and through holding on to a belief that he would one day be re-united with his loved ones. Indeed, according to Frankl (1984), those in the death camps who could find meaning and purpose to their suffering were much more likely to survive than those who fell into hopelessness and despair.

Frankl, V. E. (1984). *Man's Search for Meaning*. (revised and updated ed.) New York: Washington Square Press.

We have already explored the question of whether human beings are more orientated towards meaning or actualisation in their lives, but this assertion that meanings are 'out there' to be found raises some more interesting comparisons with the classical client-centred perspective. Could it be that, when we are talking about the actualising tendency, we are also talking about the human propensity to find meaning and purpose in every situation? Again, as with the Daseinsanalytic approach, the logotherapeutic approach tends to put more emphasis on the external characteristics of an experience than the internal ones, but it does, again, offer a novel and more 'inter-worldly' way of thinking about the actualising tendency. One key difference between the logotherapeutic and client-centred perspectives, however, is that the former places greater emphasis on an individual's responsibility to the world and to others — and consequently the possibility of more sacrifice and compromise — than the latter.

In practical terms, however, the differences between a logotherapeutic approach and a classical client-centred approach are much more substantial. Frankl was a psychiatrist, and the practice of Logotherapy has strongly directive — even manipulative — elements to it (see Frankl's case studies in Frankl, 1988). In contrast to classical Client-Centred Therapy, Logotherapy is also heavily technique-based. Lukas (1979) outlines four basic techniques:

Frankl, V. E. (1988). *The Will to Meaning: Foundations and Applications of Logotherapy*. (exp. ed.) London: Meridian.
Lukas, E. (1979). 'The four steps of Logotherapy.' In J. B. Fabry, R. Bulka, P. and W. S. Sahakian (eds.) *Logotherapy in Action*. New York: Jason Aronson.

- The first, and most authoritarian of these, is the 'appealing technique', which seems to consist of little more than insisting to clients that their lives do have meaning, or suggesting to them what that meaning might be.
- Somewhat less didactic is 'Socratic dialogue' — a technique also used in cognitive-behavioural therapies (for instance,

Dryden, W. (1999). *Rational Emotive Behavioural Counselling in Action.* 2nd ed. London: Sage.

Frankl, V. E. (1986). *The Doctor and the Soul: From Psychotherapy to Logotherapy.* 3rd ed. (Trans. R. Winston and C. Winston.) New York: Vintage Books.

Marks, I. M. (1978). *Living with Fear: Understanding and Coping with Anxiety.* New York: McGraw-Hill.

Frankl, V. E. (1986). *The Doctor and the Soul: From Psychotherapy to Logotherapy.* 3rd ed. (Trans. R. Winston and C. Winston.) New York: Vintage Books.

Längle, A. (2001). 'Old age from an existential-analytical perspective.' *Psychological Reports, 89*: 211–15.

This is an example of Längle's approach, but, unfortunately, little has yet been published in English. More detail, however, can be found at <http://www.existential-analysis.org>.

Dryden, 1999) — whereby the logotherapist engages in a debate with the client; but again principally to direct them towards a particular meaning in their life, or towards the viewpoint that their life does, intrinsically, hold some meaning.

• A third, more general technique (see Frankl, 1986), is termed 'paradoxical intention', and involves inviting the client to do — or to think about doing — the thing that he or she most fears, on the assumption that a client can take a positive attitude to even the most appalling of possibilities (again, this is a technique now used in the behavioural therapies (see, for instance, Marks, 1978)).

• Finally, there is 'dereflection', in which the client is encouraged to turn their attention away from their own problems and concerns, and instead to focus on the world around them (see Frankl, 1986). From a classical client-centred perspective, this last technique would seem particularly counter-therapeutic, given that it not only directs the client, but actively directs them away from self-reflection and self-awareness.

Before concluding this section, it should be noted that at least one of the contemporary developments of Logotherapy, Alfried Längle's 'existential-analytical' psychotherapy (see, for instance, Längle, 2001) takes a much less authoritarian and directive approach to therapeutic practice. Whilst logotherapeutic ideas, then, can be brought to the therapeutic relationship in relatively un-client-centred ways, it would also seem possible that they can be part of a less directive approach to therapy, in which the therapist is simply attentive to the client's attempts to find meaning in his or her life, and the possibilities that his or her situation might be opening out to him or her.

The existential-humanistic approach
A third 'school' of existential therapy that has emerged, primarily on the western coast of the United States, can be referred to as an 'existential-humanistic' approach. The principle driving force behind the development of this approach was the American psychologist, Rollo May, though his mentees — most notably James Bugental (1915–), Irvin Yalom (1931–) and Kirk Schneider (1956–) — have all played a major part in establishing and promoting this form of therapeutic practice. Today, there are a handful of institutions in the United States that still teach and promote an existential-humanistic approach to therapy, though existential-humanistic practitioners continue to have a major impact on the development of humanistic therapies worldwide. To a great extent, the existential-humanistic approach and classical

Client-Centred Therapy have grown up side-by-side. May, as discussed above, corresponded with Rogers; and Bugental, like Rogers, was closely involved in the development of the humanistic psychology and psychotherapy movement. Indeed, Bugental was the first president of the Association for Humanistic Psychology. Consequently, there are a number of similarities between the existential-humanistic approach and classical Client-Centred Therapy that can be identified.

First, in contrast to the more European existential approaches, the existential-humanistic approach tends to adopt a relatively individualistic perspective, in which there is an emphasis on helping clients to get in touch with their *own* needs and feelings — away from the demands and pressures of others (see, for instance, May, 1969b). Here, there is also a tendency to assert the intrinsic 'aloneness' of each human being, in contrast to the emphasis on interrelationships (see, for instance, Bugental, 1981; Yalom, 1980). There is also a strong emphasis on encouraging clients to get in touch with their 'subjective' experiences — particularly those in the here-and-now (for instance, Bugental, 1999). Clients, for instance, may be encouraged to describe how they are feeling towards their therapist in the immediacy of the therapeutic encounter, encouraged to talk about what is going on within them at a bodily level (for instance, Schneider and May, 1995), or to describe past experiences in as much detail as possible (Yalom and Elkin, 1974). Such approaches are more directive than a classical approach to Client-Centred Therapy, but there are strong similarities to the process-experiential approaches to therapy. Indeed, existential-humanistic therapists specifically draw on such techniques as focusing (Gendlin, 1996) to help their clients with this 'inner search'.

A second similarity between the existential-humanistic approaches and classical Client-Centred Therapy is that there is a great emphasis on the therapist being real and authentic in the therapeutic encounter. Yalom is probably the most ardent advocate of this, and his genuineness and transparency is evident in many of his highly acclaimed case-studies (see, for instance, Yalom, 1989, 1999). Indeed, in contrast to some classical client-centred therapists (for instance, Brodley, 2001), Yalom (2001) argues that it is nearly always helpful for therapists to share with their clients their own, personal experiences, as well as their views on the mechanisms of therapy, and their feelings towards the client in the here-and-now.

May, R. (1969b). *Love and Will.* New York: W. W. Norton and Co, Inc.
Bugental, J. F. T. (1981). *The Search for Authenticity: An Existential-Analytic Approach to Psychotherapy.* (Exp. ed.) New York: Irvington.
Yalom, I. (1980). *Existential Psychotherapy.* New York: Basic Books.
Bugental, J. F. T. (1999). *Psychotherapy isn't What You Think: Bringing the Psychotherapeutic Engagement in the Living Moment.* Phoenix, AZ: Zeig, Tucker and Co., Inc.
Schneider, K.J. and May, R. (1995). 'Guidelines for an existential-integrative (EI) approach.' In K. J. Schneider and R. May (eds.) *The Psychology of Existence: An Integrative, Clinical Perspective.* New York: McGraw-Hill.
Yalom, I. and Elkin, G. (1974). *Every Day Gets a Little Closer: A Twice-told Therapy.* New York: Basic Books.
Gendlin, E. (1996). *Focusing-Oriented Psychotherapy: A Manual of the Experiential Method.* New York: The Guilford Press.

Yalom, I. (1989). *Love's Executioner and Other Tales of Psychotherapy.* London: Penguin.
Yalom, I. (1999). *Momma and the Meaning of Life: Tales of Psychotherapy.* London: Piatkus.
Brodley, B. T. (2001). 'Congruence and its relation to communication in client-centred therapy.' In G. Wyatt (ed.) *Rogers" Therapeutic Conditions. Vol. 1:Congruence.* Ross-on-Wye: PCCS Books, pp. 55–78.
Yalom, I. (2001). *The Gift of Therapy: Reflections on Being a Therapist.* London: Piatkus.

Bugental, J. F. T. (1981). *The Search for Authenticity: An Existential-Analytic Approach to Psychotherapy.* (Exp. ed.) New York: Irvington.

Yalom, I. (1989). *Love's Executioner and Other Tales of Psychotherapy.* London: Penguin.
Schneider, K. J. (2003). 'Existential-humanistic psychotherapies.' In A. S. Gurman and S. B. Messer (eds.) *Essential psychotherapies.* New York: Guilford Press.

Rogers, C. R. (1951). *Client-Centered Therapy.* Boston: Houghton Mifflin.
Rogers, C. R. (1959). 'A theory of therapy, personality and interpersonal relationships as developed in the client-centered framework.' In S. Koch (ed.) *Psychology: A Study of Science.* New York: McGraw-Hill, pp. 184–256.

Schneider, K. J. (2003). 'Existential-humanistic psychotherapies.' In A. S. Gurman and S. B. Messer (eds.) *Essential psychotherapies.* New York: Guilford Press.
Schneider, K. J. and May, R. (1995). 'Guidelines for an existential-integrative (EI) approach.' In K. J. Schneider and R. May (eds.) *The Psychology of Existence: An Integrative, Clinical Perspective.* New York: McGraw-Hill.
Yalom, I. and Elkin, G. (1974). *Every Day Gets a Little Closer: A Twice-told Therapy.* New York: Basic Books.

A third similarity between the two approaches is that existential-humanistic therapists, like classical client-centred therapists, hold a relatively optimistic view of human nature. Bugental (1981), in particular, has written extensively about the human capacity to grow and realise 'its true potential'.

In contrast to classical client-centred therapists, however, existential-humanistic therapists tend to adopt a more challenging and proactive stance towards their clients (see, for instance, Yalom, 1989), though this appears to be lessening somewhat in recent years (see Schneider, 2003). Much of this difference in practice comes down to a fundamental difference in philosophical and psychological principles. As discussed earlier, both a client-centred and an existential approach share the belief that clients' difficulties tend to be a consequence of their denial or distortion of certain lived-experience; but where they differ, as discussed above, is their views on how these defensive processes arise. From a classical client-centred position, denial and distortion comes about because of the introjection of external values — particularly values as to what is, and what isn't, worthy of positive regard (Rogers, 1951, 1959). Here, then, if a client can experience a non-directive relationship, and one which positively values *all* of their experiences, then their need for denial and distortion should slowly dissolve. By contrast, however, an existential perspective argues that denial and distortion often arises 'internally': as human beings turn away from the inherent limitations, paradoxes and anxieties of their lives. Here, then, providing the client with a non-directive and accepting relationship may not be sufficient to dissolve their defence 'mechanisms', because it was not a dysfunctional relationship that put those defences there in the first place. Rather, here, the therapist needs to work with the client to help them challenge their internally-generated defences, and this means that the therapist may need to adopt a more challenging and directive stance. Thus, in comparison to client-centred therapists, existential-humanistic practitioners are likely to put more emphasis on pointing out to a client where they may be deceiving or blocking themselves (Schneider, 2003, refers to this as 'vivification') and also confronting them to overcome these self-deceptions. This might involve, for instance, encouraging a client to really 'stay with' feelings of anxiety or discomfort (Schneider and May, 1995), pointing out to them when they seem to be distracted from the therapeutic relationship (Yalom and Elkin, 1974), or reminding them that they always seem to talk about their feelings in the second person.

Alongside this inner search, existential-humanistic therapists, most notably Yalom (1980) and Bugental (1981), have also argued that there are certain 'ultimate concerns' that all clients need to be encouraged to acknowledge and own. Yalom outlines four: death, freedom, isolation and meaninglessness; whilst Bugental suggests six: finiteness, potential to act, choice, awareness, separateness and embodiedness. In contrast to the *principled non-directivity* of a classical client-centred approach, then, existential-humanistic therapists may tend towards encouraging their clients to explore these concerns, or perceiving their experiences and difficulties in terms of a resistance to these existential issues. If, for instance, a client appears desperate to immerse themselves in a relationship — or indeed, seems to become heavily dependent on the therapist — the therapist might suggest to them that, perhaps, they find it difficult to acknowledge their fundamental aloneness in the world.

R. D. Laing

A fourth approach to existential therapy was developed by the infamous Scottish psychiatrist, R. D. Laing (1927–89). Like May, Laing had some contact with Rogers, but the relationship between the two men was less than genial. Indeed, Laing described Rogers as 'one of the least personable people' that he'd ever met, and the kind of guy that 'wouldn't last two minutes in a Glasgow pub' (in Mullan, 1995, p. 210).

Despite this animosity, there are numerous similarities between Laing's and Rogers' approaches. As a psychiatrist, Laing was appalled by the mechanistic, inhumane way that his colleagues treated their patients, and he dreamt of a psychiatric system that would treat its users with dignity and respect. Here, like Rogers, Laing adopted a phenomenological outlook, arguing that we should try to understand the 'mentally ill' in terms of their subjective experiences, rather than in terms of 'objective' diagnoses or categories (see Laing, 1965). And if we did so, he argued, we would find a far greater intelligibility and meaningfulness in their thoughts and actions than we had previously imagined.

With respect to client-centred theory, one interesting question this raises is whether Laing is talking here about the same thing as an actualising tendency? In other words, is the belief that there is always an intelligibility and meaningfulness behind human behaviour the same as saying that human beings have an innate drive to maintain and enhance their being? To the extent that it would not be meaningful to do anything other than maintain and

Yalom, I. (1980). *Existential Psychotherapy*. New York: Basic Books.
Bugental, J. F. T. (1981). *The Search for Authenticity: An Existential-Analytic Approach to Psychotherapy*. (Exp. ed.) New York: Irvington.

Principled non-directivity is mentioned in every chapter, but see Tony Merry's Chapter 2, p. 40–2 for a brief summary.

Mullan, B. (1995). *Mad to be Normal: Conversations with R. D. Laing*. London: Free Association Books.

Laing, R. D. (1965). *The Divided Self: An Existential Study in Sanity and Madness*. Harmondsworth: Penguin.

enhance one's being, these two hypotheses are relatively similar. There are, however, two key differences. First, in contrast to the notion of an actualising tendency, there is no assumption in Laing's hypothesis that human beings have an innate tendency to act in pro-social ways. Indeed, like May, Laing was very critical of Rogers' tendency to dismiss, or minimise, the human potentiality for evil (see Mullan, 1995). Second, for Laing, this tendency to act in meaningful and intelligible ways is not something that we have the *potential* to actualise, but is something that we are actualising all the time — whether we are schizophrenic, depressed or 'normal'. So, in contrast to some readings of classical client-centred theory, it is not a tendency that can become damaged or distorted, but something that continues to manifest even when, from an external perspective, the person appears to be behaving in profoundly bizarre or unintelligible ways.

Mullan, B. (1995). *Mad to be Normal: Conversations with R. D. Laing.* London: Free Association Books.

Laing, R. D. (1965). *The Divided Self: An Existential Study in Sanity and Madness.* Harmondsworth: Penguin.

Ibid.

Laing (1965) was particularly keen to demonstrate the intelligibility behind schizophrenia. Drawing on existential philosophy, Laing argued that individuals who are predisposed to schizophrenia may experience a fundamental sense of 'ontological insecurity'. That is, they lack a 'firm sense of [their] own and other people's reality and identity' (*ibid.* p. 39). Because of this, he argued, they may experience certain fears: of engulfment by others, of imploding in on themselves, and of being depersonalised by those around them. To defend themselves against these perceived threats, he argued that they may then try to divide themselves in two, leaving an empty and compliant 'false self' on the public plane, whilst retreating to a safer private citadel of their mind. For Laing, then, schizophrenic withdrawal from 'reality' was not simply a manifestation of madness, but a particular strategy that ontologically insecure people might use to defend themselves against a world that seemed to threaten annihilation. In detaching themselves from reality, however, Laing argued that they might then begin to slip into psychosis, as they become less and less able to relate to others, and thereby less able to experience confirmation and communication with an external world. In his later writings, however, Laing (1967) emphasised the intelligibility of schizophrenia even more forcefully, arguing that it could be part of an individual's process of self-healing — or what he termed 'metanoia' — in which the individual breaks through the restrictive and false shell that they have placed around them. Again, then, we can see here many similarities to Rogers' notion of actualisation, though in a more radicalised form; and with the emphasis on the actualising tendency being fundamentally present in psychological distress, rather than corrupted or damaged.

Laing, R. D. (1967). *The Politics of Experience and the Bird of Paradise.* Harmondsworth: Penguin.

As with Rogers, too, Laing placed great emphasis on the role that environmental factors played in the development of psychological distress. For Laing (1967), schizophrenia was a particular strategy that an individual adopted to survive a particular *social* environment: more specifically, one in which a person had been presented with so many deceptions, double-binds, invalidations and disturbed means of communication that the only way they felt that they could protect themselves was by seeking refuge in their own inner world (see Laing, 1969, 1971). Here, as with Rogers, Laing put particular emphasis on the damaging effects of an unloving family environment. In contrast to Rogers, however, Laing seems to suggest that it is not so much the lack of love that is damaging, as the way that that lack of love is often covered up with pretences, lies, and double messages. Perhaps this is no more true than in Laing's own childhood, when his mother's distant and unaffectionate attitude to him was confounded by protestations of love and overtly possessive behaviours (see Burston, 1996).

Such an understanding of the aetiology of psychological distress also led Laing to explore the realm of 'metaperceptions' (see Laing, Phillipson and Lee, 1966): how one person thinks someone else perceives them, and how well that corresponds to that other person's actual perception. Here, the hypothesis was that, the more closely an individual's meta-perceptions correspond to another person's actual perceptions of them, the more psychologically functioning that person, and their relationship, is likely to be. So, for example, if I think you see me as weak and incompetent, but you actually see me as arrogant and brutish, then problems are likely to emerge in our relationship. Here, then, Laing goes beyond the client-centred idea that psychological distress is related to intra-personal (i.e. within an individual) incongruence, to suggest that it can also emerge from *inter*-personal incongruence.

Laing wrote little about the actual practice of therapy, but, from the accounts of his clients and supervisees, it seems that his approach was not particularly dissimilar to a classical client-centred practice (see, for instance, Resnick, 1997; Semyon, 1997). He put great emphasis on listening and being present to clients, and would often go through whole sessions without saying a word, though his psychoanalytic background meant that he was somewhat more prone to interpretations and reflections on 'transference' issues. Like Rogers, Laing also fundamentally rejected the use of therapeutic techniques; emphasising, instead, the importance of a genuine meeting between two human beings, in which the client could begin to trust in the possibility of real

Ibid.

Laing, R. D. (1969). *Self and Others.* (2nd ed.) London: Penguin.
Laing, R. D. (1971). *The Politics of the Family and Other Essays.* Harmondsworth: Penguin.

Burston, D. (1996). *The Wing of Madness: The Life and Work of R. D. Laing.* Cambridge, MA: Harvard University Press.

Laing, R. D., Phillipson, H. and Lee, A. R. (1966). *Interpersonal Perception: A Theory and a Method of Research.* London: Tavistock.

Resnick, J. (1997). In B. Mullan (ed.) *R. D. Laing: Creative Destroyer.* London: Cassell.
Semyon, M. (1997). 'Mina Semyon.' In B. Mullan (ed.) *R. D. Laing: Creative Destroyer.* London: Cassell.

Mullan, B. (1995). *Mad to be Normal: Conversations with R. D. Laing*. London: Free Association Books.

Thompson, M. G. (1994). *The Truth About Freud's Technique: The Encounter with the Real*. New York: New York University Press.

Now in its second edition: van Deurzen, E. (2002). *Existential Counselling and Psychotherapy in Practice*. 2nd ed. London: Sage.

DuPlock, S. (ed.) (1997). *Case Studies in Existential Psychotherapy and Counselling*. Wiley Series in Existential Perspectives on Psychotherapy and Counselling. Chichester: John Wiley.

van Deurzen, E. (2002). *Existential Counselling and Psychotherapy in Practice*. 2nd ed. London: Sage.

human engagement. Indeed, with respect to congruence, Laing probably went further than most client-centred therapists, and could be brutally honest with his clients. He reports, for instance, 'I might say "do you realize that by virtue of what you've just said you are treating me like your father. Now I want to point out to you that I'm not your fucking father"' (Mullan, 1995, p. 319). In terms of a genuine encounter, it also seems that Laing had little time for externally-imposed boundaries or rules. Rather, at the heart of his practice was a willingness to encounter his clients in a spontaneous and unpremeditated way. Indeed, like Rogers, Laing believed that the decisive moments in therapy were often unpredictable, unique, unforgettable, always unrepeatable and often indescribable.

The British School of Existential Analysis

Within the United Kingdom, followers of Laing have tended to move in one of two directions. First are those who have returned to the more psychodynamic roots of Laing's work (for instance, The Philadelphia Association, Thompson, 1994); second are those who have extended and developed the more existential elements of his work. This latter group can be roughly referred to as the 'British school' of existential analysis, and has primarily emerged through the work of Emmy van Deurzen (1951–) (formerly van Deurzen-Smith). Van Deurzen established the first UK-based training course in existential therapy in 1982; establishing the Society for Existential Analysis in 1988; and, in that same year, publishing the first edition of *Existential Counselling in Practice*, which has gone on to be one of the key texts of existential therapeutic practice.

As with Laing, there are many similarities between the classical client-centred approach and the general practice of British-based existential therapists (see DuPlock, 1997, for a range of examples of existential therapeutic practice). There is an emphasis on relating to clients over-and-above therapeutic techniques; a tendency to work descriptively — helping clients to 'unpack' their lived experiences — rather than interpretatively; and a commitment to seeing clients as intelligible, meaning-orientated beings, rather than in terms of their pathologies. This is where the general commonalities tend to end, however, because of all the 'schools' of existential therapy, the British school is probably the most diverse and heterogeneous. Indeed, as van Deurzen writes: 'The movement has its own history of splitting and fighting and there is a healthy disagreement about what existential work should be' (2002, x). In this section, then, I will focus primarily on the work of two of its foremost theorists: Emmy van Deurzen and Ernesto Spinelli.

In contrast to existential psychotherapists like Yalom (1980) and Bugental (1981), who focus on such grand existential issues as meaningless and death, van Deurzen's approach has a more everyday-orientation — perhaps because it comes from a counselling background rather than a psychotherapeutic one. Like many existentialists, van Deurzen's starting point is that life is an 'endless struggle where moments of ease and happiness are the exception rather than the rule' (van Deurzen, 2002, p. 132); and that 'problems in living' (not 'pathologies') arise when people are reluctant to face the reality of their imperfect, dilemma-ridden and challenging existences. Hence, the aim of therapy is to help clients 'wake-up' from their self-deceptions, and come to terms with their life in all its imperfections and complexities.

Yalom, I. (1980). *Existential Psychotherapy*. New York: Basic Books.
Bugental, J. F. T. (1981). *The Search for Authenticity: An Existential-Analytic Approach to Psychotherapy*. (Exp. ed.) New York: Irvington.

van Deurzen, E. (2002). *Existential Counselling and Psychotherapy in Practice*. 2nd ed. London: Sage.

Here, then, is an interesting contrast with a classical client-centred approach, which has a more idealistic notion of how life could be. Indeed, from a van Deurzen-ian position, one could argue that client-centred notions of actualisation and the good life — if transmitted to clients, either explicitly or implicitly — could actually be quite counter-productive, leading clients to think that a 'perfect life' is just around the corner, if only they can be more actualised, or more spontaneous, or more in touch with their inner process. In other words, rather than coming to accept, engage with, and celebrate their life as it actually is, the client may be enticed into a position in which they are constantly looking for something better: deferring their engagement with life until the moment in which they are fully-functioning or healed.

Like most practitioners within the British school, van Deurzen's (*ibid.*) therapeutic approach is primarily descriptive. Clients are encouraged to talk about their lives: to clarify their thoughts, feelings and experiences, and to develop a deeper insight into how they have come to experience their world in the way that they do. In contrast to a more non-directive perspective, however, van Deurzen does suggest that clients should be actively encouraged to explore *all* aspects of their lives — not just the ones they tend to — and she outlines four 'dimensions' of worldly-being (the physical world, the personal world, the social world and the world of values and meanings) that clients can be helped to examine. Here, then, is a more challenging approach than the client-centred perspective, and it is again based on the assumption that people have a reluctance to face up to the reality of their lives — though van Deurzen talks about 'reluctance' rather than the

Ibid.

more strongly-worded 'resistance' — and that this reluctance is not just a consequence of external forces.

In contrast to a client-centred perspective, there is also a more philosophical element to van Deurzen's (*ibid.*) therapeutic approach. For her, the values and meanings that we adopt in life — for instance, that we should be able to live a life without discomfort or suffering — are as central to our being as our feelings or emotions. Hence, it is not only important to explore how a client feels towards their world, but also how they think about their world and their lives. In this respect, then, van Deurzen's approach to therapy is less of a psychological exploration, and more of a philosophical exploration, in which a client's beliefs, meanings and values are brought to the fore, examined, and possibly revised. In contrast to a classical client-centred approach, too, the role of the therapist here, according to van Deurzen, is not necessarily a non-directive one. For whilst van Deurzen believes that it is essential that clients should come to their own values and beliefs, she also suggests that therapists should not hold back on what they believe to be true. Indeed, in direct contrast to a non-directive approach, she writes that the therapist should be like a 'guru' or 'tutor' to the client (van Deurzen, 2002): someone who brings to the therapeutic encounter their own knowledge and experience, such that the client can consider a wider range of standpoints than just their own. At times, then, the therapeutic approach that van Deurzen advocates is less of a personal exploration, and more of a general, philosophical dialogue, in which guidelines for living are distilled, and strategies for meeting the challenges of life are identified.

In contrast to van Deurzen's approach, Ernesto Spinelli's theory and practice of therapy (see Spinelli, 1994, 1997, 2001) is much closer to a client-centred standpoint. Exactly like Rogers (1959), Spinelli (1994) suggests that a client's psychological difficulties tend to arise when their self-structure becomes incongruent with their lived-experiences; and he puts particular emphasis on the way that individuals may attribute their experiences to others as a means of psychological defence. Coming from a phenomenological background, Spinelli (1994) also puts considerable emphasis on the importance of staying with a client's lived-experiences (what he terms 'being with' the client) and of being willing to stand in the client's shoes to experience this world as they experience it (what he terms 'being for' the client). Spinelli's approach is also one of the most non-directive of the existential therapies, and he puts particular emphasis on the therapist adopting

van Deurzen, E. (2002). *Existential Counselling and Psychotherapy in Practice.* 2nd ed. London: Sage..

Ibid.

Spinelli, E. (1994). *Demystifying Therapy.* London: Constable.
Spinelli, E. (1997). *Tales of Un-Knowing: Therapeutic Encounters from an Existential Perspective.* London: Duckworth.
Spinelli, E. (2001). *The Mirror and the Hammer: Challenges to Therapeutic Orthodoxy.* London: Continuum.
Rogers, C. R. (1959). 'A theory of therapy, personality and interpersonal relationships as developed in the client-centered framework.' In S. Koch (ed.) *Psychology: A Study of Science.* New York: McGraw-Hill, pp. 184–256.

a stance of 'un-knowing' towards their clients (Spinelli, 1997), in which they strive to hold in abeyance fixed beliefs, values and assumptions.

Where his approach differs from a classical client-centred perspective, however, is in his fundamental commitment to an '*intersubjective*' world-view. This has a number of consequences. First, whilst he argues that therapists should adopt a stance of un-knowing towards their clients, he does not in any way suggest that they should attempt to be non-directive; for, from an intersubjective standpoint, we will inevitably and ineradicably influence those that we are in relationship with. From this perspective, then, it is less important to make concerted efforts *not* to direct our clients in any way, and more important to note how we might be trying to influence our clients, and to possibly try and make this explicit. Second, Spinelli (2001) argues that it is not only important to explore the client's experiences and relationships, but also how his or her behaviours might impact on the experiences and relationships of others (after all, from an intersubjective standpoint, all these things are related). In working with a client who is about to leave his wife, then, Spinelli suggests that the work is not simply finished when the client has come to understand his feelings and experiences, but may also require an exploration of how this could impact on his wife and his children, as well as their relationships to each other and him. Third, Spinelli suggests that the therapeutic encounter affords the client a particular opportunity to explore their 'relational realms' — how they experience themselves and others in relationship — and also how their relational realms might interact with those of another person; in this case, their therapist. Finally, like classical client-centred therapists, Spinelli believes that it is the relationship that is of foremost importance to therapy, above and beyond any content or techniques. He states: 'My clients remind me over and over again that what they take from me is, first and foremost, the me who they experience being there with them. What I say to them, what we discuss, what knowledge I have is way down the line in terms of its significance to their lives' (2002, personal communication).

Research

Given its tendency towards anti-scientism, it should come as no surprise that there have been few attempts to empirically validate the efficacy of existential therapeutic practice. Indeed, a review of the relevant research by Walsh and McElwain (2002) fails to cite a single study in which the existential approaches to therapy

Spinelli, E. (1997). *Tales of Un-Knowing: Therapeutic Encounters from an Existential Perspective*. London: Duckworth.

Intersubjectivity is the belief that human beings are intrinsically interrelated.

Spinelli, E. (2001). *The Mirror and the Hammer: Challenges to Therapeutic Orthodoxy*. London: Continuum.

Walsh, R. A. and McElwain, B. (2002). 'Existential Psychotherapies.' In D. J. Cain and J. Seeman (eds.) *Humanistic Psychotherapies: Handbook of Research and Practice*. Washington, DC: American Psychological Association.

Bugental, J. F. T. (1976). *The Search for Existential Identity: Patient-Therapist Dialogues in Humanistic Psychotherapy*. San Francisco: Jossey-Bass.

DuPlock, S. (ed.) (1997). *Case Studies in Existential Psychotherapy and Counselling*. Wiley Series in Existential Perspectives on Psychotherapy and Counselling. Chichester: John Wiley.

Spinelli, E. (1997). *Tales of Un-Knowing: Therapeutic Encounters from an Existential Perspective*. London: Duckworth. Yalom, I. (1989). *Love's Executioner and Other Tales of Psychotherapy*. London: Penguin.

Yalom, I. (1999). *Momma and the Meaning of Life: Tales of Psychotherapy*. London: Piatkus.

Hubble, M., Duncan, B. L. and Miller, S. D. (1999). *The Heart and Soul of Change: What Works in Therapy*. Washington, DC: American Psychological Association.

Norcross, J. (ed.)(2002). *Psychotherapy Relationships that Work: Therapists Contributions and Responsiveness to Patients*. New York: Oxford University Press.

have been directly tested. Nevertheless, there are in existence several collections of case studies of existential therapeutic practice, which testify to the potential value that such an approach can have (see Bugental, 1976; DuPlock, 1997; Spinelli, 1997; Yalom, 1989, 1999). Furthermore, at an indirect level, there is considerable evidence to support an existential approach to therapeutic practice. Walsh and McElwain, for instance, point to the well-established research finding that 'successful psychotherapy as understood by clients involves a process of self-reflection, considering alternative choices of action, and making choices' (2002, p. 261). They also point to the ever-increasing body of research which suggests that a warm, empathic and honest relationship is a key factor in the successfulness of therapy (see Hubble, Duncan and Miller, 1999; Norcross, 2002), second only to a client's commitment, drive and willingness to explore their experiences. It should be noted, however, that such findings are generic to a whole host of therapeutic disciplines — most directly, Client-Centred Therapy — and in no way support an existential approach over-and-above other practices. All of the key existential hypotheses, then, remain to be tested: for instance, that it is therapeutically beneficial to help clients talk about death, or that helping clients to find meaning in their lives is of substantial value.

Conclusion

At the beginning of this chapter, it was suggested that the relationship between an existential approach to therapy and a classical client-centred one was complex and multi-faceted, and I hope to have shown that this is the case. To conclude this chapter, however, I want to make some very broad generalisations about the similarities and differences between these two approaches.

On the whole, both approaches tend to:
• emphasise the uniqueness and individuality of each client, and of each therapeutic encounter;
• understand the client in terms of their 'subjective', lived-experiences, rather than from an external, diagnostic perspective;
• see psychological problems as a result of the distortion or denial of experiences, and holds that an acknowledgement of one's true being can lead to a greater intensity and fullness of living;
• reject the use of techniques in therapy, emphasising instead the importance of a genuine, spontaneous, human encounter;
• emphasise the importance of accepting and validating the client, however bizarre or maladaptive their behaviour might seem.

Conceptually and practically, however, there also tends to be a number of differences between the existential approaches to therapy and the classical client-centred one. In general, the existential approaches:

• place more emphasis on the role of choice and agency in human change; such that the practice may be more likely to engage with clients at the level of conscious deliberation, as well as at the level of feelings and senses;

• puts less emphasis on the client's inherent tendency to find the answers that are right for them, such that the therapist may be more likely to adopt a directive or educational role;

• sees distortion and denial as arising from 'internal' sources as well as external ones, such that challenge and confrontation — as well as unconditional positive regard — may be seen as necessary to help clients face up to the truth of their being;

• holds that limitations, struggles and discomforting feelings are intrinsic to the human condition, such that therapy is more about helping clients to 'come to terms with' these aspects of their being than moving beyond them;

• makes more assumptions about what the 'real', underlying issues are for clients, such that the practice adopts a more directive standpoint;

• conceptualises human existence in less individualistic and individual-centred terms (and also doesn't believe that human beings are inherently pro-social), such that the therapist may specifically encourage clients to consider the needs, feelings and demands of others, rather than just their own.

There are similarities and differences, then, between the existential approaches to therapy and classical Client-Centred Therapy, but none of these differences would appear insurmountable. Indeed, many of them would seem enormously fertile grounds for exploration, dialogue and growth. Rather than see these two approaches as competing, then, I would see them as having a great potential to complement each other. Perhaps this is because, as I suggested in a previous paper,

> despite the divergences in philosophical and psychological opinion, both approaches are fundamentally committed to understanding human beings in the most dignified, respectful, and validating way possible. (Cooper, 2003, p. 54)

Cooper, M. (2003). 'Between freedom and despair: Existential challenges and contributions to person-centered and experiential therapy.' *Person-Centered and Experiential Psychotherapies, 2*(1): 43–56.

Resources

Introductory overviews
Cooper, M. (2003). *Existential Therapies*. London: Sage.

Existential Philosophy
Cooper, D. E. (1999). *Existentialism*. Oxford: Blackwell.
Society for Phenomenology and Existential Psychology:
<http://www.spep.org/>.

Daseinsanalysis
Boss, M. (1979). *Existential Foundations of Medicine and Psychology*. New York: Jason Aronson.
Swiss Society for Daseinsanalysis:
<http://www.daseinsanalyse.ch/>.

Logotherapy
Frankl, V. E. (1986). *The Doctor and the Soul: From Psychotherapy to Logotherapy*. 3rd ed. (Trans. R. Winston and C. Winston.) New York: Vintage Books.
Viktor Frankl Institute Vienna:
<http://www.logotherapy.univie.ac.at/>.

Existential-Humanistic Approach
Yalom, I. (1989). *Love's Executioner and Other Tales of Psychotherapy*. London: Penguin Books.
Existential-Humanistic Institute:
<http://www.existentialhumanisticinstitute.com>.

Laing
Laing, R. D. (1965). *The Divided Self: An Existential Study in Sanity and Madness*. Harmondsworth: Penguin.
Laing, R. D. (1969). *Self and Others*. 2nd ed. London: Penguin.

British School of Existential Analysis
van Deurzen, E. (2002). *Existential Counselling and Psychotherapy in Practice*. 2nd ed. London: Sage.
Spinelli, E. (1997). *Tales of Un-Knowing: Therapeutic Encounters from an Existential Perspective*. London: Duckworth.
Society for Existential Analysis:
<http://www.existentialanalysis.co.uk/>.

integrating with integrity

richard worsley 6

Introduction

Unlike most authors in this book, I am not writing about a 'school' or particular approach within the family of person-centred and experiential psychotherapies. Rather, I am writing about the way I, as an individual, want to think of putting theory into practice. I am happy to call this way *integrative* in that I seek to build into my awareness as a person-centred therapist a broad canvas of theory together with a consistent and, I intend, faithfully person-centred way of being and practising. I do not represent anyone else in this, but seek to be me. I invite others to work out, in the light of this, what it is to be themselves as person-centred practitioners. Person-centred practice is idiosyncratic: I seek to be uniquely who I am with my clients — and beyond.

My starting point is the view that the Person-Centred Approach is a basic philosophy of living, and not a technique for therapy. This is challenging. There is nowhere that I do not meet the person-centred challenge and vision in life. (In this it seems to parallel quite closely my Christian faith.) While this is demanding, it is also immensely freeing. I am free to work out what it is to be person-centred for me. I have a community of people on similar journeys to help me in this. I own the word integrative of my practice not because I belong to something called an *integrative school of thought*, but because I want to integrate into my therapeutic work as much of life's experience as possible. I want to be as much present for my clients as I can be. Integration is about the stretching of my boundaries and presuppositions to allow into my experiencing as much as I can about the world as I see it. I want to trust that, when people are in contact with me, they experience me as vivid, engaged, searching, as well as attentive, open, accepting, loving.

What is integration?

Three very different meanings of integration occur to me. An integrative approach to Person-Centred Therapy involves a clear grasp of how these three fields of meaning function.

See 'Freeing the Therapist', Ch. 8 of my book *Process Work in Person-Centred Therapy*. Worsley, R. (2002). London: Palgrave.

'The person-centered approach, then, is primarily a way of being that finds its expression in attitudes and behaviors . . .' C.R. Rogers (1986). 'A Client-Centered/ Person-Centered Approach to Therapy.' In I.L. Kutash and A. Wolf (eds.) *Psychotherapist's Casebook*. San Francisco: Jossey-Bass, pp. 197–208.

'Idiosyncratic' is used by Rogers to signify the qualities of a functional relationship — Rogers, C.R. (1977). *Carl Rogers on Personal Power*. New York: Delacorte, pp. 205–6

Tony Merry writes that the approach is rooted in the therapist's '*quality of presence*, meaning . . . the underlying attitudes and values of the counsellor that help clients feel safe enough to explore difficult, even painful experiences.' Merry, T. (1999). *Learning and Being in Person-Centred Counselling*. Ross-on-Wye: PCCS Books, p. 85.

In this respect it would be true to say that all of the person-centred approaches to therapy outlined in this book integrate 'as much of life's experiences as possible'.

This may not seem immediately relevant, but I put it forward as an important analogy for a healthy way of integrating theory and practice.

See Tony Merry, 'Self Theory', p. 26 this volume.

'The Therapist's View of the Good Life: The Fully Functioning Person.' In C.R. Rogers, (1961). *On Becoming a Person.* Boston: Houghton Mifflin, pp. 183–96.

Constructs are the whole ideas with which we think.

I see the person-centred movement as less a 'school' than a community. Within it we explore this process of integrating the new. I find I want to say to colleagues, at times: You are very different from me, but I recognise the full integrity of your stance. To other colleagues I want to say: Your stance feels to me to be tinged with the defensive! And yet even this defensiveness is for me an understandable response to the popularising of quick-fix, directive therapies.

Meta-theory is the theory of how theories link together and are validated. Dryden, W. (ed.) (1992). *Integrative and Eclectic Therapies: A Handbook.* Buckingham: Open University Press.

For instance, Park Lane College, Leeds, offers an integration of person-centred and psychodynamic perspectives.

The key question for the integrative psychotherapies is the nature of the process of integrating elements from two or more apparently disparate models of therapy.

Hales, J. (1999). 'Person-Centred Counselling and Solution-Focused Therapy.' *Counselling, 10* (3).

The first meaning is used by a number of schools of therapy to describe the process of healing within the client. In Carl Rogers' terms, the individual becomes more fully functioning as she integrates into her awareness and symbolises to herself all that she experiences. She then ceases to deny those parts of her experience which are at odds with her self-concept. She begins to see herself as fundamentally safe in being open to new experiencing.

In a similar fashion, schools of psychotherapy are also prone to a level of dysfunction in which they develop a strong and rigid self-concept, often signalled by what language and *constructs* are acceptable and what are not. They reject large elements of experience in the world, and particularly those offered by other approaches. It is a ghetto-mentality. Responsible integration within the Person-Centred Approach aims at an imaginative use of various theories and philosophies of therapy to stimulate an increased openness to experience within the therapist. However, this is neither naïve nor uncritical — to be responsible is to link back the process of integration to the basic philosophy so as to demonstrate coherence. To be integrative, in the sense that I aspire to, is to be open so that as a movement we model a fuller functionality.

The second meaning of integration concerns those who work towards new models of therapy based on an amalgamation or a transcending of current models. This is a task that can be done more or less responsibly, but it is simply not the task that I am concerned with here. Psychotherapy integration in this sense involves developing a set of principles, a *meta-theory*, by which elements of the constituent theories can be drawn together. There is a complex and technically challenging range of ways of being integrative in this sense. A number of diploma training courses offer integrative training in this sense of the word. Some of these use elements of the Person-Centred Approach.

Integrative therapy is a perfectly respectable pursuit. It is simply not what I am referring to when I describe my own practice as integrative. I eschew integration in this sense because I believe that the integration of the Person-Centred Approach often involves a radical misunderstanding of the core principles of the model. Two examples serve to illustrate. Jonathan Hales (1999) offers an interesting argument that there is a real synergy between Person-Centred Therapy and solution-focused therapy. He has much useful to say. However, within the constraints of a short article, his comparing of the two models misses the holistic nature of the Person-Centred Approach. He argues that there is a particularly person-centred way of offering a solution-focused approach, and in this he works in a way that I have sympathy with. However, he equates being person-centred with 'listening and acknowledging' and then adds in solution-focused features which seem to me to be rescuing of the client from her own experience. So, I question that he fully integrates the *key principles* of person-centredness, because he fails to trust the 'negative' experiencing of the client.

While Hales attempts to be person-centred, but arguably misses the mark, Leslie Greenberg, together with his colleagues, Laura Rice and Robert Elliott, offer a magisterial integration of the *theory* of Carl Rogers and Fritz Perls, together with research into cognitive-affective psychology, in the first half of their book, *Facilitating Emotional Change,* but then use it in a way that is highly *process-directive.* Their integration of Rogers with Perls leaves them with an account of dysfunction under six major headings. They then develop six 'basic treatment principles' to correspond to these. They believe: if the client processes dysfunctionally, first diagnose the dysfunction and then implement the corresponding treatment. While the authors insist that the therapist should have a firm grasp of the underlying principles of the models involved, I am still unsure as to why this differs from technical eclecticism.

I believe that Greenberg, Rice and Elliott make a key logical error here. In developing their complex and informative description of dysfunction, they divide dysfunction into six categories — a *taxonomy.* There is a problem with taxonomy. When we list the categories into which things fall, we can make the logical error of treating these categories as if they are real in the outside world. They are not. They are our constructs. They are useful and they are approximate. The world which they represent is not in categories at all. Thus it is not possible to use our taxonomic categories as the basis for person-centred intervention, because we are mistaking our own constructs for objective realities in the client. The eclectic counsellor aspires to this. The person-centred counsellor does well to value her not-knowing for longer, and thus to trust the client's expertise in her own process needs.

The third meaning of integration is the one which governs my own practice. In order to be open to experience and wisdom, I seek to be in dialogue with:
• new ways of conceiving person-centred theory,
• theory and insights from other models,
• conceptualisations generated by humanistic and other

Process direction is minimally the giving of a suggestion or instruction to the client: 'Try that again, but make it a lot louder.' However, David Rennie (1998). *Person-Centred Counselling: An Experiential Approach.* London: Sage, p. 81, points out that this *may* involve a radical change of stance by the therapist. 'When process-directing, counsellors take charge. They assume the role of expert — an expert on process.'

Greenberg, L.S., Rice, L.N. and Elliott, R. (1993). *Facilitating Emotional Change: The Moment-by-Moment Process.* New York: Guilford. See also Worsley, R. (2002). *Process Work in Person-Centred Therapy.* London: Palgrave, Chapter 13.

Technical eclecticism is therapy that tries to diagnose and then match treatment to problem — a rational, 'tool bag' approach.

Ibid.

Taxonomy is the assigning of individual items to logical classes. It has been an important part of science, for instance in the classification of plants and animals in natural history. Underlying the question of our constructs is a complex and important debate about the social construction of all therapy. See McNamee, S. and Gergen, K.J. (1992). *Therapy as Social Construction.* London: Sage.

Note, for example, the difference between Rogers' (1957) seven stages of process in psychotherapy — 'seven-ness' is his construct — and the underlying reality that each client changes in a unique way. C.R. Rogers (1961). 'A Process Conception of Psychotherapy.' In *On Becoming a Person.* Boston: Houghton Mifflin, pp. 125–59

This is a preliminary listing. I do not want to prejudge what can and cannot be integrated, and by what methods.

Such openness to the new is a natural development for person-centred theory, one directly related to Rogers' own stance as an empiricist for whom the question was often: What does my theory promote in new research and understanding? (See Rogers' paper 'The Actualising Tendency in Relation to "Motives" and to Consciousness.' In M.R. Jones (ed.)(1963). *Nebraska Symposium on Motivation.* Lincoln: University of Nebraska Press, pp. 1–24.)

Thorne, B. (1992). *Carl Rogers.* London: Sage, pp. 90–4. See also Barrett-Lennard, G.T. (1998). *Carl Rogers' Helping System: Journey and substance.* London: Sage, Chapter 16.

I note that all such characterisations are stereotypical, and can be used to bad-mouth others. This is not within the spirit of the movement.

The purist's conservatism is described by Merry — 'The "Classical" Position: an Overview', p. 43 this volume.

This debate has been recently outlined by Germain Lietaer's paper: 'The Client-Centered/Experiential Paradigm in Psychotherapy: Development and identity.' In J.C. Watson, *et al.* (2002)(eds.) *Client-Centered and Experiential Psychotherapy in the 21ˢᵗ Century: Advances in theory, research and practice.* Ross-on-Wye: PCCS Books, pp. 1–15.

psychologies,
• philosophical knowledge which might inform therapy,
• other therapeutic practices (but with caution).

Integration in sense three is not about the creation of a new model of therapy, whereas integration in sense two demonstrates responsibility by a mapping of the process of integration on to a meta-theory. Integration in sense three does this by testing out this process against the core concepts of person-centred theory.

In the remainder of this chapter, I will look at some examples of material which might be integrated into person-centred practice, in order to explore the dynamics and consequences of integration. This list is incomplete. What is to be integrated is life's experience as a whole! If the practitioner of the classical, client-centred model protests that they also do this, then I am delighted.

The idea of integration

At the heart of this book is the classical position set out by Tony Merry. Experiential psychotherapy differs from the classical stance in various ways and can be seen as the other end of a classical-experiential continuum. The debate between the different strands of the movement has often been acrimonious. Brian Thorne (Thorne, 1992) likens it to the encounter of religious orthodoxy with heresy. However, the question of integration does not fit onto the classical-experientialist continuum. To force it into this construct would be to risk allying it with experiential psychotherapy. As an integrative practitioner, I find myself wanting to remain close to — but also separate from — the classical stance, and at times critical of the experientialists for throwing out the baby with the bathwater.

To understand the question of integration, a parallel continuum has to be imagined. It ranges from a purist approach to a liberal-integrative approach. I characterise the purist stance as very reluctant to move beyond the formulations of theory and practice offered by Carl Rogers, while the liberal-integrative stance is open to new theory and practice with a low threshold of critical engagement. (I see myself as near to the mid-point on this continuum, and believe that neither extreme is responsible.) What is at stake in this continuum is the openness to integration and the rigour of testing of the integrity of the process of integration. Thus, the key questions for the integrative, person-centred practitioner are: What can be integrated? How can this be tested, and with what effect on practice?

The classical, client-centred key ideas or hypotheses

When looking at the CCC/experiential continuum, it is possible to ask of any particular position, of any member of the person-centred paradigm's family: how are you in relation to the key ideas of the classical stance? Any other stance can then describe similarities and differences in terms of these key ideas. By contrast, integrative practice, as I aspire to it, allocates to these key questions a different role or function.

In integrating a particular concept into theory or practice, be it in the quiet of my study or the hurly-burly of the therapy room, I am always testing out the basic question: In thinking and doing and in being, am I remaining person-centred, or am I in danger of departing from the essence of the vision of the movement? The method of testing which I will demonstrate in the latter portion of this chapter is to enter into dialogue with the CCC hypotheses. The hypotheses are and remain touchstones for my practice, even where I might want to dissent from them.

Far more frequent than outright dissent is a response that says: I strive to remain with these hypotheses, but I choose to put them into practice in my own particular way. Yet the process of checking out remains: how am I with the CCC hypotheses?

Against this background, I want to make a key distinction between the first and fourth — the actualising tendency, and non-directiveness — on the one hand, and the second and third — the causes of dysfunction and the tasks of therapy — on the other. The first hypothesis, the actualising tendency, is at the root of the movement, what Jerold Bozarth (Bozarth, 1998) has called its foundation block. If this is not sufficiently the case to be a valid working hypothesis, then there is no Person-Centred Approach. The concept of non-directivity flows from it. They are necessary to the Person-Centred Approach.

The second and third hypotheses are not, I believe, necessary, but rather are contingent upon observation and research. For example, the concept of conditions of worth is at the heart of person-centred theory, but if it were demonstrated that other concepts were important, even essential, to our understanding of dysfunction, this would not be a fatal flaw in the CCC. Other mechanisms might explain other sorts of dysfunction. They could be accommodated.

These hypotheses are set out in Tony Merry's Chapter 2.
1. What motivates us? The actualising tendency.
2. Theory of personality — self-structure, introjection, incongruence, distortion and denial of experience.
3. Theory of therapy — the release from conditions of worth.
4. The essence of therapy as non-directive.

The word *hypothesis* is an important one for understanding Rogers. In science, a hypothesis is a 'first guess' which is then tested out against reality. Rogers invites us to adopt his theory by testing it out, rather than as fixed or prejudged ideas. See Rogers, C.R. (1951). *Client-Centered Therapy.* Boston: Houghton Mifflin, pp. 35–6.

I reject the notion that the CCC hypotheses imply any particular way of expressing them in practice, even though empathic response must remain by far the most common. What is key is that the agency, and in particular the meaning-generating agency of the client is paramount. See Brodley, B.T. (2002). 'Observations of Empathic Understanding in Two Client-Centered Therapists.' In J.C. Watson *et al.* (eds.) *Client-Centered and Experiential Psychotherapy in the 21ˢᵗ Century: Advances in theory, research and practice,* Ross-on-Wye: PCCS Books, pp. 182–203.

Bozarth, J. (1998). *Person-Centred Therapy: A revolutionary Paradigm,* Ross-on-Wye: PCCS Books, Chapter 4. Germain Lietaer, an experiential therapist, does not agree that the actualising tendency is the 'foundation block' of the approach. He puts it as a 'second order'* apect of the client-centred/experiential paradigm. (Lietaer, G. (2002). 'The Client-Centered/Experiential Paradigm in Psychotherapy: Development and identity.' In Watson, J.C., Goldman, R.N. and Warner, M.S. *Client-Centered and Experiential Psychotherapy in the 21st Century: Advances in theory, research and practice.* Ross-on-Wye: PCCS Books, pp. 1–15.)
* See appendix, this volume, sidenote on pages 154 and 155.

But see Tony Merry, 'The Six Conditions Work Together', pp. 38–40, this volume.

Campbell Purton (2002). 'Person-Centred Therapy without the Core Conditions.' *CPJ*, March, pp. 6–9, and my response, Worsley, R. (2002). 'Client Process and the Core Conditions.' *CPJ*, May, pp. 18–20.

Dissonance is a mismatch or clash of meanings. The word suggests a musical metaphor or disharmony. In client work it is the dissonance between experience and the self-concept which is sometimes noticed or felt, and can lead to a reducing of incongruence.

Grant, B. (1990). 'Principled and Instrumental Non-Directiveness in Person-Centered and Client-Centered Therapy.' *Person-Centered Review*, 5: 77–88. Reprinted in D. J. Cain (ed.)(2002). *Classics in the Person-Centered Approach.* Ross-on-Wye: PCCS Books, pp. 371–7.

The notion of efficacy in therapy is becoming increasingly linked with empirically supported therapies which claim to be able to determine with accuracy which treatments match which dysfunctions. This appeals to American medical insurers but is anathemous to the Person-Centred Approach.

See, for instance, the instrumental use of the two-chair technique in Greenberg, L.S. *et al.* (1993). *Facilitating Emotional Change: The Moment-by-Moment Process.* New York: Guilford, Chapter 11, or in Rhonda Goldman's (2002). 'The Two-Chair Dialogue for Inner Conflict.' In J.C. Watson, *et al.* (eds.) *Client-Centered and Experiential Psychotherapy in the 21st Century: Advances in theory, research and practice.* Ross-on-Wye: PCCS Books, pp. 427–47.

Indeed, Campbell Purton (2002) has already argued that the notion of conditions of worth is not a useful way to describe the dysfunction manifested in post-traumatic stress. I have come to believe that a relationship rooted in the core conditions is corrective of a number of dysfunctional processes, of which conditionality is but one.

In short, the therapist's commitment to the client's actualising tendency and thence to the therapy as non-directive (in an appropriate sense) are core hypotheses against which to test any process of integration. Major *dissonance* is to be taken with utmost seriousness. By contrast, the second and third hypotheses are important (but not essential) parts of the testing process, and dissonance may indicate a need to refine person-centred thought rather than to depart from it.

Non-directivity: principled or instrumental?

Barry Grant's distinction between principled and instrumental non-directivity (Grant, 1990) is a crucial one, for it affects the way integration happens, and reflects the underlying motivation for integration. Grant argues that principled non-directiveness is founded upon the inalienable right of the client to self-determination, and therefore the absolute commitment of the therapist to provide a relationship in which this can happen. Principled non-directivity is an essentially ethical commitment. By contrast, instrumental non-directivity is based upon a commitment by the therapist to provide the client with significant change. Thus non-directivity is one tool in this. It is only reasonable to be non-directive when this is efficacious. Otherwise the therapist may depart from non-directive interventions.

Either stance provides a feasible base from which to think integratively. However, the effect of each is hugely different. If the therapist takes an instrumental stance, then it is likely that integration becomes a taking on board of more useful tools and interventions for those occasions when the classical, non-directive approach is judged by the therapist to be either non-efficacious or less so than a directive intervention. This basis for intervention drifts ineluctably in the direction of integration, sense two, or more likely in the direction of technical eclecticism — the selection of useful interventions that match the diagnosed need of the client. Principled non-directivity results in a very different process of integration. To this I am committed. It is a matter of my belief in the right of the client to a relationship that is radically trusting in both their autonomy and their creativity.

However, this commitment to principled non-directivity gives to me a new freedom. If a relationship is non-directive *in principle*, then the relationship has to be viewed holistically. By contrast, instrumental thinking tends to reduce the relationship to a set of discrete interventions, some of which are 'non-directive' and some of which are not. To see the relationship as a whole, as an evolving and living whole, is crucial. Once the whole relationship becomes the focus of attention, rather than individual interventions, then I am freed to take reasonable risks and to negotiate these with my clients as appropriate. I will want to test out honestly with myself the power structure of a relationship and then know that, if my client is genuinely in possession of the work, that I may be with her in a number of ways that I think of as non-conventional.

It is for me a matter of principle that in the early part of therapy, or when clients are particularly vulnerable, or have a markedly externalised locus of evaluation, non-directive, tracking responses are key. However, with a client who is moving beyond this state to a greater functionality, I have learned that she can be met more fully and more often from my own frame of reference. Occasionally I judge such to be a worthwhile risk even in the earliest stages of work. I recently worked with a client who had firmly fixed in her mind, after conversations with her psychiatrist, that her dysfunctional thinking had to change. This injunction had merely set up a new cycle of failure, but also seemed to me to hold in place a conscious block against listening to her feelings. I therefore asked her permission to explore this, saying that I did not often do this but that I felt it was important. I then engaged with her in an exercise of visualising an emotively significant scene, and asked her to distinguish thinking from feeling responses to it. I shared my own responses as very different. At that point, we talked about how change happens. I invited her to be open to the fact that listening to her feelings may be just as important as changing thinking patterns. I then swiftly checked with my supervisor that this was valid psycho-education rather than my acting out a concealed competitiveness with the psychiatrist.

Even at an early stage in the relationship, I felt — exceptionally — that it would free the client if I were congruent about my disagreement with her cognitive emphasis, while empathising with the experience of feeling her thinking as she did. It was a risk, but well worth taking as long as the relationship remains otherwise firmly rooted in her experience and my tracking of it.

I integrate from a position of principled non-directivity. This roots

I believe that principled non-directivity is well-exampled in the work of Margaret Warner, who integrates models of dysfunction into a largely classical approach. See, for example, Warner, M. (2002). 'Luke's Dilemmas: A Client-Centered/Experiential model of processing with a schizophrenic thought disorder.' In J.C.Watson *et al.* (eds.) *Client-Centered and Experiential Psychotherapy in the 21st Century: Advances in theory, research and practice.* Ross-on-Wye: PCCS Books, pp. 459–72.

Non-directivity is a principle which cannot be fully attained, except from a holistic view of the relationship. See Worsley, R. (2002). *Process Work in Person-centred Therapy.* London: Palgrave. pp. 68–73, for a fuller version of this argument.

Marge Witty commented: 'There is a great deal of variation in the ways client-centred practitioners interact with their clients — as much variation as there are persons . . . In the mature form of Client-Centred Therapy (meaning practice in which the therapist is freely him or her self in the situation) many possible implementations of the attitudes may emerge.' Witty, M. (2002). *Contested questions between client-centred and experiential therapies.* A paper given to the BAPCA conference, Durham, UK, September. Published on Allan Turner's website <www.allanturner.co.uk.>.

It is arguable that there is a difference between being directional — stating my disagreement and hence pointing to possible directions of movement — and being directive — 'Let's do this now because it is useful.' I am yet to be convinced that this difference is more than a matter of degree.

Raskin noted that Carl Rogers acted in one of two ways — empathic responding or 'a freely functioning client/person-centered therapist'. The former can be taught, up to a point, as a portrayed skill. The latter happens when we bring the whole self to the client. Raskin, N.J. (1998). 'Responses to person-centered versus client-centered.' *Renaissance*, 5, pp. 2–3.

C.R. Rogers (1961). 'To Be That Self Which One Truly Is: A Therapist's View of Personal Goals.' In *On Becoming a Person*. Boston: Houghton Mifflin, pp. 163–82.

I act spontaneously when I am guided by fast but out-of-awareness processing. I am reflexive when I refer my doing back to conscious thinking processes. For a fuller description of spontaneity and reflexivity, and its relationship to the research of Greenberg *et al* (1993), see Worsley, R. (2002). *Process Work in Person-centred Therapy*. London: Palgrave, pp. 192–200.

my practice in a faith in the client's actualising tendency; keeps me away from the equation of *engaging* process with process *direction*; frees me, in seeing non-directivity as a quality of the whole relationship, to take risks congruently, as I want to.

Therapist spontaneity and reflexivity — a way of being

The last four words — as I want to — feel like a real hostage to fortune. At least the experiential psychotherapist claims to make an objective judgement about how treatment might be responsibly matched to diagnosis. The CCC practitioner often exhibits a close care to respond consistently from within the client's frame of reference. Surely to do 'as I want' is pretty irresponsible stuff?

Indeed, doing what I want could be massively chaotic. As a person-centred therapist, I see myself as responsible towards my clients and towards the whole profession, and test this act of responsibility time and again against the CCC hypotheses as outlined by Tony Merry. However, psychotherapy is for me the meeting of souls. I aim to bring my whole self to my client as best I can. Sometimes this feels risky. It is. But to confine the self is untherapeutic: I want to bring as much as possible of who I am, how I think and learn and feel, to my relationship with the client, and to accept that I will from time to time make mistakes in doing this. Below I will explore a number of examples of integration, sense three. In these, feeling and understanding become part of me, and then I respond as naturally as possible from this knowing.

Carl Rogers points out that to be fully functioning is to be open spontaneously, freely and uninhibitedly to the self, to thinking but above all to feeling (Rogers, 1961). This healthy functioning moves along a continuum from *spontaneity* to *reflexivity*. In other words, I am often free in that I can experience my self, my feelings, my contact with the world at the edge of awareness, uninhibited by processes of distortion and denial. At other times, my freedom subsists in a full and conscious focus upon appropriate and often challenging material. How and when I access each of these modes of processing is also an indication of how functional I am.

A simple example may help here. A couple of weeks ago, my daughter asked me for some money to help her buy her first car. My spontaneous first reaction to her request was an internal feeling that this would be a really nice thing to do, and I would enjoy getting it fixed. I could stretch out to her in love at that point. My reaction was healthy because it expressed a core love for her; it could have been unhealthy if introjects to do with buying love or to do with my need to control money rigidly had come into play. Spontaneity uninhibited by introjected material was, and felt, good. However, at that point, I needed to say: But let's talk about how to do this, and whether it really is a good idea. This reflexive response was (I hope!) fatherly wisdom looking to check out the practical consequences of her and my actions. It had to be reflexive — consciously considered, measured. However, I note that my reflexive checking out could bear a marked resemblance to my introjected need to control money. Spontaneity and reflexivity, healthy function and dysfunction interweave in a tantalising fashion.

The key difference between integration as I understand it and the sort of integration-cum-technical-eclecticism which Greenberg et al., (1993), exhibit is this. An experientialist like Greenberg intervenes with the client's process is a way that is diagnostic, is designed to bring about specific change, but above all is simply designed. It is reflexive, and thus tends to be directive in the sense that at this point the therapist assumes a consciously expert role. By contrast, I suggest that the ideal of an integrative approach is to bring to the client the spontaneous awareness and resourcefulness of the therapist, using reflexivity as the mode for supervision and reflection. While I do not preclude absolutely the occasional and critically assessed use of a piece of designed and negotiated process work — see my first example of integration below — my aim is to take all material that is integrated into the approach, together with material that is at the heart of the approach, and hold it within me so that my spontaneous and engaged self may access it as it needs to. New learning does not lead to newly designed interventions. I hold within me what I know, in alertness, but passively, until I find that it seems therapeutic for my knowing to influence my way of being. Above all, I seek to be spontaneous, creative and idiosyncratic with my client, taking and assessing risks but always guided by principled non-directivity.

The question now remains: what can be integrated and how? The following categories are neither authoritative nor exhaustive, but simply examples of what I take to be reasonable practice.

Cognitive-behavioural interventions

Cognitive-behavioural therapy is philosophically far removed from the Person-Centred Approach. The behavioural aspect is about the changing of behaviour through a process of conditioning

Greenberg, L.S., Rice, L.N. and Elliott, R.(1993). *Facilitating Emotional Change: The Moment-by-Moment Process*. New York: Guilford.

Even David Rennie's more moderate approach claims that it is instrumentally useful for the therapist to assume, after negotiation, the agency on behalf of the client, in process direction. Rennie, D. (1998). *Person-Centred Counselling: An Experiential Approach*. London: Sage, p. 12.

'At its very core, the flow of therapy should be spontaneous, forever following unanticipated river beds . . .' Yalom, I.D. (2002). 'Create a New Therapy for Each Patient.' In *The Gift of Therapy*. London: Piatkus, pp. 33–6.

Two useful introductions in this area are: Weishaar, M.E. (1993). *Aaron T. Beck.* London: Sage; and Trower, P., Casey, A. and Dryden, W. (1998). *Cognitive-Behavioural Counselling in Action.* London: Sage.

Significant psychological change is what Rogers predicted to be the necessary outcome of the implementation of the six conditions of therapy — **Rogers, C. R. (1957).** 'The necessary and sufficient conditions of therapeutic personality change.' *Journal of Consulting Psychology* 21: 95–103.

Bozarth, J.D. (1998). *Person-Centered Therapy: A Revolutionary Paradigm.* Ross-on-Wye: PCCS Books, pp. 128–32. Jerold Bozarth has examined the use of psychological instruments as adjuncts to Person-Centred Therapy; this is one example of a *sub-contract* to do work which appears to be in and of itself outside of Person-Centred Therapy.

learned patterns. The cognitive aspect centres on the alteration of thinking, in the belief that emotions will follow this. These two aspects differ markedly from each other, but together might seem to be anathema to any depth psychotherapy. I want to tackle this area of possible integration, firstly just to illustrate what can be at stake and secondly because a number of new person-centred practitioners see cognitive behavioural interventions as an appealing way to appear effective with difficult client groups. There is obvious conflict between the person-centred view of the personality, rooted in its need for positive regard and congruent functioning, and the cognitive view, which assigns the same dysfunctions to 'irrational' thinking. What are the implications for integration?

A client comes to me with panic attacks. She is nine days away from her philosophy final examinations. She is breathing irregularly, feeling disorientated, and with chest pains. It is clear to me that this is not the normal level of stress in the face of university examinations (although it is fairly frequent). I am under no illusion that to dispose of the distressing symptom will be the end of the matter. Panic is actually a highly functional state, if the danger is real and immediate enough. What is her danger? It might well be that the possibility of failure is wholly and deeply feared by her. Why? As a therapist, I know that the crux of the matter will be heard over a number of weeks of close tracking of her, in an acceptant and open ethos. In therapy, the underlying causes will resolve. Yet the examinations are a few days away. Significant psychological change will normally take longer than this.

One option that may be negotiated with the client is a short-term piece of work to alleviate the symptom by behavioural means (see Bozarth, 1998). In this, I would favour a brief discussion of the nature of panic as largely functional, and then the careful teaching of relaxation. What are the pros and cons of such a sub-contract?

The most obvious advantage is that the client is relieved of a debilitating symptom in time for her exams. However, there is a problem. Symptoms are useful signposts, just as the pain of appendicitis is both agonising and life-saving. To cure a symptom can be dangerous. At best, the client will experience temporary relief; at worst, her self's protest at the underlying incongruence will be neglected to the detriment of her future mental health. Except where the client experiences a pressing need, I have come to believe that even seemingly useful behavioural interventions risk distorting the client's contact with her own experiencing and its purposes. I leave well alone as long as possible, and normally find that whatever I contemplated as a useful engaging with symptoms becomes irrelevant. Person-centred therapists work to accept the whole of their client's experience.

A behavioural intervention is possible but needs caution. By contrast, the cognitive intervention — the challenging and altering of patterns of belief — conflicts more directly with Person-Centred Therapy. Cognitive challenge can be radically unempathic, in that it seeks to *alter* and *not to understand* what the client thinks. In classical cognitive-behavioural work, this challenge is rooted in the belief that the irrational thinking is at the core of the client's problem. However, from a person-centred perspective, this is simply not the case. The cognitive issues are again symptoms of a deeper distortion of experience.

Greenberg *et al.* (1993). *Facilitating Emotional Change: The Moment-by-Moment Process.* New York: Guilford, has challenged, from an in-depth consideration of cognitive science and emotion schemes, the CBT prioritising of cognition over emotion.

From time to time I find myself wanting to reflect back to a client the incongruences I hear in their thinking processes. This is not *always* wrong, but I notice that for every occasion that the client derives useful feedback as to how they habitually operate, there are other occasions when they detach from my 'findings', until I can reach where they really are. However empathic, however congruent, cognitive challenge from within a person-centred framework is to be carefully judged. My key question is this: in challenging a particular thinking process in the client, have I evidence that this is empathic of the reactions to this of other parts of the client's perceiving self?

Cognitive-behavioural interventions are unlikely material for integration within the Person-Centred Approach. They are rightly treated with great caution. However, they may have some place, not least because the behavioural — but not the cognitive — element stands at a safe distance from depth therapy.

Configurations of the self

It might seem odd to move from a piece of theory as far removed from person-centred thought as is cognitive-behaviourism to an aspect of person-centred theory itself. Dave Mearns began to develop his concept of configurations of the self in the mid-1990s, and continues to do so with other practitioners (see Mearns and Thorne, 2000). The person-centred tradition is a living and changing entity. Although new aspects of theory, even if clearly person-centred, need to be integrated into the body of thinking and practice, there are theoretical and practical tensions.

Mearns, D. and Thorne, B. (2000). *Person-Centred Therapy Today.* London: Sage, Chapters 6 and 7.

Mearns and Thorne note that the normal experience for people is to experience themselves as a number of what John Rowan has described as sub-personalities or, as Mearns preferred, configurations of the self. Each of these is a voice or aspect of the self which has, to some degree, characteristic and independent functioning. Each configuration has a personality of its own. Together these form a gestalt, sometimes simple, sometimes very complex, which is the Self. The first example which Mearns worked with was his client, Elizabeth, who came to think of herself as either a Little Girl or a Nun. The first was put upon by the second. The Little Girl carried the burden of the Nun's conditional regard for her. In this fairly simple gestalt, healing came in the reconciliation of the two configurations. Mearns' key point for practice is that empathy has to be extended to the whole of the client, and as he noted, person-centred therapists find it so much easier to empathise with the Little Girl than the Nun.

Each configuration, as it emerges, is a phenomenon which exists within the client's frame of reference. Configurations are personal to each individual. Only the client can know whether a particular configuration belongs to her or not. Indeed, how we conceive of our configurations will change from time to time. At heart the concept is phenomenological at least at first sight. Mearns' point about empathising holistically is well made and not at all controversial. He likens it to the process of empathising with both partners in person-centred couples work (Mearns, 1994a and b).

However, beneath this surface simplicity there are at least two areas of challenge in integrating the concept into the Person-Centred Approach. In practice, working with configurations of self requires the same judgement as working with any other mental images and metaphors. Firstly, the therapist has to decide whether it is phenomenologically sound for the specific image or configuration to be offered by the therapist, or whether images should only be worked with if offered by the client. When the therapist *first* designates the image, then there is a danger that this will trespass upon the client's frame of reference in a major way, being at worst abusive. However, it is far from clear to me that all therapist-originated images are unhelpful. Ask yourself: Is the image I have empathic, an embodiment of my understanding of the client's experience? Can it be shared with the client in a way that will allow the client to own it or to reject it? (The latter question is about both the way it is shared and the degree of externalisation of the client's locus of evaluation at the time.)

All concepts referred to or cited here are drawn from the compact introduction to this constellation of ideas in Mearns, D. and Thorne, B. (2000). *Person-Centred Therapy Today.* London: Sage, pp. 101–8, unless otherwise referenced.

Self-pluralism is a universal and healthy phenomenon, and not to be confused with the pathological dissociative states. However, it is possible that dissociative states may exist as one end of a continuum of which normal configurations of the self are also a part.

Mearns, D. (1994a). *Developing Person-Centred Counselling.* London: Sage, Chapter 4.
Mearns, D. (1994b).'The Dance of Psychotherapy.' *Person-Centred Practice, 2* (2). Reprinted in T. Merry (ed.)(2000). *The BAPCA Reader.* Ross-on-Wye: PCCS Books, pp. 77–86.

See O'Leary, C.J. (1999). *Counselling Couples and Families: A Person-Centred Approach.* London: Sage.

Dave Mearns exemplifies abusive work as trespassing upon the client's very self-concept in his article: Mearns, D. (1999). 'Person-Centred Therapy with Configurations of Self.' *Counselling,10* (2): 125. Rugby: British Association for Counselling.

Nor is it simply a matter of deciding to work with client-generated images only. In my experience, the more risk I am prepared to take in using imagery in my reflecting, the more this becomes part of the common language of the therapy. To be too rigorously abstemious is to inhibit the client's imaginative processes and language, for language does not come from one party only, but is in the long run socially constructed. By way of example, I worked with a middle-aged man, a social worker, who saw himself as strung out between a proficient self and a sad and depressed self. He was attached to the former. It helped his career. The latter he despised. In the end, I asked him to remain for a while with his depressed self. 'I am wondering how old that part of you feels?' With amazement, he replied, 'About four years old!' The baseline image — depressed over against proficient — was mainly his, although emerging in shared conversation. The internal conviction that he had not fully grasped his own image, in despising part of himself, was clearly mine. The question allowed him to test out my image against his phenomenal field. He could own that part of the image that was mine. (I felt I was in the room with a little boy.) The owning of the image as his was the beginning, however uncertain, of a move towards self-love. Not only the therapist needs to extend empathy to all aspects of the client.

See, for a full discussion of the notion of therapy as social construction, McNamee, S. and Gergen, K.J. (1992). *Therapy as Social Construction*. London: Sage.

There are practical issues in the use of imagery, but considered and courageous integration makes for good therapy, because it goes beyond the afraid, the conservative and moves towards the intuitive, for which Carl Rogers so powerfully argued in the last years of his life.

There are also a number of theoretical issues around the integration of Mearns' concept into the Person-Centred Approach. Unlike the practical issues, these are for gradual consideration by the whole person-centred community, rather than for decision by each practitioner. The issues spread far and wide to the major question of the interface of humanistic and psychodynamic theories.

Rogers, C.R. (1986). 'Rogers, Kohut and Erickson: A personal perspective on some similarities and differences.' *Person-Centered Review, 1* (2). May, cited in D.J. Cain (2002)(ed.) *Classics in the Person-Centered Approach*. Ross-on-Wye: PCCS Books, pp. 61–70.

As person-centred theory emerges, it must be integrated into the tradition and its practice. While the issues look so different from the integration of a behavioural intervention, the process of openness and caution, of seeking integrity, is much the same.

Other developments in person-centred theory

The Person-Centred Approach is generating a number of new models on a par with Mearns and Thorne's configurations of self.

Warner, M. (2002). 'Luke's Dilemmas: A Client-Cenetred/Experiential model of processing with a schizophrenic thought disorder.' In Watson, *et al.* (eds.)(2002). *Client-Centered and Experiential Psychotherapy in the 21ˢᵗ Century: Advances in theory, research and practice*. Ross-on-Wye: PCCS Books, pp. 459–72.

'Metafacts and metacauses serve very poorly in the formation of traditional causal logics, but they work quite powerfully as "handles" for [Luke's] intuitive sensing of his overall responses to situations', *ibid*. p. 462.

See Worsley, R. (2002). *Process Work in Person-Centred Therapy*. London: Palgrave, Chapters 6 and 7 for a fuller consideration of this argument.

In particular, these are of importance when they explicate states of mind in the client which are challenging to the therapist. One useful example of this sort of material is Margaret Warner's description of her work with Luke, a young schizophrenic (Warner, 2002). Warner uses material from the thinking of both Eugene Gendlin and Garry Prouty in their work with psychotic states. She notes that Luke, her young client, tends to think in ways that are both too loose and too tight compared with normal logical thinking. Warner terms the constituents of Luke's processing 'metafacts' and 'metacauses'. These show a swift alternating between left and right hemisphere processing, with the result that they sit somewhere between the literal and the metaphorical. Once seen from this point of view — the client's process-frame of reference — then disordered thinking can take on a new meaning and moreover seems to be more functional in constructing a world-view than seems to be the case on the surface.

Warner's model gives her access to the way the client actually processes. Her concepts, 'metafacts' and 'metacauses', when held within her, help her to hear the client more accurately, and so lead to accurate empathy. I will argue below, that, as long as adequate attention is given to the nature of the insight, all insights, humanistic, psychodynamic and others, which aid empathy can be integrated into person-centred work.

From other humanistic therapies

Other therapies from the humanistic approach can be very beguiling. I will consider here brief aspects of Transactional Analysis (T.A.) and of Gestalt Therapy. As a teacher of counselling, I found that some students could find each of these appealing, because they offer what the Person-Centred Approach allegedly does not — a way of being effective and powerful with the client! I have found that those who like neat systems of thought find great satisfaction in T.A., with its systematic classification of interactions and motivations, and with its unmatchable ability to make dull parties more enjoyable. Similarly, those who long to do something really helpful for their clients cannot wait to get their hands on the appropriately well-judged misunderstanding of Gestalt Therapy. Of course, at best these distortions are simply a stage in the development of some person-centred counsellors, journeying through free exploration towards a principled trust in the client. This journey is a long way removed from a responsible understanding of these therapies.

So the first thing I want to urge is that other therapies have to be properly understood, *and not just in outline*. Whatever is then drawn down from them needs to be filtered through the fundamental philosophical stance of the Person-Centred Approach. In this spirit, I want to look at the use of two constructs, one from T.A. and one from Gestalt.

TA theory parallels the PCA concept of conditions of worth with two linked ideas — injunctions and counter-injunctions. The former consists of 'commands' which are introjected normally in early childhood. The idea is perhaps narrower and more rigid than conditions of worth. However, in formulating the notion of counter-injunctions, Eric Berne made an important phenomenological observation: some of a client's introjects seem to be out of the client's awareness, while others are inwardly audible by the client as if an alien voice were speaking to them.

I too notice how my clients differ markedly in how they contact their conditions of worth. Some seem to be able to render them accessible to their reflexive and conscious processing; others never do this, and resist any unwise speculations by the therapist as inappropriate interpretation. In seeking to understand my clients, Berne's construct helps me to hear more clearly the differences in the ways clients contact the past. However, I remain open to the notion that the differences in processing styles may be more varied, idiosyncratic and complex than Berne's hypothesis allows for. Berne's phenomenological observation of clients is a valued insight, aiding attention and empathy, while I remain neutral as to the value of his derived concepts.

The second construct is at the heart of Gestalt Therapy. Gestalt's genius has been to describe human awareness in detail and systematically. This description differs from Rogers', but has much in common with person-centred theory. One aspect of the Gestalt theory of awareness is the Cycle of Experience. In any experience, for instance, eating an apple, that experience can be seen as a cycle of engagement, arousal, contact and satisfaction, with a return to the ground state, the fertile or fallow void, before another experience can be had. To complete the cycle is to be functional. Dysfunction is in the interruption of this cycle.

Each phase of the cycle has its own characteristic kind of interruption. This description of experience I take to be a useful generalisation, not a hard-and-fast rule.

The texts I have most valued for T.A. and Gestalt are:
• As an introductory text: Stewart, I. and Joines, V. (1987). *TA Today*. Nottingham: Lifespace.
• For a learned consideration of TA: Clarkson, P. (1992). *Transactional Analysis Psychotherapy: an integrated approach*. London: Routledge.
• For an accurate but accessible description of Gestalt: Sills, C., Fish, S. and Lapworth, P. (1995). *Gestalt Counselling*. Bicester: Winslow.
• Still the main and authoritative source on the theory underlying Perls' work: Perls, F.S., Hefferline, R.A. and Goodman, P. (1973). *Gestalt Therapy: Excitement and growth in the human personality*. Harmondsworth: Penguin.

Berne hypothesised that the latter — counter-injunctions — stem from later childhood, are consciously derived from parental messages and actions, and are an attempt by the organism to come to terms with the more primitive injunctions.

For an inspired attempt at an integration of Rogers' and Perls' theory, see Greenberg *et al.* (1993). *Facilitating Emotional Change: The Moment-by-Moment Process*. New York: Guilford, pp. 1–95.

See Worsley, R. (2002). *Process Work in Person-centred Therapy*. London: Palgrave, pp. 115–17, or
Sills, C., Fish, S. and Lapworth, P. (1995). *Gestalt Counselling*. Bicester: Winslow, pp. 48–70.

How might the cycle of experience be useful? I find that being aware that some clients interrupt their own experience helps my empathy. Yet, from time to time making this explicit is helpful. On one occasion, a client had worked over an extended period on his communication with his partner. There was a sense of the growth in him of confidence to communicate. He was both more congruent and less defended against underlying fears of personal and sexual criticism. Near the end of the therapy, I shared the idea of the cycle of experience. He seemed to find the notion useful that during sex he was interrupting himself. The concept provided a way for him to explore his own experiencing as it was happening for him. He returned swiftly to normal functionality.

Again, the concept from Gestalt acts as an item of language by which to understand experiencing. It was my client's actualising tendency which allowed him, in his own way, to discover his many layered needs in the complexities of his relationship, and to seek to satisfy them. 'Useful tools' can inhibit this process. It was important to have waited until late enough in the therapy to facilitate the behavioural change which correlated with the deeper shifts in his personality. It was facilitated by making available to my client a conceptual device which enabled him to hear his own process. It was not done to him or for him. The intervention accords with the four CCC hypotheses, adding only a conceptualisation of how conditions of worth can cause the client to interrupt their own experience.

We might ask *why* I did this. I did it because the idea of interrupted experience was within me. My client had been talking about interrupted experience. I was reaching out in empathy. 'Here is what I am thinking. How is it for you?' It is thus like a language, a way of searching for a new understanding.

The language itself comes from my frame of reference — but that is true for all language we use. My client had the opportunity to seize upon it or not. The CCC practitioner might feel that this is a tool: take this and use it because it will make you better. Rather I see it as a mode of communication, a mutually con-structed way of thinking, begun by me but owned by us both, through which I and my client can strive to understand how it was for him. In this understanding he discovered his own way of changing.

So far, I have discussed the integration of concepts into person-centred practice, whether those concepts be from within the PCA, like Margaret Warner's model of schizophrenic processing, or from other humanistic therapies. The integration of concepts into practice is relatively conservative. The remaining three categories concern the boundaries between the PCA and other approaches to therapy. While the discussion here is necessarily brief, it is also merely the tip of the iceberg. There are large radical debates to be had about the interface of the PCA with experiential psychotherapy, with aspects of the psychodynamic movement, and with existential therapy.

Engaging with process

In listening to a client, I am aware simultaneously of three aspects of her self-presentation: (i) the manifest content and narrative of what she says, together with its underlying constructs and ideas; (ii) the explicit emotions together with implicit emotions and underlying affect-structures; (iii) her process. Process is often out of her awareness, but can be rendered into awareness: 'I notice you clench your fist as you talk about your brother.' What we call process is in fact a whole range of interlocking events within the person which relate to the How? rather than the What? of experiencing. On the continuum which runs between CCC and experiential psychotherapy, the key issue is how to engage with process. The issues are broad and complex. However, an engagement with the views of David Rennie (1998) serves as a useful example.

I begin with the case of Andy:

Andy, whom I have known for a nearly two years, is talking about a new sense he has that he has a self which can exist, and is stable. 'I feel that I am no longer dirty. I am real. I don't have to think all the time that other people will find out how despicable I am. I can even stand up to my younger brother — well, sometimes.'

He seems to tell me this with surprised delight! He is animated. He looks me in the eye. He talks of his mother, who sexually abused him over some three years until he was taken into care, and does so with patent rage/outrage. His body is alive with anger. It is still a struggle for me to come anywhere near to deep empathy with this experience. 'It has damaged me as a man,' he said often enough. But I can draw near to his pain. But now, so different. Fluent — one of my favourite words of clients. Fluency is about having found some wholeness along the way.

'I know the memories still sear into you. I know how you must hate her. I can feel something of your anger as I listen, and I want to say, it feels good to hear it, as well as painful. I can still picture you with your hands hidden behind your back in those early sessions, like you dare not let them be seen to show what they felt. I really admire the flow of your anger.'

Maybe I don't say it quite like that. I spread out my empathic responding and my observing over time, but this summary will do. (Worsley, 2002, p. 47)

In this moment of therapy, I strove to empathise with Andy, making contact with his process as well as all else that he was expressing. It was important to me that I should engage openly and congruently

Key texts here are Worsley, R. (2002). *Process Work in Person-Centred Therapy*. London: Palgrave. **Rennie, D. (1998)**. *Person-Centred Counselling: An Experiential Approach*. London: Sage. Greenberg *et al*, (1993). *Facilitating Emotional Change: The Moment-by-Moment Process*. New York: Guilford. A particularly useful introduction is Germain Lietaer's article, 'From Non-Directive to Experiential: A Paradigm Unfolding.' In B. Thorne and E. Lambers, (eds.) (1998). *Person-Centred Therapy: A European Perspective*. London: Sage, pp. 62–73.

Worsley, R. (2002). *Process Work in Person-centred Therapy*. London: Palgrave.

Expressing pleasure with a client's healing is tricky. It can be read as praise which invites an exporting of the client's locus of evaluation to the therapist — at worst to the /
cont. over

/cont . . . expert therapist. Such reflection needs to sit in the context of a developed relationship in which the therapist can trust how the client will manage her responses.

Rennie, D. (1998). *Person-Centred Counselling: An Experiential Approach.* London: Sage.

I used my understanding of Andy's process — pointing to his fluent anger — to reflect his feelings, and the contrast with his sitting on his hands in the past. This process reflection also enables me to express my pleasure, my reaction to what is going on in the room.

Sometimes, in working with clients with very distorted processing and an urgent need — such as imminent exams — I will intervene directively. In essence, this can be seen as a cognitive-behavioural intervention, as above.

with the fact that he was doing anger so differently from earlier in therapy, and that I got a genuine satisfaction from this. However, my engagement with Andy's process was empathic and as such was in line with the four hypotheses of the CCC. I view the client's process as one aspect of their frame of reference. To engage with process is not very different from other ways of engaging with the client. In particular in long-term therapy, it is not my aim to change the client's process by interfering with it. (It is my fantasy that Andy would have reacted badly to such interference. He had already been abused by someone who should have cared for him! Clients with a history of abuse are prone to experience therapist error as threatening, often replaying the abuse.)

By contrast to my own view, David Rennie sets out a cogent enough argument for process direction (Rennie, 1998). While I disagree with him, some of his observations are most valuable. He begins from the stance that the conditions of therapy are 'necessary and *probably* sufficient' — thereby ducking the issue, but expressing well his moderate experiential stance. He stresses the role of the client as agent, a concept which does some justice to the actualising tendency. He then observes that the client's agency, which is often trustworthy, can be damaged beyond the point that it is self-sustaining. Rennie also notes that humans function in two registers — the spontaneous and the reflexive. (This is useful. It means that for some clients process reflection can be a real aid to their healing, because they work well from the reflexive register.) However, his next step is the one I find controversial. He concludes that there are times when the client's agency is at such a low ebb that it is necessary for the therapist to take it in hand by some process direction.

This last point is controversial for a number of separate reasons. It is not clear to me that the client's agency is ever damaged to the extent that directivity is the healing factor. Rennie takes no account of the counter-argument that it is precisely at the time when agency feels vulnerable that the therapist is required to trust it rather than overwhelm it with kindness. Rennie believes that the client is expert on her content and feelings but that the therapist is expert on process. The client, it seems to me, *is* expert on her own process. The therapist is by contrast expert on the content, feeling and process of clients in general, but not of any one client. Rennie confuses the sense in which it is proper for person-centred therapists to claim expertise.

However, unlike the CCC therapist, I do not find it obviously and in principle wrong to be process-directive on each and every occasion. (See above my argument that principled non-directivity allows for carefully judged directive interventions on some occasions.) It falls to me to be critically aware of the impact and rationale of those rare occasions when I judge process direction to be a worthwhile risk. In this I differ from Rennie. He believes that process direction is *necessary* at times when clients are too vulnerable to look after themselves. By contrast, I will tend to use a process-directive intervention cautiously, agnostically, and preferring those occasions when the client is strong enough to meet me in this way.

As I have become increasingly confident in my clients' robust actualising tendency I have seen it as less and less necessary to take responsibility for them in a Rennie-like way; yet, in trusting in this robustness, I find that I can take risks. Responsible integration, for me, subsists in a careful thinking through of the pros and cons of all risks. The illusion of risk-free therapy leads to constricted, fearful therapy conducted in bad faith.

Transference and other shibboleths

Psychodynamic psychotherapy is rich in both theory and imagery. It is also the point of departure for the major humanistic therapies. This has made for tricky relationships between therapists of different persuasions. Person-centred therapists have a tendency to regard the psychodynamic with suspicion, and thereby throw out the baby with the bathwater.

This interface between psychodynamic theory and practice and the PCA will be a point of growth in the coming years. Some of the theoretical debates are already under way. Dave Mearns and Brian Thorne (2000, p. 105) have already noted the similarity of their theory of configurations of self to object relations theory. Above all other parts of psychodynamic theory, transference marks out both the openness and the ghetto-mentality of the PCA. A shibboleth is a sign of tribal identity. The word literally means, in Hebrew, an ear of corn. However, the meaning does not matter. The word was difficult to pronounce for non-Hebrew speakers, and so its articulation was a test of racial belonging. Sometimes I feel that the whole argument about transference is a test of purity, regardless of meaning.

In February 1987, John Shlien published an article in the influential journal, *Person-Centered Review,* entitled 'A Countertheory of

While person-centred therapists are understandably reluctant to use the word 'expert', in fact our training gives us hard-won expertise on the process of therapy and upon the use of the self within it. It is the client who we meet as amateurs (love-ers).

Worsley, R. (2002). *Process Work in Person-Centred Therapy.* London: Palgrave, pp. 203–5, offers a fuller discussion of the taking of this risk.

The relationship between a timorous non-directiveness and trust in the client's robustness is made by Maria Villas-Boas Bowen (1996), in 'The Myth of Non-Directiveness: the case of Jill.' In B.A. Farber, D.C. Brink and P.M. Raskin (eds.) *The Psychotherapy of Carl Rogers: Cases and Commentary.* New York: Guilford, pp. 84–94.

Mearns, D. and Thorne, B. (2000). *Person-Centred Therapy Today.* London: Sage.

Shlien, J.M. (1987). 'A Countertheory of Transference.' *Person-Centered Review, 7* (2): 15–49. The article and the key responses to it are reproduced in Cain, D.J. (ed.) (2002). *Classics in the Person-Centered Approach.* Ross-on-Wye: PCCS Books, pp. 414–80. The 1987 version was a revision of the original published in Levant, R.F. and Shlien, J.M. (eds.) (1984). *Client-Centered Therapy and the Person-Centered Approach.* New York: Praeger, pp. 153–81.

Rogers, C.R. (1951). *Client-Centered Therapy.* Boston: Houghton Mifflin, pp. 198–218.

Many modern object relations therapists would sympathise with Rogers' caution, even if disagreeing with his disavowal of the therapeutic use of transference. See, for instance Scharff, J.S. and Scharff, D.E. (1992). *Scharff Notes: A Primer of Object Relations Therapy.* New Jersey: Aronson, pp. 113–14 and 137.

Shlien, J.M. (1987). 'A Countertheory of Transference.' In Cain, D.J. (ed.) (2002). *Classics in the Person-Centered Approach.* Ross-on-Wye: PCCS Books, p. 427.

Worsley, R. (2002). *Process Work in Person-Centred Therapy.* London: Palgrave, Chapter 12.

Transference'. Shlien was being deliberately provocative. The article is a fine one, with much good sense in it, not least on the love-like quality of empathy. However, his basic contention was that transference is a construct developed by therapists to protect themselves from the real, and from responsibility in relating.

Any worthwhile psychodynamic therapist will know and understand Shlien's point: transference can be used abusively. However, it is a long step from this to the conclusion that transference does not exist. I take it that there are transferential phenomena, and that Carl Rogers' brief thinking about them (Rogers, 1951) is very much to the point. Rogers noted that transferences should be moved through towards the real relationship. Therefore, transferential and counter-transferential phenomena will not be used in the PCA either interpretatively, or, more to the point, as an assertion of therapist expertise. How then might transferential phenomena be useful?

First of all, I take Shlien's point that transference has to be loosely enough defined to free it from the theoretical context of psychoanalysis. I regard transference as a general tendency to replay patterns of relating, in such a fashion that the current relationship is distorted. It is an acting out of introjects within a gestalt of relating. Sometimes it is benign and sometimes a problem for the client. In a relationship with a former supervisor, I recognised that I was struggling to be congruent, particularly about the psychological boundaries of the relationship. I came gradually to recognise that I was inhibited in particular by a sense of having at all costs to avoid being hurtful. I know this area of myself. It is the pattern of emotions I lived out with my mother in adolescence and early adulthood. I had done work on it, but here it was again! It was in part down to me, and in part down to my supervisor's view of me as 'a good son'.

Transference is, as Shlien says, a shorthand for a whole set of complicated dynamics, with the thread of the recycling of relational patterns running through (Shlien, 1987). To take transference seriously, to integrate it into the PCA, is to listen carefully to those patterns of recycling. Listening for what might be transferential is another form of empathising with the client's processing.

In my published case of Hilary (Worsley, 2002), the client slowly came to recognise that her mother had constructed for her a persona, a number of configurations of self, which she then played out in relation to both men in authority and to sexual partners.

The recognition of transference-patterns helped me empathise with Hilary. In recognising that Hilary showed both a behavioural pattern and a deep puzzlement at her own motivation, I could begin to feel the sense of her introjected material, from mother. I did not need to decide to do anything at all. I kept the possibility within me that this pattern was powerful and crushing for Hilary. That was enough. It is really important to see patterns of transference and counter-transference as possibilities rather than facts, until they emerge into the client's self-understanding for confirmation. To see them as emergent facts too soon is to drift into a wrong power dynamic.

However, Hilary was a client who clearly benefited from working within herself reflexively. She soon saw the transference herself. It was a shared dawning awareness between us. Seeing it became a temporary source of safety. It was a handle by which she could grasp her own fears and maladaptive behaviours under pressure, until therapy obviated the need for such self-conscious processing.

It is important to be aware that any theoretical concept can be misleading. I listened to Alistair for a long while, convinced that there must be an emotional pattern in his past which forbade him to care for his own needs. It did not emerge. I felt my own frustration. What prevented him from facing this? In the end, I simply asked him. As far as he was aware, there was no such injunction from earlier life. However, there was one from his current partner!

Transference, as a general concept freed from its Freudian past, is like any other theoretical concept. I need to ask: What does it point to in the world or in the client's awareness? How do I empathise better if I hold this meaning-structure within me? Do I ever point openly to it? How might it be misleading me or narrowing my awareness?

The existential dimension

Existential philosophy is a diverse movement united only by the question: What is Being? Some of the more pragmatic philosophers of the analytic school call into doubt whether this question even has meaning. It is at the root of existential psychotherapy, itself a diverse movement. The aim of the existential therapist is to help the client confront within their own living, inauthenticity and self-ignorance, and to move towards a greater trust in their inner self and reality.

I was tempted for a while to try and answer my own questions. The point is that there are not universal answers, for me, to these questions, but rather a process of vigilance in therapy. How do *all my concepts* (including the PCA ones) affect me?

The methodology of existential therapy is close to the PCA in some respects, but far more challenging and directive than most PCA practitioners would want to be. It is built on an assumption that the therapist has a peculiar expertise, in philosophy and living. It is not obviously compatible with the PCA.

However, the philosophical basis of person-centred theory, phenomenology, is closely allied with existentialism (van Deurzen-Smith, 1988). Moreover, Rogers entered into dialogue with some of the key English-speaking existentialists of his day — most notably Martin Buber, Rollo May and Paul Tillich. This overlap between the PCA and existentialism is often ignored. Exploring it is one of the more important pieces of work still to be done. Yet, however tentatively, the question of integration can be faced here too.

Person-centred thinking has a clear idea of what it is to be human, and sees dysfunction as a departure from these qualities. However, the outline qualities tend to focus upon psychological health — avoiding the introjection of conditions of worth, for example — and so are partial and pragmatic. Existentialism also gives an account of what it is to be human. What sort of partnership can it have with person-centred theory?

The answer to this question could be a whole book, but here must be a single paragraph standing for my personal hypothesis. Existential philosophy deals with the question of meaning in Being. It suggests that some very general categories of Being, such as inauthenticity or the refusal to take self-responsibility, are not appropriate. As such, it could be used grossly directively. However, it is also part of a person's health, psychological and spiritual, to engage with meaning. I therefore hypothesise that, for some clients, but by no means all clients, near the end of therapy when the therapist can trust the robustness of the client to make their own life-decisions over against other views, it is possible to engage in conversation which facilitates meaning generation within conscious awareness. Such a conversation would look rather different from the normal practice of most PCA practitioners. It would be more of a Socratic and less of a Rogerian dialogue.

With this tantalizing tidbit, the subject must rest. I believe that it will be a major area of development in person-centred theory and practice in the coming decade. The result of further reflection will be integrated into the PCA.

van Deurzen-Smith, E. (1988). *Existential Counselling in Action*. London: Sage, p.162.

Mick Cooper points out that few contemporary existential thinkers would want to make judgements about which ways of being are appropriate or inappropriate. Even Heidegger states several times that he does not intend to suggest that authenticity is a more advanced way of being than inauthenticity. However, Richard replies that, in his view, terms such as 'bad faith' and 'inauthentic' have a rhetoric of their own and point to places where we would not want to head ourselves.

By this I mean that the therapist would be more willing to engage the client in debate, and feel less need to give her main attention to tracking the client. Both Rogers and Socrates were engaged in experiential education, but whereas Rogers speaks from his own frame of reference relatively infrequently, Socratic dialogue is the engagement of two people in a 'comparing' of world views.

See 'Heather', my case study, Worsley, R. (2002). *Process Work in Person-Centred Therapy*. London: Palgrave, pp. 175–7.

Conclusion

To know a concept is to be enlightened or deluded. I can never be sure which. Yet each concept is a lens to look through. It may clarify or distort. It may affect the way I am or what I do, or it may simply assist my empathic waiting, a loitering with loving intent.

To integrate new material into the PCA is not the same as being an integrative or eclectic practitioner. It is far more conservative, but it also frees the therapist to be herself and to take appropriate risks. All the while, the yardstick of CCC hypotheses needs to be in the background.

I would be arrogant to say that I was more free (better?) than the CCC therapist. All I have is my own experience that, for me at least, some of my freedom subsists in my integrative approach to Person-Centred Therapy.

My plea is to be ourselves, to take the risks and to allow our minds to render our hearts attentive.

Resources

This chapter is a statement of a personal view of being person-centred. As I said at the beginning, it does not represent a school of thought or a movement. Therefore the resources which specifically elucidate what I have written are few.

As far as websites are concerned, I recommend Peter Schmid's site <www.pfs-online.at>. Peter is open to much, not least in his integration of therapy and theology and pastoral practice.

Besides my own book, detailed above, there are factual contributions like: Thorne, B. (1998). *Person-Centred Therapy: A European Perspective* London: Sage.

I would also recommend any of the articles written by Margaret Warner, who is indubitably a good, person-centred practitioner, with a talent for integrating her understanding of dysfunction into therapy.

For example: **Warner, M.S. (2000).** 'Person-Centred Therapy at the difficult edge: A developmentally based model of fragile and dissociated process.' In D. Mearns and B. Thorne (2000). *Person-Centred Therapy Today.* London: Sage, pp. 144–71.
Warner, M.S. (2002). 'Luke's Dilemmas: A Client-Centered/Experiential model of processing with a schizophrenic thought disorder.' In Watson, *et al.* (eds.) (2002). *Client-Centered and Experiential Psychotherapy in the 21st Century: Advances in theory, research and practice.* Ross-on-Wye: PCCS Books, pp. 459–72.

mapping person-centred approaches to counselling and psychotherapy

appendix
pete sanders

Midway through the conference, someone said to me on the stairway (Garry Prouty, it was) 'Doesn't seem very client-centered, does it?' Just what I had been thinking.
John Shlien.

Introduction

Art Bohart recently described an American problem: he suggested that such was the decline in Client/Person-Centred Therapies in the United States, that no one ever called themselves a client or person-centred therapist any more. Yet, he asserted, most practitioners (from cognitive to analytical), when asked, declared their belief in the primacy of the relationship, the importance of empathy, and never once acknowledged Rogers. It occurred to me that in the United Kingdom, we suffer the inverse problem, namely that according to some estimates, the majority of counsellors identify themselves as person-centred, yet scrutiny of their practice, however, reveals a very different story.

Let me start by saying that if you have been practising client-centred, person-centred or experiential psychotherapy for any appreciable length of time, you will have read much of this before. I am not making any claims for ground-breaking analysis. Nor am I making apologies for repetition in the first part of this paper since it is, in my view, imperative that this community of practitioners that identify with the Person-Centred Approach continues to present itself with the issues raised today. You may know of many members of this community who have made attempts to tackle this issue — some scholarly, some brave, most in good heart trying to work towards resolution.

I deliberately side-step theoretical issues, and focus on who we are and what we call ourselves, while acknowledging the interrelatedness of these areas. The present paper concerns itself with strategy and vocabulary rather than theory and practice.

Shlien, J. M. (1994/2003). 'Untitled and Uneasy.' Paper presented at the Third International Conference on Client-Centered and Experiential Psychotherapy, Gmunden, Austria, published in J.M.Shlien (2003). *To Lead an Honorable Life.* Ross-on-Wye: PCCS Books.

Bohart A.C. Keynote address at the fifth International Conference on Client-Centered and Experiential Psychotherapy, Chicago, June 2000.

As a general sidenote, some readers may know that this paper was presented at the fifth International Conference on Client-Centered and Experiential Psychotherapy, Chicago, June 2000. Quite independently, Germain Lietaer presented a paper with similar aims at the same conference: 'The Client-Centered/ Experiential Paradigm in Psychotherapy: Development and identity'. Peter Schmid's keynote presentation was also warmly inclusive: 'The Necessary and Sufficient Conditions of Being Person-Centered: On identity, integration and differentiation of the paradigm.' Both are published in J.C. Watson, R.N. Goldman and M.S. Warner (eds.)(2002). *Client-Centered and Experiential Psychotherapy in the 21ˢᵗ Century: Advances in theory, research and practice.* Ross-on-Wye: PCCS Books.

This appendix is adapted with permission from Sanders, P. (2000). 'Mapping person-centred approaches to counselling and psychotherapy.' *Person-Centred Practice*, 8 (2): 62–74.

A matter of identity

Bohart, A.C. (1995). 'The Person-Centered Psychotherapies.' In A. Gurman and S. Messer (eds.) *Essential Psychotherapies: Theory and Practice.* New York: Guilford, pp 85–127.

Bohart (1995) described a widely-held view when he wrote:
> Person-centered therapy is an umbrella term chosen to refer to the variety of approaches grounded in a theoretical view of the nature of human beings and their interactions originally developed by Carl Rogers in the 1940s and 1950s . . . (p. 85)

Discussion regarding the range of approaches claiming to be 'person-centred' has been ongoing for many years in books, journals, unpublished papers, seminars, and cafes, not to mention hotel bars at international conferences. At recent meetings of person-centred practitioners in the UK, many have expressed the need for some defining statement which would help them work more proactively with the situation referred to by Merry in 1990:

Merry T. (1990). 'Client-Centred Therapy: some trends and some troubles.' *Counselling, Journal of the British Association for Counselling, 1* (1): 17–18.

> . . . I am troubled by two things. One is the way the term 'person-centred' is becoming widely used to describe situations which do not do justice to the spirit or the original meaning of that term — 'person-centred hypnotherapy', for example. The other . . . is the growing, but mistaken view, that Client-Centred Therapy has no distinct or unique identity, but is simply a means of providing a psychological climate in which other techniques, methods and approaches can be applied. (p. 17)

Merry's troubles, were, even in 1990, merely the latest in a line of complaints. In one of the biggest-selling English-language counselling textbooks ever published, Dave Mearns and Brian Thorne (1988) lament:

Mearns, D. and Thorne, B. (1988). *Person-Centred Counselling in Action.* First Ed. London: Sage.

> We are little short of horrified by the recent proliferation of counselling practitioners, both in America and Britain, who seem to believe that by sticking the label 'person-centred' on themselves they have licence to follow the most bizarre prompting of their own intuition or to create a veritable smorgasbord of therapeutic approaches which smack of eclecticism at its most irresponsible. (p. 2)

I wonder whether any of the tens of thousands of readers world-wide who bought that book imagined that the authors might be talking about *them*? Two years previously, Wood (1986) had voiced another concern, typical of the time, when he wrote:

Wood, J.K. (1986). 'Roundtable Discussion.' *Person-Centered Review, 1* (3): 350–1.

> Most people repeat vacuously the cliché: 'I believe that Rogers' conditions are necessary but not sufficient.' Some of Rogers' closest colleagues use hypnosis, guided fantasies, paradoxical statements, dream analysis, exercises, give homework assignments and generally follow the latest fads to supply their missing deficiency. (p. 351)

In 1988, the ADPCA newsletter, *Renaissance*, published the views of Barbara Brodley, Nat Raskin, Peggy Natiello, Elio Nacmias, Curtis Graf and Marlis Pörtner in a debate entitled 'Person-Centered versus Client-Centered'. Six practitioners, person-centred all, yet no two of them could agree. Two years earlier the 'Roundtable Discussion' from which I quoted Wood, above, asked for written replies to the question 'What is most essential to the continued development of the theory and application of the Person-Centered Approach?' Twenty-three notable practitioners' responses were printed and although many were concerned about the future of the therapeutic application of the approach, there was little agreement on solutions.

Tony Merry's words (above) encapsulate some of the many layers of the problem. Firstly there is the tension between the umbrella term 'Person-Centred Approach' and the more narrow term used by Rogers (1951) for therapeutic settings; 'Client-Centred Therapy'. Secondly there is a lack of clarity and lack of agreement over the definition of either term. Although apparently Rogers consistently stated that there was no difference in theoretical position between the two terms it is clear that there has been, as Shlien put it in 1986, ('Roundtable Discussion') '. . . a haemorrhage of meaning from the words "person-centered"'. He rails against the term 'Person-Centered Approach' saying 'What is it? It is only an "approach" — not a defined practice or theory. "Approach" signifies influence, not identity.' Then individual practitioners try to claim some basis for their own practice by differentiating between *types* or sometimes *degrees* of person-centredness. And so practitioners who could be supporting each other find themselves at war.

Other therapeutic approaches active in the UK are defining their principles, identifying their methods, researching their effectiveness and obtaining funding for their practice. They have an identity, or in the current idiom, they have created a brand image and they are selling it. (Some will assert that the PCA — or at least Carl Rogers and Client-Centred Therapy — did this successfully in the USA in the period 1950–1970.)

I agree with Hutterer (1993), (although the present paper has a different emphasis) that this is an issue of identity — or lack of it. I concur with his view that the Person-Centred Approach has largely failed to establish an identity, or if we were to couch it in terms of our theory, a 'self' if you like. The features of a healthy 'self' in terms of client-centred personality theory include 'an

ADPCA — Association for the Development of the Person-Centered Approach <www.adpca.org>.

Renaissance, (1988). Volume 5, Numbers 3 and 4. *Responses to Person-Centered vs Client-Centered.* ADPCA.

Rogers, C.R. (1951). *Client-Centered Therapy.* Boston: Houghton Mifflin.

Shlien J.M. (1986). 'Roundtable discussion: What is most essential to the continued development of the theory and application of the person-centered approach?' *Person-Centered Review, 1* (3): 334–52.

Hutterer, R. (1993). 'Eclecticism: An identity crisis for person-centred therapists.' In D.Brazier (ed.) *Beyond Carl Rogers.* London: Constable.

Rogers, C.R. (1951). *Client-Centered Therapy.* Boston: Houghton Mifflin.

organised, fluid, but consistent conceptual pattern of perceptions of characteristics and relationships of the "I" or the "me", together with the values attached to these concepts' (Rogers, 1951, p. 498).

So, I argue, it is *our* lack of a definition that permits misunderstanding and misrepresentation of the approach, i.e. this lack of definition from within the person-centred/client-centred community invites others to appropriate the terms and 'misuse' them.

In our professional lives as person-centred yherapists we are constantly having to wrestle with definitions of the approach that are foisted upon us from outside the approach. Worse still, the conditions that prevail in the professional world of counselling and psychotherapy in the year 2000 are exactly those which we would understand as 'conditions of worth'. The client-centred tradition is of no value, has no worth today if it cannot introject the solution focused, quick-fix values of this world driven by a hellish cocktail of accountants and mandarins fixated upon evidence-based practice. Brian Thorne (1996) wrote:

Thorne, B. (1996). 'The Cost of Transparency.' *Person-Centred Practice, 4* (2): 2–11.

> If we therefore capitulate to the culture [elsewhere in this coruscating paper he refers to it as the 'culture of contempt'] and are concerned only to win favourable judgements, to court the approval of government, or conform to the increasingly strident demands for quick-fixes and the production of stress-fit work-addicts, we shall, in effect, become psychologically disturbed ourselves and by definition incapable of offering the core conditions to our clients. (p. 10)

Without a stated shared identity, enabling us to define our practice and our values from within, we cannot hope to establish a position for our theory and practice of therapy in the wider world of counselling and psychotherapy. Instead of a clear identity simply stated, we have a fragmented professional identity with the fragments frequently arguing. To return to Rogers' words, 'fluid' we may be, but 'consistent' we are not, and I hardly dare breathe the word 'organised'. Yet nowhere in our theory is it suggested that disorganisation is a good thing. In fact, quite the opposite. The organism, we are told, reacts as an *organised whole* to its phenomenal field (Rogers, 1951) and congruence (which is likely to manifest itself in a sense of self-belief) is when the organism's experiences are in accord with its concept of itself. Disorganisation and incongruence — these qualities would not be in my top ten if I wished to secure the professional standing of the Person-Centred Approach and Client-Centred Therapy in the new millennium.

Rogers, C.R. (1951). *Client-Centered Therapy.* Boston: Houghton Mifflin.

We have our own values. Let us not disappear by default — we practise a principled, humane approach badly needed by the world. Let us stay fluid, let us agree on our consistencies and let's get organised. Urgent action is necessary to maintain the integrity of the approach and to restore the ownership of the approach to its practitioners. However, I believe there are further factors within the world of Person-Centred Therapy which help to maintain the approach in a state of crippling inactivity, delaying the achievement of a clear identity and maintaining the situation wherein Person-Centred Therapies fail to make it on to approved lists for funding in the USA and across Europe:

• Carl Rogers' fabled reticence to be prescriptive in his definition of the approach or as Hutterer (1993, p. 274) put it '. . . the strong anti-dogmatism of Rogers' approach'.

• The widely-held view that Person-Centred Therapy practitioners must *always* uncritically accept *all* views for fear of not being person-centred. (This view is, in my experience, frequently held by many non-person-centred practitioners and seems to be based on mistaken notions of the non-judgemental element of UPR.) This has, on occasions, led to the failure on the part of the Person-Centred Therapy community to challenge and rectify misinterpretations and misunderstandings of the core theoretical principles of the approach.

• An 'inclusivism' held as a value by some Person-Centred Therapy practitioners, whereby it becomes a major offence to propose the exclusion of certain practices from beneath the 'umbrella'.

• A view held by some that 'chaos' is good. I believe this is a hotchpotch of misunderstandings of the mathematical model of chaos theory and applying the subsequent erroneous metaphor either to a state of organisation of personality, and/ or as a directive to *never* organise ourselves as an approach or movement with a clear identity.

These last two factors conspire to leave us with not even a sense that we are allowed to evaluate, let alone have any *strategy* for the evaluation of developments, modifications, extensions and variations to theory and practice, where the innovation might seem to violate a principle of the Person-Centred Approach.

A matter of strategy

I suggest that without an identity which describes the '. . . pattern of perceptions of characteristics and relationships . . . together with the values attached to them' (Rogers, 1951), Person-Centred Therapy has difficulty in positioning itself in the world of

Hutterer, R. (1993). 'Eclecticism: An identity crisis for person-centred therapists.' In D.Brazier (ed) *Beyond Carl Rogers.* London: Constable.

It is worth mentioning that there have been notable, if infrequent, exceptions to this lack of response and rebuttal, e.g. Bozarth, J.D. (1995). 'Person-Centered Therapy: A misunderstood paradigmatic difference.' *The Person-Centered Journal, 2* (2): 12–17.
Brodley, B. T. (1986). *Client-centered psychotherapy — What is it? What is it not?* Unpublished paper presented at 1st annual meeting of the Association for the Development of the Person-Centered Approach. Chicago, Il.
Barrett-Lennard, G.T. (1993). 'Understanding the Person-Centered Approach to Therapy: A "reply" to questions and misconceptions.' *The Person-Centered Approach and Cross-Cultural Communication: An International Review, 2*: 99–113.
Merry, T. (1995). 'Editorial.' *Person-Centred Practice, 3* (2):1–5.

Rogers, C.R. (1951). *Client-Centered Therapy.* Boston: Houghton Mifflin.

professional helping. I believe that it is, therefore, increasingly important that we define the principles of Person-Centred Therapy, understand when these principles have been violated and establish an identity that is inclusive of those supporting the core principles and — and here is the difficult part — decide what to do when a theoretical position or practice does not support the core principles. I believe that this has not happened previously because we have lacked three essential ingredients:

• A vocabulary that all Person-Centred or Client Centred Therapists can share and use when describing the approach and positions within it, both inside and outside the Person-Centred Therapy community.

• An open process within which the definition of principles, identification of positions and consideration of strategy can take place.

• An enthusiasm within the approach to rigorously develop a clear definition of core principles.

The remainder of this appendix is a series of suggestions. As I write elsewehere in this appendix, these suggestions are intended to provoke debate regarding strategy for the consolidation of the family of therapies identifying themselves as 'person-centred'. Firstly a set of principles for Person-Centred Therapies is suggested. Secondly I will make suggestions for the beginnings of a vocabulary for the positions within Person-Centred Therapy, and finally I will suggest a process we can share — namely the development and adoption of a position statement. We will need to be understanding and respectful of others identifying with the approach, whilst we all openly share our positions. This paper is an invitation to all those interested, to enter into purposeful dialogue with the aim to corporately develop, adopt, and promote the adoption of, a unitary vocabulary and statement of principles.

On reflection, this is an impracticable suggestion. It would not be possible for a position statement to emerge and exist independently of individuals and organisations. The point I was trying to make is that the statement should be, and be percieved to be, non-partisan.

Germain Lietaer and Peter Schmid independently have addressed the same problem of identifying the irreducible principles or criteria of the Person-Centred Approach and applying them to the tribes of the nation.
Lietaer suggests first and second order

I further propose that after a period of consultation that the vocabulary and principles be eventually published as a 'position statement'. It is important that the statement is not associated with one person or organisation. The purpose of publication will be to distribute it world-wide to individuals, institutes and associations with an invitation to adopt it. (Adoption of such a position statement will be discussed later in this appendix.)

A matter of principles

I am proposing two levels of principle which would require commitment to all principles in the primary group, and permit practitioners to select principles from the secondary group.

The primary principles of person-centred therapies

- The primacy of the actualising tendency — it is a therapeutic mistake to believe, or act upon the belief, that the therapeutic change process is *not* motivated by the client's actualising tendency.
- Assertion of the necessity of therapeutic conditions (1957 and 1959) and therapeutic behaviour based on *active inclusion* of these — it is a therapeutic mistake to *exclude* any of the conditions. *Passive* inclusion, assuming that such conditions are always present in all relationships, is also insufficient. This primary principle, which declares the paramount importance of the relationship in Person-Centred Therapy, requires active attention to the provision of these conditions.
- Primacy of the non-directive attitude *at least* at the level of content but not necessarily at the level of process. It is permissible for the therapist to be an 'expert' *process*-director — it is a therapeutic mistake to direct the content of a client's experience either explicitly or implicitly.

The secondary principles of person-centred therapies

- Autonomy and the client's right to self-determination — it is a therapeutic mistake to violate the internal locus of control.
- Equality, or non-expertness of therapist — it is a therapeutic mistake to imply that the therapist is an expert in the direction of the content and substance of the client's life.
- The primacy of the non-directive attitude and intention in its absolute and pure form as elaborated by, for example, Barbara Brodley. Shlien (2000) suggests that such a principle be called *inherently non-directive* — it is a therapeutic mistake to wrest control of change process from the client's actualising tendency in any way whatsoever.
- Sufficiency of the therapeutic conditions proposed by Rogers (1957 and 1959) — it is a therapeutic mistake to *include* other conditions, methods or techniques.
- Holism — it is a therapeutic mistake to respond to only a part of the organism.

This is not intended to be an exhaustive list and some have reasonably criticised me for appearing to emphasise negative cases (i.e. 'it is a *mistake* . . .'). Also, I have refrained from referencing these principles since I am hoping that the reader will understand that not only are these principles clearly contained in the bulk of Rogers' work from 1950–1961, they remain at the heart of the

aspects of identity of person-centred and experiential therapy: **First order:**
- focus on the experiencing self
- moment-by-moment empathy
- a high level of personal presence
- an egalitarian dialogical stance
- a belief that the Rogerian therapist conditions are *crucial.*

Second order:
- holistic person-centeredness
- emphasis on self-agency and self-actualizing process
- self-determination and free choice as human possibilities
- pro-social nature of the human being
- autonomy and solidarity as existential tasks. See Lietaer, G. (2002). 'The Client-Centered/Experiential Paradigm in Psychotherapy: Development and identity.' In J.C. Watson, R.N. Goldman, and M.S. Warner (eds.) *Client-Centered and Experiential Psychotherapy in the 21ˢᵗ Century; Advances in theory, research and practice.* Ross-on-Wye: PCCS Books.

Schmid, however, describes a person-centred image of the human being and three distinguishing characteristics of a Person-Centred Approach:
- client and therapist spring from a fundamental 'We'
- the client comes first
- the therapist is present.
He elaborates these statements in an ethical, political and therapeutic framework.
See Schmid, P. (2003). 'The Characteristics of a Person-Centered Approach to Therapy and Counseling.' *Person-Centered and Experiential Psychotherapies, 2* (2): 104–20.

Shlien, J.M. (2000). Personal communication.

Rogers, C.R. (1957). 'The Necessary and Sufficient Conditions for Therapeutic Personality Change.' *Journal of Consulting Psychology, 21* (2): 95–103.
Rogers, C.R. (1959). 'A theory of therapy, personality and interpersonal relationships as developed in the client-centered framework.' In S.Koch (ed.) *Psychology: The Study of a Science, Vol. 3.* New York: McGraw-Hill, pp. 184–256.

Bozarth, J.D. (1998). *Person-Centred Therapy: A Revolutionary Paradigm.* Ross-on-Wye: PCCS Books.
Mearns, D. (1996). 'Working at relational depth with clients in person-centred therapy.' *Counselling, 7* (4): 306–11.
Thorne, B. and Lambers, E. (1998). *Person-Centred Therapy: A European Perspective.* London: Sage.

It is worth repeating that this appendix was written in an effort to stimulate a strategy in the CCT/PCA world to move towards a unified vocabulary. In other words a set of terms, definitions, labels which we could all agree upon. Of course, the whole project is deeply flawed: people may call themselves what they wish. At another level, though, therapy (CCT/PCA included) is rightly ridiculed for its befuddling array of therapeutic approaches and terms. I contend that clients and therapists would both be better served if we could agree on what we called ourselves and that we did more or less what it says on the tin.

Wood, J.K. (1986). 'Roundtable discussion: What is most essential to the continued development of the theory and application of the person-centered approach?' *Person-Centered Review, (1)* 3: 334–52.

work of contemporary writers clearly identified with Person-Centred Therapies today (e.g. Bozarth, 1998; Mearns, 1996; Thorne and Lambers, 1998).

To reiterate; in order to be included in the family of therapies identified as 'person-centred', theory and practice must be based on all of the primary principles. They are *necessary*. Secondary principles can then be held as the basis for theory and practice as required (see *self-exploration, self-evaluation and self-inclusion*, below).

A matter of vocabulary

If one of the missing ingredients is the lack of a shared vocabulary, I suggest that this community of practitioners sets about developing one without delay. The process has to start somewhere, so here I offer the beginnings of a debate about the terms we use to describe some of the variations of practice within the approach. It is deliberately incomplete since it is an opening contribution to a dialogue, and other practitioners are invited to contribute terms and meanings. I believe, though, that if we cannot work towards widespread agreement on the meaning of titles and terms, the project is lost.

At the heart of my personal motives is the desire to have a term I could apply to my own practice. Sometimes I wish I was a process-experiential therapist, then at least I would know what to call myself and others would have a fair idea about my theory and practice. I think it is time that the community of person-centred therapists developed a parsimonious vocabulary that embraces the range of practice acceptable within the principles outlined above.

First comes a triplet of terms which are aimed at moving towards a clarification of the confusing, and for some, false dichotomy of Person-Centred and Client-Centred Therapy.

Person-Centred Approach
In the Roundtable Discussion of 1986, Wood said 'There is no *the* person-centered approach . . . In short it is everything and nothing. What could be most essential to its development? Only Shakespeare could imagine.' Yet in the same discussion, others (e.g. Brian Thorne) referred to the Person-Centred Approach as though there was a consensus of understanding of its meaning.

At least in the UK, this term has come to refer to the whole range of settings in which the principles (in various states of dilution) of the PCA can be implemented, such as education, management, custodial care, care-taking in the service of people with a disability, the management and delivery of healthcare, etc. Although the principles have not been defined anywhere, various writings allude to the notion that the PCA is a way of being as a teacher, manager, nurse, etc. which has at its heart the three 'core' conditions of empathy, unconditional positive regard and congruence. These core conditions are held and enacted in forms that are adapted to the situation and activity and emerge variously as respect, understanding, warmth, equality, honesty, authenticity, acceptance and love.

Person-Centred Therapy/counselling

Hitherto this term has enjoyed general use and is the cause of most cases of confusion, misapplication and offence. I suggest that the person-centred community gives a more particular meaning to this overused term to prevent its misappropriation by all-and-sundry. I propose that its meaning should be construed in close relation to *classical Client-Centred Therapy* (below) and the characteristics which discriminate the two might, for example, be the liberality of the interpretation of the principles of the approach in their *content*, but not in their *extent*. Such characteristics would include the definition of empathy and, thereby, the constitution of empathic responses, and so on. Although, as I mentioned above, Rogers made no distinction between Person-Centred and Client-Centred Therapy, I believe the time has come to do so. Indeed some practitioners in the UK have already begun to differentiate their position by adopting the appellation *classical client-centred therapist*.

Classical Client-Centred Therapy/counselling

Although not used by these writers, the term most closely fits the position described by Brodley (1986, 1999), Bozarth (1998) and Merry (1998). Classical Client-Centred Therapy is used to identify theory and practice closest to the original tenets of Client-Centred Therapy as described by Rogers in 1951, 1957 and 1959. It adopts the principles in their 'classical' form, and often puts the non-directive attitude (for example, Raskin 1948, Brodley 1999, Merry, 2000) at the centre of its theoretical position and practice.

Next comes a collection of terms describing approaches with *experiencing* at the core of the therapeutic process. Some writers have argued against their exclusion from the Person-Centred

Brodley, B. T. (1986). 'Client-centered psychotherapy — What is it? What is it not?' Unpublished paper presented at 1st annual meeting of the Association for the Development of the Person-Centered Approach. Chicago, Il.

Brodley, B.T. (1999). 'About the nondirective attitude.' *Person-Centred Practice, 7* (2): 79–82.

Bozarth, J.D. (1998). *Person-Centred Therapy: A Revolutionary Paradigm.* Ross-on-Wye: PCCS Books.

Merry, T. (1998). 'Can the core principles of person-centred counselling be described?' *Person-Centred Practice, 6* (2). Reprinted in T. Merry (ed.). *Person-Centred Practice: The BAPCA Reader.* Ross-on-Wye: PCCS Books, pp. 14–16.

Merry, T. (2000). 'Editorial.' *Person-Centred Practice, 8* (1): 1–3.

Raskin, N. (1948). 'The development of non-directive psychotherapy.' *Journal of Consulting Psychology, 12*: 92–110.

Prouty, G. (1999). 'Carl Rogers and Experiential Therapies: A Dissonance?' *Person-Centred Practice,* 7 (1): 4–11.
Warner, M.S. (2000). 'Person-Centered Psychotherapy: One nation, many tribes.' *The Person-Centered Journal,* 7 (1): 28–39.

Gendlin, E.T. (1978). *Focusing.* New York: Everest House. (New British edition, London: Rider, 2003.)
Gendlin, E.T. (1996). *Focusing Oriented Psychotherapy.* New York: Guilford Press.

Rice, L.N. (1974). 'The Evocative Function of the Therapist.' In D.A.Wexler and L.N.Rice (eds.). *Innovations in Client-Centred Therapy.* New York: John Wiley and Sons.
Greenberg, L.S., Rice, L.N. and Elliott, R. (1993). *Facilitating Emotional Change: The Moment-by Moment Process.* New York: Guilford Press.

Readers are reminded that they should consider all of the terms used by me here to be *my own inventions* for use as examples. It is important that practitioners individually and in groups or associations, identify themselves.

Hutterer, R. (1993). 'Eclecticism: an identity crisis for person-centred therapists.' In D.Brazier (ed.). *Beyond Carl Rogers.* London: Constable.
Rogers, C.R. (1951). *Client-Centered Therapy.* Boston: Houghton-Mifflin.

Worsley, R. (2002). *Process Work in Person-Centred Therapy: Phenomenological and existential perspectives.* Basingstoke: Palgrave.

Therapy umbrella on a theoretical basis (lately Prouty, 1999) and others for their inclusion on the basis of practice (Warner, 2000). Without commenting on whether such approaches should be included or excluded, they include:

Focusing-oriented psychotherapy
After Gendlin (1978, 1996) and others, this term is applied to a strand of theory and practice that has as its central tenets the importance of experiencing, the articulation of that experiencing and the role of the therapist as an expert process-facilitator.

Process-experiential psychotherapy
With its roots in the work of Rice (1974) and more recently Greenberg *et al.,* (1993), this strand derives from an integration of an experiential approach, information-processing theory, gestalt psychotherapy and client-centred theory. The aim is for the therapist to be the expert director of the client's process of experiencing cognitive-affective information.

Lastly, at least in this paper, there are therapeutic approaches which are integrative in nature. It is sometimes not clear on what basis some of these approaches claim to be 'person-centred', and, for the moment, I am not commenting on whether they should be included or excluded. These I have called:

Person-centred integrative therapies
What is acceptable integration? Hutterer (1993) presents a thorough series of arguments against eclecticism and concludes with an insight which encapsulates the dilemma: 'I think we must accept that no school of therapy will ever reach the whole truth. But I think it is also true as Rogers said back in 1951: "Truth is not arrived at by concessions from differing schools of thought" (Rogers, 1951, p. 8)' (Hutterer, 1993, p. 284).

I have used the term *person-centred integrative therapies* in an effort to describe initiatives which attempt to integrate Person-Centred Therapy with other sympathetic orientations at a level of theory and philosophy (theoretical integration — see technical eclecticism, below) whilst clearly explaining how the primary principles of Person-Centred Therapy are upheld within the integrative theory and practice. In other words, no concessions are made at the level of primary principles. Some UK practitioners have attempted to do this, for example Worsley (2002).

Self-exploration, self-evaluation and self-inclusion

If I were to imagine for a moment that these principles were accepted and adopted by a wide range of individuals, associations and institutes that identify with the Person-Centred Approach and/or Client-Centred Therapy, then it would be possible to invite all such practitioners, associations and groups to firstly 'adopt' the statement of principles and positions, then secondly state the basis on which they believe themselves to be included. The reader might well ask 'who will be doing the inviting?' My answer is simple: one consequence of *my* adopting these principles must be to describe how they apply to *my* theoretical position and the way *I* practise. This process, then, will be one of *self*-scrutiny, *self*-description and *self*-inclusion.

In order to include myself in the 'person-centred family' I must hold, and base my practice on, the primary principles. I may then 'pick and mix' from the secondary principles.

The issue here is whether I accept the invitation to explore my understanding of theory and then declare what behaviour limits my own practice. Do I think that anything goes, and that all behaviour is acceptable as person-centred practice? The answer for me is 'No', so I then ask myself what would I do and what would I not do? What principles flow from my practice, and what practice flows from my principles?

If I can be honest with myself in this self-evaluation, and if after supervision and consultation with my peers, I am happy with my understanding of theory and implementation in my practice, then I will be able to exclude myself or include myself as appropriate. Parenthetically, I have begun to wonder whether Person-Centred Therapy can be so attractive a proposition in the professional world of the twenty-first century that anyone would want to be included when so many commentators declare that all the evidence is set against it?

Inclusion — some examples

• *Classical Client-Centred Therapy* may be characterised by an acceptance of and an attempt to adhere to all of the principles at both levels. Interpretation of the principles would be precise and faithful to Rogers' early writings, with the discriminating characteristic of classical Client-Centred Therapy being its *inherently* non-directive position. Therapeutic conditions might

When I first wrote this it seemed a very risky thing to do — to say what I thought should and should not be included in a definition of CCT, and more widely, the PCA. As it happens, no great storm broke. What I wrote was largely ignored until it was picked up a couple of years later by Richard Worsley in his (2002) *Process Work in Person-Centred Therapy.* Basingstoke: Palgrave. And then later by Paul Wilkins (2003). *Person-Centred Therapy in Focus.* London: Sage.

It is still my hope that practitioners will be brave enough to say what they do and call it what it is. An interesting contribution to the debate is the courageous book edited by Suzanne Keys (2003). *Idiosyncratic Person-Centred Therapy: From the personal to the universal.* Ross-on-Wye: PCCS Books.

be considered to be attitudes, but defined by a set of limiting behaviours.

• *Person-Centred Therapy* may be characterised by a similar acceptance of all of the principles at both levels, but with a more liberal interpretation possibly exemplified by Rogers' later writings, and possibly whereby the conditions-as-attitudes position is exemplified by a greater range of acceptable behaviours.

• *Focusing-oriented Psychotherapy* might accept the primary principles and all of the secondary principles with the exception of the primacy of the non-directive attitude. Many Focusing-oriented therapists would take the role of active process-facilitator, whilst some might hold Gendlin's theory of experiencing and process of therapy at the theoretical level, *informing* their practice and understanding of the client's process, without moving them to actively direct the client.

• *Process-experiential psychotherapy* might be characterised by an acceptance and adherence to the primary principles but only some of the secondary principles, e.g. accepting the client's autonomy, but rejecting both absolute non-directivity and the non-expertness of the therapist.

Richard Worsley however argues for the sufficiency of the therapeutic conditions by seeing what is integrated as an expression of these conditions. He emphaises the attitudinal nature of the core conditions (see above, p.160: 'Person-centred therapy').

• *Person-centred integrative approaches* would accept the primary principles and perhaps all but one of the secondary principles — rejecting the secondary principle of sufficiency of the therapeutic conditions. A possible systematic pattern of acceptance and rejection of secondary principles might be based on a theoretical justification for including additional therapeutic elements. In essence, any theoretical justification would need, at least in part, to be argued on the basis of including extra elements to facilitate the actualising tendency and how this would work.

Exclusion — some examples

Egan, G. (1987). *The Skilled Helper: Models, Methods and Skills for Effective Helping,* 3rd ed. Monterey, CA: Brooks/Cole.
Hermansson, G. (1998). *Eclectic Counselling: Working with an integrated model,* 2nd ed. Palmerston North: Inside-out Books.

• *Technical eclecticism* (Egan, 1987; Hermansson, 1998; and others) in contrast to theoretical eclecticism (see 'Person-centred integrative approaches' above) is where an attempt is made to create a model at the level of method or technique on a pragmatic basis. It is not uncommon for trainings or graduates of trainings in the UK based on a problem-solving or problem-management model to describe themselves as 'person-centred'. Although we might recognise the integrity of the effort in the development of these approaches, such approaches are excluded because they violate practically all of the principles of Person-Centred Therapy and share none of the theory of personality or change.

In fact some have no theory at all (e.g. in my view, Egan, 1987) and operate entirely on an unevidenced pragmatic basis.

• *Haphazard eclecticism* a somewhat derogatory term coined by Dryden (1994) to most charitably describe an quasi-intuitive model 'I use whatever makes sense to me and whatever I feel comfortable with' (Lazarus, 1981 — though I hasten to add that Lazarus was not writing in support of this approach!) Such practice would seem to have no theoretical integrity and is a subjective assembly of theories informed solely by the intuition of the therapist. Perhaps this style of approach is based on a misunderstanding of Rogers' references to intuition in his later writings.

• *Medical-mimicry* is the attempt to use a pseudo-scientific justification for the application of a range of approaches according to what the therapist diagnoses as the client's need. So it is a 'diagnosis — selection of method — application of method' model and sometimes, advocates of such an approach will cite themselves as 'person-centred' since they believe that they offer the person-centred 'core conditions' as an underpinning to the model. Dryden (1994.) refers to this approach disparagingly as 'hat-rack eclecticism', where, in one variation, practitioners wear different 'hats', e.g. '. . . a Gestalt hat with one client, a psychoanalytic hat with another, and so on' (p. 351) again depending upon the practitioner's analysis/ assessment/diagnosis of the client's needs. They are excluded on the basis (from diagnosis onwards) that they are essentially unprincipled assemblies of techniques, especially after Bozarth (1998a and b) has argued so persuasively against the 'specificity myth'.

• *Marriages of convenience* are models which are based on trainings where (possibly because of staff expertise) the first part of the training is roughly person-centred in content and the second part of the training is, for example, roughly psycho-dynamic in content. Graduates of such trainings in the UK commonly declare themselves to be 'person-centred/psycho-dynamic', never having addressed the potentially antagonistic philosophical roots, theoretical orientations and practices of the two approaches. These 'models' may not even be considered to be models and are excluded since they are also unprincipled, often accidental, marriages of two approaches with little regard for the principles of either.

• *We are all doing the same thing really* models are versions of integrative models that exist in some training establishments in the UK. They arise, I understand, from trainings that encourage comparative approaches in theory and practice. The model goes

Egan, G. (1987). *The Skilled Helper: Models, Methods and Skills for Effective Helping.* 3rd ed. Monterey, CA: Brooks/ Cole.

Dryden, W. (1984). *Individual Therapy in Britain.* London: Harper & Row.
Lazarus, A.A. (1981). *The Practice of Multimodal Therapy.* New York: McGraw-Hill.

Dryden, W. (1984). *Individual Therapy in Britain.* London: Harper & Row.

Bozarth, J.D. (1998a). 'Playing the Probabilities in Psychotherapy.' *Person-Centred Practice, 6* (1): 9–21.
Bozarth, J.D. (1998b). *Person-Centred Therapy: A Revolutionary Paradigm.* Ross-on-Wye: PCCS Books.

something like this, after comparing Person-Centred Therapy with psychoanalysis, we can see that on a theoretical level the Rogerian self-concept is really the Freudian superego and at a practice level empathic listening is really free association, so we are all doing the same thing really. Graduates of such trainings feel free to call themselves psychodynamic or humanistic or person-centred as they choose.

Such a view also attempts to take the self-identified intellectual high ground of the post-modernist, i.e. that there are no meta-models or paradigms. To advocate one model or paradigm in the year 2000 (e.g. a person-centred one [see Ellingham, 1999]) is to be intellectually naïve or backward. Postmodernist thinking requires us, we are told by some, to believe that all therapists are doing the same thing really.

Adopting the position statement

And so, finally, I invite individuals, associations and institutes to adopt the position statement (comprising the vocabulary, principles and examples of inclusion and exclusion). By 'adopt' I mean that the association or institute in question will make a statement in their publicity such as 'The British Association for the Person-Centred Approach adopts the position statement', or 'The Manchester Training Institute adopts the position statement when describing its training programmes' and in the case of an individual practitioner, 'Pete Sanders is a classical Client-Centred Therapist as defined by the position statement'.

The consequences of adopting the position statement could be, for example, that the organisation includes the statement in its constitution, or bases membership categories on acceptance of the principles. As an individual, I would implicitly agree to base my practice on a position described in the statement. Following my declaration of adoption, my clients, my employers and fellow professionals would have a ready reference point to help them define my practice. Furthermore, this definition would be one shared by hundreds if not thousands of therapists world-wide.

The PCA would have an identity which could be declared in professional circles and defended where necessary. When authors from other therapeutic orientations publish work which misrepresents the PCA by definition, individual practitioners may correct this misrepresentation by appeal to the shared consensual nature of the statement within the Person-Centred Therapy community. Practitioners obliged to register practice with

Ellingham, I. (1999). 'On Transcending Person-Centred Postmodernist Porridge.' *Person-Centred Practice, 7* (3): 62–78.

This is not rocket science. I am simply suggesting that all practitioners select a descriptor from a consensually approved list and practise (given their personal idiosyncrasies) within its rough limits. The practitioners themselves do the selecting. All we might ask, in such a framework of self-regulation, is that we openly declare our practice and practise reflexively. Other professionals might then be better able to make referrals, clients might be better able to choose and practitioners might understand the parameters of their own practice better.

regulatory or professional bodies can ask that the professional body adopts the position statement in its definitions.

Having found our identity, it should not be set in stone. I would hope that developing and maintaining a flexible yet consistent position statement should be the major project of any national or world organisation for the therapeutic application of the Person-Centred Approach.

As an endnote to this chapter and indeed this book, I believe that the new World Association for Person-Centered and Experiential Psychotherapy and Counseling (WAPCEPC) represents some of the best efforts to bring to gether, and constructively address the differences between, the tribes of the person-centred nation.

index

directivity 61, 111
dissociated process 18
dissociation xvi
Dryden, W. 112, 134, 161
Duncan, B.L. 122
DuPlock, S. 118, 122
Dymond, R. 4

E

eclecticism
    haphazard 161
    technical x, 127, 160
edge of awareness 67, 74, 83
Egan, G. 160
Elkin, G. 113, 114
Ellingham, I. 162
Elliott, R. 10, 63, 81, 91, 92, 127, 133, 158
Ellis, A. 14
Embleton-Tudor, L. 75
emotion schemes 81–2
empathic
    attunement 83
    conjecture 84
    exploration 84
empathy/empathic understanding 6, 31–4, 37–8, 42, 75,
        83–5, 103
empty chair dialogue 84
    procedure 60
encounter groups 13
ethical activity 18
Ethical Framework (BACP) 67
evocative
    function of the therapist 83
    responding 60
existence
    as a process 97
    as embodied 103
    as freely-choosing 97
    as future- and meaning-orientated 98
    as in-the-world 101
    as limited 100
    as unique 96
    as with-others 102
    tragedy of, 104
existential
    dimension 145
    neuroses 110
    philosophy see 'existentialism'
    therapy x, 95
    view of human being 96
    -humanistic approach 112, 114, 124
existentialism 4–5, 96–106, 145–6
experiencing 51, 54, 56, 87
    -level 64

lived 103
experiential
    psychotherapy x, 10
    responses 70
    shift 50
    track 91
expertness (of therapist) 78, 80, 86
expressive therapy xi–xii
expressivity 74

F

Farson, R. 11, 12
felt
    experiencing 69
    meaning 70, 71, 75
    sense 46, 54, 58, 67, 70–1, 74, 77, 103
Feynman, R. 12
Fish, S. 139, 140
Focusing Institute xvii, 65
focusing x, 1, 8–9, 49, 59, 84, 113
    instructions 49
focusing-oriented
    psychotherapy 45, 49, 60–1, 63, 67, 160
    response 58
following responses 84
fragile process 18
Frankl, V. 95, 110, 111, 112, 124
Freiberg, H.J. 98
Freud, S. 54, 96, 107
Friedli, K. 44
Friedman, M. 109
fully functioning person 69

G

Garfield, A.E. 81
Gellman, M. 12
Gendlin, E.T. 7, 8, 9, 10, 11, 45, 46, 47, 48, 49, 50, 51, 52,
        54, 55, 56, 57, 59, 60, 65, 69, 72, 73, 74, 77, 83,
        89, 91, 103, 113, 138, 158
genuineness 113
Gergen, K.J. 127, 137
Gestalt Therapy 138, 139, 140
getting a distance 60
Glass, G.V. 63
Gloria 14
goal directed 23, 27
Goldman, R.N. 149
Goodman, P. 130, 139
Grant, B. 19, 41, 62, 92, 130
Graw, K. 64
Greenberg, L.S. 10, 78, 81, 83, 89, 90, 91, 92, 127, 130,
        132, 133, 135, 139, 158
groups 12
    encounter 13

moment-by-moment empathy 87
moral choice 41
Ms G. (case of) 33, 34
Mullan, B. 115, 116, 118

N

Natiello, P. 74
necessary and sufficient conditions 31, 134
necessity of therapeutic conditions 155
Nietzsche 96, 103, 106
nineteen propositions 27
non-directive
    attitude 35, 40, 91–2, 155
    therapy 2, 9, 10, 21
non-directivity 40–1, 61–2, 68, 92, 130
    instrumental 41, 62, 92, 130
    principled 41, 62, 92, 130, 131
non-
    expertness of therapist 155
    invasive 40
    judgemental 43 (see also 'unconditional positive
      regard')
Norcross, J. 122
environmental factors 40

O

O'Hara, M. 95
O'Leary, C.J. 136
ontological insecurity 116
organismic experiencing 26
Orlinsky, D.E. 64

P

paradoxes 100
paradoxical intention 112
Parks, B.K. 64
Peace Project, 13
Perls, F.S. 14, 127, 139
Person-Centered Review 14
Person-Centred Practice 44
personality change 55
phenomenology 4, 5, 94, 95
Phillipson, H. 117
pluralistic self 18, 30, 102 (see also 'configurations of
    self')
Polanyi, M. 11, 12
Pörtner, M. xv, 17, 32, 74
position statement 162
positivism 6
potentials 24
pre-expressive self xv
pre-symbolised experience 69
Pre-Therapy xii, xiv, xv, xvi, 17, 32
presence 15, 16, 87

principles (of person-centred therapies) 154
    primary 155
    secondary 155
process 98, 140
    conception of psychotherapy 8, 46
    direction 79, 84, 87, 127
    identification 79
    model 52
    skipping 56
    -oriented psychotherapy 10, 81–5
Process Scale 75
process-experiential
    approaches 113
    psychotherapy 158, 160
Prouty, G. xiv, xv, 17, 32, 68, 69, 71, 73, 74, 75, 92, 157
psychodynamic psychotherapy 143, 144
psychological
    contact xiv, xvi, 6, 31
    disturbance 55, 56
    maladjustment 28
    self-determination 39, 43
psychotic symptoms xv, xvi
Purton, C. 10, 56, 65, 67, 73, 130

R

Rank, O. 3
Raskin, N.T. 3, 4, 21, 132, 157
referent 77
reflection 35
reflexive/reflexivity 75, 78
Rennie, D. 75, 78, 79, 80, 91, 127, 133, 141, 142
research 43–4, 63–4, 121–2
Resnick, J. 117
responds to the environment 30
Rice, L.N. 10, 60, 81, 83, 91, 92, 127, 133, 158
Rogers, C.R. vii, x, xiv, 2, 3, 4, 5, 6, 7, 8, 11, 12, 13, 15,
    17, 21, 23, 25, 26, 27, 31, 33, 34, 35, 36, 37, 39,
    43, 45, 46, 47, 48, 49, 53, 57, 61, 68, 72, 75, 76,
    89, 95, 97, 98, 103, 104, 105, 108, 114, 120, 125,
    126, 127, 129, 132, 134, 137, 139, 144, 150, 151,
    152, 153, 155, 158
Rogers, N. xiii, xiv
Russell, D. 5, 7, 13, 47

S

Sachse, R. 64
Sanders, P. xv, xvii, 32, 43, 93
Sartre, J-P. 5, 96, 97, 98, 100, 110
scale for 'experiencing level' 48
Scharff, D.E. 144
Scharff, J.S. 144
schizophrenia 7, 44, 48, 74, 116, 117, 140
Schmid, P. 18, 102, 147, 149, 154, 155
Schneider, K.J. 113, 114